GED Connection®

Social Studies & Science

LiteracyLink® is a joint project of PBS, Kentucky Educational Television, the National Center on Adult Literacy, and the Kentucky Department of Education. This project is funded in whole, or in part, by the Star Schools Program of the USDE under contract #R203D60001.

Social Studies: **by Victoria Cox Kaser**
Science: **by Marion Castellucci**

Acknowledgments

Content Design and Workbook Editorial Development
Learning Unlimited,
Oak Park, Illinois

Design and Layout
By Design,
Lexington, Kentucky

Project Consultant
Milli Fazey, KET,
Lexington, Kentucky

Production Manager
Debra Gibson,
Copywrite,
Lexington, Kentucky

This project is funded in whole, or in part, by the Star Schools Program of the USDE under contract #R203D60001.

PBS LiteracyLink, LitTeacher, LitLearner, LitHelper, and PeerLit are registered marks of the Public Broadcasting Service.

Printed in the United States of America.
ISBN 978–1–881020–40–0

LiteracyLink® Partners
LiteracyLink is a joint project of:
Public Broadcasting Service
Kentucky Educational Television
National Center on Adult Literacy
The Kentucky Department of Education

Contents

Program 22: Passing the GED Science Test

Program 23: Life Science

Program 24: Earth and Space Science

Program 25: Chemistry

Program 26: Physics

Reference Handbook

GED CONNECTION
consists of these
educational tools:

39 VIDEO PROGRAMS

shown on public
television and in adult
learning centers

ONLINE MATERIALS

available on the
Internet at
http://www.pbs.org/literacy

THREE COMPANION
WORKBOOKS

Language Arts, Writing
and Reading; Social
Studies and Science;
and Mathematics

GED Connection Orientation

Welcome to the *LiteracyLink*® system. This workbook is part of a multimedia educational system for adult learners and educators that includes both *GED Connection* for GED preparation and *Workplace Essential Skills*, targeted at upgrading the knowledge and skills needed to succeed in the world of work.

Instructional Programs

GED Connection consists of an orientation program and 38 instructional programs. Each GED topic can be approached in three ways—through video, print, and online. For example, Program 19 is *Economics*. To study this topic, you can watch the *Program 19* video lesson, work in the *Program 19* workbook lesson in this book, and go online to http://www.pbs.org/literacy and then to the GED *Social Studies* module.

Getting Started with the System

You will make the best use of *LiteracyLink* if you use all of the components. At http://www.pbs.org/literacy, you will establish your Home Space, which is your starting point for working through the Internet portion of *LiteracyLink*.

For additional practice, visit *LiteracyLink* online at http://www.pbs.org/literacy.

Making the Best Use of the Workbook

Before you start using this workbook, take some time to preview its features.

1. The **GED Pretest** will help you decide which GED areas you need to focus on. You should use the evaluation chart, provided after the pretest answer key, to develop your study plan.
2. Each workbook lesson corresponds to a video program and Internet activities.

   The **Before You Watch** section orients you to the video program:

   > **Objectives** form the focus for each video, workbook, and online lesson
   > **Sneak Preview** provides an introductory exercise, answers, and feedback
   > **Program Summary** explains what you are about to see in the video
   > **Vocabulary** defines key content area terms

   The **After You Watch** section covers key GED content and skills:

   > **Key Points** to think about and **GED Tips**
   > **Lesson Segments** that provide core instruction
   > **Skill Practice** to reinforce what you have learned
   > **Connection** to another GED subject area
   > **GED Practice** with items similar to those on the GED Test

3. The **GED Practice Test** helps you evaluate your GED readiness.
4. The **Answer Key** consists of answers and explanations.
5. A **Reference Handbook** provides additional resources for GED preparation.
6. The **Glossary** and **Index** help you find the information you need.

For Teachers

Portions of *LiteracyLink* have been developed for adult educators and service providers. LitTeacher is an online professional development system that provides a number of resources including PeerLit, a database of evaluated websites. You can also access LitTeacher at http://www.pbs.org/literacy.

Who's Responsible for LiteracyLink®?

LiteracyLink was developed through a five-year grant by the U.S. Department of Education. The following partners have contributed to the development of the *LiteracyLink* system:

 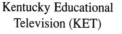 

| PBS Adult Learning Service | Kentucky Educational Television (KET) | The National Center on Adult Literacy (NCAL) of the University of Pennsylvania | The Kentucky Department of Education |

All of the *LiteracyLink* partners wish you the very best
in passing the GED and meeting all of your educational goals.

Social Studies Pretest

DIRECTIONS: Choose <u>the one best answer</u> to each question.
<u>Questions 1 through 3</u> refer to the following passage.

By the 1770s, many American colonists were troubled by their relationship with Great Britain. The colonists felt they were not adequately represented in Britain's government. In 1774, representatives from all the colonies but one met in Philadelphia. They agreed to no longer trade with Great Britain. They hoped that this would make Great Britain's government change some of its policies toward the colonies.

But Great Britain did not change its policies. So, colonial representatives decided that it was time to be free of British rule. On July 4, 1776, they approved the Declaration of Independence. This document, written by Thomas Jefferson, explained why the colonists had decided to break away from Great Britain. This is part of what it said: "We hold these truths to be self-evident, that all men are created equal, that they are endowed by their Creator with certain unalienable rights [rights that cannot be taken away], that among these are Life, Liberty, and the pursuit of Happiness,—That to secure these rights, Governments are instituted among Men, deriving their just powers from the consent of the governed, —That whenever any Form of Government becomes destructive of these ends, it is the Right of the People to alter or to abolish [end] it..."

1. Which statement <u>best</u> explains the purpose of the Declaration of Independence?
   (1) to declare war on Great Britain
   (2) to separate the American colonies from Great Britain
   (3) to separate the United States into the North and the South
   (4) to set the border between the United States and Canada
   (5) to make the United States part of Great Britain

2. Which of these slogans support the beliefs stated in the Declaration of Independence?
   (1) Power to the King!
   (2) Power to Great Britain!
   (3) Power to the People!
   (4) Power to the Colony!
   (5) Power to God!

3. How did the colonists first try to solve their problems with Great Britain?
   (1) They declared independence.
   (2) They moved farther west.
   (3) They refused to buy British goods.
   (4) They fought the Revolutionary War.
   (5) They elected the first U.S. President.

<u>Question 4</u> is based on the circle graph.

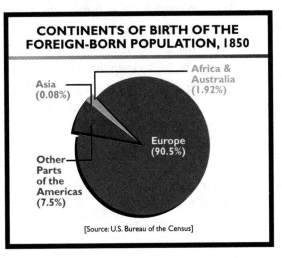

CONTINENTS OF BIRTH OF THE FOREIGN-BORN POPULATION, 1850

Asia (0.08%)
Africa & Australia (1.92%)
Europe (90.5%)
Other Parts of the Americas (7.5%)

[Source: U.S. Bureau of the Census]

4. Based on the graph, which statement is the <u>best</u> conclusion about U.S. residents in 1850?
   (1) Few Germans lived in the United States.
   (2) Everyone living in the United States was a citizen.
   (3) Few were foreign-born.
   (4) More immigrants came from Europe than from any other continent.
   (5) Since 1850, the number of immigrants to the United States has dropped.

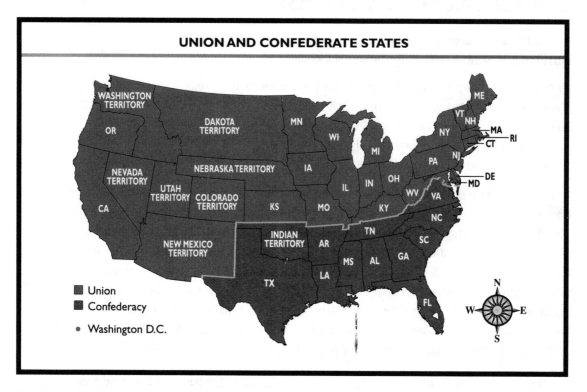

UNION AND CONFEDERATE STATES

5. The Confederate states broke away from the United States partly because they feared the U.S. government would end slavery. Trying to keep these states from breaking away led to the Civil War. In which part of the United States did most slave owners live?
   (1) in the Northwest
   (2) in the North
   (3) in the Southwest
   (4) in the Southeast
   (5) near California

6. Whether slave owners could bring slaves to the Western territories was one issue that deeply divided northerners and southerners. Southerners were eager to bring slaves to warm regions where cotton could be grown. Which Western territory do you think was most attractive to slave owners?
   (1) Washington Territory
   (2) Dakota Territory
   (3) Nevada Territory
   (4) Colorado Territory
   (5) New Mexico Territory

7. Which conclusion about the Civil War is best supported by the map?
   (1) Most of the nation stayed with the Union.
   (2) Most of the nation became Indian Territory.
   (3) Most of the territories belonged to the Confederacy.
   (4) Oregon and California were the westernmost states in the Confederacy.
   (5) The Confederacy lost the Civil War.

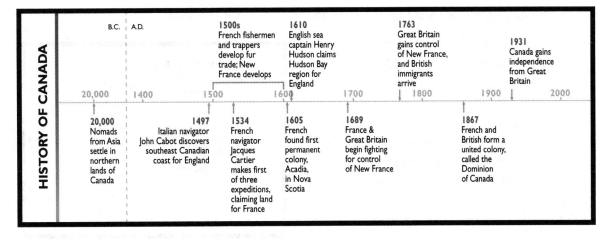

HISTORY OF CANADA

1500s French fishermen and trappers develop fur trade; New France develops	**1610** English sea captain Henry Hudson claims Hudson Bay region for England	**1763** Great Britain gains control of New France, and British immigrants arrive	**1931** Canada gains independence from Great Britain		

B.C. | A.D.

20,000 | 1400 | 1500 | 1600 | 1700 | 1800 | 1900 | 2000

20,000 Nomads from Asia settle in northern lands of Canada

1497 Italian navigator John Cabot discovers southeast Canadian coast for England

1534 French navigator Jacques Cartier makes first of three expeditions, claiming land for France

1605 French found first permanent colony, Acadia, in Nova Scotia

1689 France & Great Britain begin fighting for control of New France

1867 French and British form a united colony, called the Dominion of Canada

Questions 8 through 10 refer to the timeline above.

8. England and France both made early claims for land in Canada. Based on the information in the timeline, what was the main attraction that drew colonists to this part of the Americas?
   (1) the land's natural resources
   (2) freedom to worship as they pleased
   (3) discovery of gold
   (4) escape from the king's rule
   (5) the right to vote

9. During which period does it appear that tensions between British colonists and French colonists in Canada were mostly resolved?
   (1) between 1534 and 1605
   (2) between 1605 and 1610
   (3) between 1610 and 1689
   (4) between 1689 and 1763
   (5) between 1763 and 1867

10. In which century did Canada become an independent nation?
    (1) the 1500s
    (2) the 1600s
    (3) the 1700s
    (4) the 1800s
    (5) the 1900s

Questions 11 and 12 refer to the diagram.

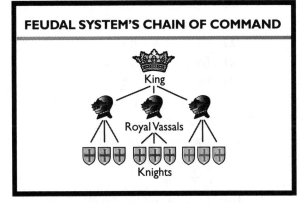

FEUDAL SYSTEM'S CHAIN OF COMMAND

King

Royal Vassals

Knights

11. Which statement **best** explains the chain of command in Europe's feudal system?
    (1) The king directs the royal vassals, who supervise the knights.
    (2) Each vassal is in charge of the same number of knights.
    (3) The king is at the top of the feudal system.
    (4) The knights command the royal vassals, who direct the king.
    (5) Poor people should appear at the bottom of the diagram.

12. With which opinion would a feudal king most likely agree?
    (1) The poor should report directly to the royal vassals.
    (2) Authority should be evenly distributed.
    (3) Vassals are the most powerful people in the kingdom.
    (4) Knights' decisions are equal to kings' decisions.
    (5) Kings are the ultimate authority.

Questions 13 through 15 are based on the following passage and graph.

Medicare is the name of a health insurance program established by the United States government in 1965. Its purpose is to provide health insurance for people who are 65 years old or older. Medicare works by helping older Americans pay for medical bills. In 1995 the government spent $159.9 billion on Medicare. In 1996 it spent $174.2 billion on Medicare. In 1997 Medicare cost estimates were $194.3 billion.

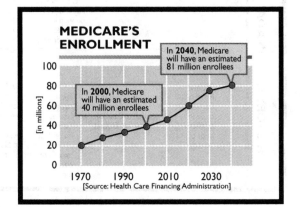

13. Based on the information above, what prediction can you make about the future cost of Medicare?
    (1) The cost will go up.
    (2) The cost will go down.
    (3) The government will pay a smaller part of the insurance costs for older Americans.
    (4) The government will replace Medicare with less expensive programs.
    (5) The cost will remain about the same.

14. What is the most likely explanation for the expected rise in Medicare enrollment?
    (1) The population of the United States is projected to drop during the next 20 years.
    (2) More people are expected to get sick in the future.
    (3) Private insurance companies will go out of business in the future.
    (4) There will be more doctors to serve elderly patients in the future.
    (5) The number of people reaching the age of 65 is expected to grow.

15. What headline would you expect to see on a newspaper printed in 2010?
    (1) Number Getting Medicare Benefits Falls Sharply
    (2) Medicare Costs Drop Drastically
    (3) Government Expands Benefits of Medicare Program
    (4) Medicare Cuts Benefits Due to Budget Limits
    (5) Medicare Minimum Age Dropped to 30

Question 16 is based on the following graph.

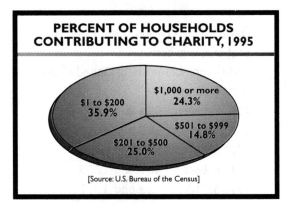

16. Which statement does the circle graph best support?
    (1) About 80 percent of all U.S. households give money to charity.
    (2) Giving money to charity is the most important expenditure in 25 percent of U.S. households.
    (3) Most Americans contribute less than $501 to charity every year.
    (4) Most Americans receive more than $500 in charity every year.
    (5) The amount of money Americans give to charity is rising.

Question 17 refers to the following passage.

In 1957 six western European nations—Belgium, France, Italy, Luxembourg, the Netherlands, and West Germany—decided to create the European Economic Community (EEC). The goal of the EEC was for member nations to work together to free up trade and eventually dispose of tariffs and quotas, thereby creating the free flow of goods and capital between nations.

In 1970 the idea of having all EEC members use just one currency, or kind of money, was introduced. The currency would make it both easier and cheaper to buy and sell products across national borders.

By 1999 the European Economic Community had become the European Union (EU), and its membership had grown to 15. On New Year's Day of that year, 11 of the 15 members introduced a new currency called the euro.

Countries deciding to use the euro agreed to give up some authority that is usually handled by individual nations. For example, each country's government could no longer make independent decisions about issues like trade, public spending, and tax rates. In addition, the countries would no longer print their own money, and a country's money is part of its identity. However, countries using the euro hoped to find themselves part of one of the greatest economies in the world.

17. In what way are countries of the European Union like the states of the United States?
    (1) All the members are part of one big nation.
    (2) There is a free flow of people and products across borders.
    (3) Each member prints its own money.
    (4) All the members believe in a single religion.
    (5) No member can make any decision independently of the group.

Question 18 refers to the following passage.

The three basic economic systems are:

Capitalism: an economic system in which the means of production, distribution, and exchange are privately owned

Socialism: an economic system in which the government owns and controls many of the nation's most important industries

Communism: an economic system in which the means of production, distribution, and exchange are owned and controlled by the government

18. Which conclusion do the definitions support?
    (1) Individuals have the most economic freedom under capitalism.
    (2) Individuals make the fewest economic decisions under capitalism.
    (3) Socialism and communism are the same.
    (4) Socialism is the world's most popular economic system.
    (5) People are happiest living in a communist country.

Questions 19 and 20 are based on the following passage.

There are two ways to become an American citizen. One way is by birth. Anyone born in the United States is automatically an American citizen, whether or not the parents are American citizens. Also, anyone born to American parents is an American citizen, no matter where that person is born. The second way to become a citizen of the United States is by a process called naturalization. Those who are not born citizens must live in the United States for at least five years. They must also pass a test to show that they have an understanding of the principles of the nation's government as well as the ability to read, write, and speak basic English. If a person meets these qualifications, he or she then takes an oath of allegiance and receives a certificate of naturalization.

19. How do people from other countries become United States citizens?

(1) They give birth to their children in the United States.

(2) They go through the naturalization process.

(3) They enter the country and stay.

(4) They learn English.

(5) They take the GED Test.

20. Which person would <u>not</u> be an American citizen?

(1) the person who was born in Arizona of Mexican parents

(2) the person who was born in Paris of parents who are U.S. citizens

(3) the Albanian immigrant who became naturalized

(4) the person whose parents both were born in Utah

(5) the Japanese immigrant who returns to Japan

Questions 21 and 22 are based on the following passage and cartoon.

The United States relies on the nation's bureaucracy, the vast network of agencies and departments that help the U.S. President do the work of government. The 2.8 million bureaucrats who get their paychecks from the government do everything from working for the Veteran's Administration to running the Social Security Administration to overseeing air flight regulations. Bureaucracies are known for their red tape: the inability to take action until all procedures or routines have been completed.

"It's called 'The Bureaucracy Game'. The first player that moves loses."

["The Bureaucracy Game" by Tim Tyler. Reprinted with permission.]

21. What is the purpose of the nation's bureaucracy?

(1) to help carry out the government's work

(2) to help the president write laws

(3) to defend the United States

(4) to run the nation's court system

(5) to work with other countries

22. What does the cartoon imply is a problem of the bureaucracy?

(1) There are too many bureaucrats.

(2) The bureaucracy plays political games.

(3) The bureaucracy is slow to do anything.

(4) Only men are bureaucrats.

(5) Bureaucrats are not elected.

Questions 23 and 24 are based on the following document.

JUROR SUMMONS

SUMMONS FOR JURY SERVICE
IN THE
STATE OF TEXAS   COUNTY OF WELLINGTON

WELLINGTON COUNTY COURTHOUSE
1001 PEARL STREET
BEAUMONT, TX 77701

MARY ANN JONES
3902 MAIN ST
BEAUMONT, TX 77703

State Of Texas
County of Wellington

JUROR BADGE

JUROR NO. 47346   PANEL NO. 95060501

THIS COURT SUMMONS YOU TO APPEAR FOR JURY DUTY AT THE TIME AND PLACE SHOWN BELOW.

YOUR REPORTING DATE IS:			
JANUARY	11	XXXX	8:00 AM
Month	Day	Year	Time

You will serve in the Courthouse located at: SEE MAP ON BACK
CENTRAL JURY ROOM
1001 PEARL STREET
BEAUMONT, TX 77701

Recorded Message Phone #:   1-800-555-1234

23. Which assumption can you make from reading the summons?
  (1) The judicial branch is responsible for writing laws.
  (2) People from one state can be called to serve on juries in other states.
  (3) A courthouse is where the executive and legislative branches meet.
  (4) People are called to serve on juries in their own regions.
  (5) Mary Ann Jones is under arrest.

24. Which part of the Juror Summons indicates the use of recent technology in the judicial process?
  (1) the summons itself
  (2) the juror badge
  (3) the map on the back
  (4) the reporting date
  (5) the badge's county seal

Question 25 refers to the following information.

In the United States, the Miranda Rights are given to people placed under arrest: "You have the right to remain silent. Anything you say can and will be used against you in a court of law. You have the right to talk to a lawyer and have one present with you while you are being questioned. If you cannot afford to hire a lawyer, one will be appointed to represent you before any questioning, if you wish one."

25. Police read these rights to people they arrest and accuse of a crime. With which opinion would the writer of the Miranda Rights most likely agree?
  (1) Once arrested, a person is better off talking to the police before anyone else.
  (2) Convicted criminals should have few rights.
  (3) If you haven't done anything wrong, then you don't need a lawyer.
  (4) The police have your best interests at heart.
  (5) Everyone should have the right to legal representation.

Questions 26 and 27 are based on the following map and passage.

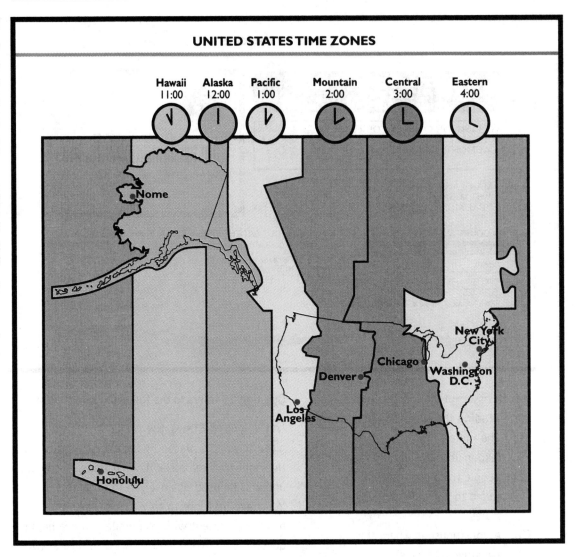

UNITED STATES TIME ZONES

Hawaii	Alaska	Pacific	Mountain	Central	Eastern
11:00	12:00	1:00	2:00	3:00	4:00

Nome

New York City

Chicago

Denver

Washington D.C.

Los Angeles

Honolulu

Our day and night are created when Earth rotates, or turns, on its axis. It takes Earth 24 hours to make one complete rotation. This means that if it is 1:00 P.M. in New York, it will take 24 hours of turning, or rotating, before it is 1:00 P.M. again in that part of the world.

To make time standard in the world, scientists have divided Earth into two dozen segments, or time zones. For every zone, time changes by one hour. So when it is 10:00 A.M. in Oregon, it is 9:00 A.M. in Alaska, which is one segment farther west, in the next time zone.

26. According to the map, the 50 states within the United States fall within how many time zones?
    (1) two
    (2) three
    (3) four
    (4) five
    (5) six

27. If it is 3:00 P.M. in New York City, what meal are people probably eating in Los Angeles?
    (1) breakfast
    (2) mid-morning snack
    (3) lunch
    (4) dinner
    (5) bedtime snack

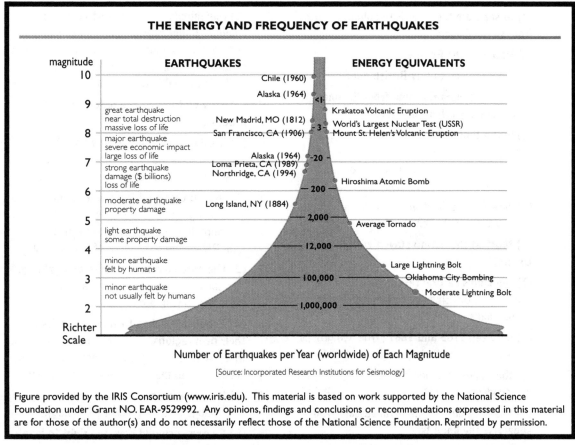

THE ENERGY AND FREQUENCY OF EARTHQUAKES

EARTHQUAKES

ENERGY EQUIVALENTS

Chile (1960)

Alaska (1964)

Krakatoa Volcanic Eruption

great earthquake
near total destruction
massive loss of life

New Madrid, MO (1812)

World's Largest Nuclear Test (USSR)

San Francisco, CA (1906)

Mount St. Helen's Volcanic Eruption

major earthquake
severe economic impact
large loss of life

strong earthquake
damage ($ billions)
loss of life

Alaska (1964)
Loma Prieta, CA (1989)
Northridge, CA (1994)

Hiroshima Atomic Bomb

moderate earthquake
property damage

Long Island, NY (1884)

light earthquake
some property damage

Average Tornado

minor earthquake
felt by humans

Large Lightning Bolt

Oklahoma City Bombing

minor earthquake
not usually felt by humans

Moderate Lightning Bolt

Richter
Scale

Number of Earthquakes per Year (worldwide) of Each Magnitude

[Source: Incorporated Research Institutions for Seismology]

Figure provided by the IRIS Consortium (www.iris.edu). This material is based on work supported by the National Science Foundation under Grant NO. EAR-9529992. Any opinions, findings and conclusions or recommendations expresssed in this material are for those of the author(s) and do not necessarily reflect those of the National Science Foundation. Reprinted by permission.

28. Which statement does the diagram best support?
- **(1)** Most earthquakes give off only small amounts of energy.
- **(2)** Earthquakes occur mainly in Asia.
- **(3)** In the United States, only Californians should fear earthquakes.
- **(4)** Human-made explosions release more energy than any earthquake does.
- **(5)** Humans can feel almost all the earthquakes that Earth experiences.

29. Which assumption can you make based on the diagram?
- **(1)** Most earthquakes occur in the Americas.
- **(2)** Most people will die because of earthquakes.
- **(3)** Many people are afraid of earthquakes.
- **(4)** All earthquakes give off some amount of energy.
- **(5)** Earthquakes will eventually separate California from the United States.

Question 30 is based on the following quote.

"...The sanddrifts now lay before us like a boundless sea, and it was not without sundry misgivings that we entered this forbidding realm... We suffered most from the July heat, which at midday rose to 113 Fahr. in the shade, and at night was never less than 73. No sooner did the sun appear above the horizon than it scorched us mercilessly. In the daytime, the heat enveloped us on all sides, above from the sun, below from the burning ground...The air, too, was terribly dry; no dew fell, and rain-clouds dispersed without sending more than a few drops to earth..."

30. From this description, where do you assume the author was traveling?
- **(1)** through a forest
- **(2)** on vacation
- **(3)** across many rivers
- **(4)** across a desert
- **(5)** in the mountains

Social Studies Pretest Answers and Explanations

1. **(2) to separate the American colonies from Great Britain**

2. **(3) Power to the People!**

3. **(3) They refused to buy British goods.**

4. **(4) More immigrants came from Europe than from any other continent.**

5. **(4) in the Southeast** Based on the map and passage, you can deduce that most slave owners lived in the Confederates states, in the Southeast region of the United States.

6. **(5) New Mexico Territory** It is a warm area in the West, next to Texas—a slave state.

7. **(1) Most of the nation stayed with the Union.**

8. **(1) the land's natural resources** Both the French and British saw economic advantages to the land's resources of fur and fish.

9. **(5) between 1763 and 1867** The two groups formed a union of their colonies.

10. **(5) the 1900s** Canada gained its independence in 1931.

11. **(1) The king directs the royal vassals, who supervise the knights.**

12. **(5) Kings are the ultimate authority.**

13. **(1) The cost will go up.** The text indicates that costs are currently going up, and the graph indicates that the number of enrollees is climbing, which would cause the cost of Medicare to rise.

14. **(5) The number of people reaching the age of 65 is expected to grow.**

15. **(4) Medicare Cuts Benefits Due to Budget Limits** This is a likely effect of the sharp rise in Medicare enrollment projected for 2010.

16. **(3) Most Americans contribute less than $501 to charity every year.** More than half (60.9%) contribute less than $501 to charity.

17. **(2) There is a free flow of people and products across borders.**

18. **(1) Individuals have the most economic freedom under capitalism.** Both socialism and communism include a level of government control over industries, thus limiting the role of the individual in the economy.

19. **(2) They go through the naturalization process.**

20. **(5) the Japanese immigrant who returns to Japan** This is the only option that describes a person who would not be an American citizen.

21. **(1) to help carry out the government's work** The passage states, "The United States... relies on the nation's bureaucracy... [to] help the U.S. President do the work of government."

22. **(3) The bureaucracy is slow to do anything.** The cartoon says that any bureaucrat who takes action will lose the game.

23. **(4) People are called to serve on juries in their own regions.** The document shows that Mary Ann Jones, from Beaumont, Texas, has been called to the courthouse in Beaumont.

24. **(2) the juror badge** The bar code on the juror badge indicates recent technology.

25. **(5) Everyone should have the right to legal representation.** The Miranda Rights are read to anyone who is arrested. They focus on the right of the accused to have a lawyer.

26. **(5) six** The continental United States is within four time zones, but Alaska is in a fifth time zone, and Hawaii is in a sixth time zone.

27. **(3) lunch** It would be 12:00 noon in Los Angeles, a time when most people eat lunch.

28. **(1) Most earthquakes give off only small amounts of energy.** Almost all of the earthquakes are a magnitude 2.

29. **(4) All earthquakes give off some amount of energy.**

30. **(4) across a desert** The words *sanddrifts, heat, scorched,* and *terribly dry* all apply to deserts.

Circle the question numbers that you got incorrect. Use this information to determine the skills and content areas in which you need more work.

	Comprehension	Application	Analysis	Evaluation
U.S. History	3	2	1, 4, 5, 6	7
World History	8, 10		9, 11	12
Economics		15	13, 14, 17	16, 18
Civics and Government	19, 21, 22	20, 24	23, 25	
Geography	26	27	29, 30	28

In this program, you'll meet a GED graduate whose return to school led to a successful career in politics. You'll get some tips on how to read maps and graphics and find out what other kinds of knowledge and skills you'll need to pass the GED Social Studies Test.

BEFORE YOU WATCH

16

Passing the GED Social Studies Test

OBJECTIVES

1. Examine the types of questions and graphics on the test.

2. Determine the number of items and how long you will have to take the test.

3. Explore the social studies content areas on the test.

You may live in a huge city or a tiny village. Good jobs may be plentiful in your area, or they may be scarce. Local politicians may or may not be doing a good job running your community. Geography, economics, and government play huge roles in your home and work lives.

Geography, economics, and government are three of the topics covered by the GED Social Studies Test. In addition, the Social Studies Test covers U.S. history and world history. Knowing about history is important because it helps us better understand the present.

The GED Social Studies Test assesses your ability to use what you already know about social studies, what you read on the test, and your critical thinking skills to correctly answer questions. It is not a test of recalling facts.

How can you prepare for the GED Social Studies Test? First, use the video, workbook, and online lessons to familiarize yourself with the test. Take the practice tests to see how well you do and in what areas you need improvement. You can also prepare by paying closer attention to the news to learn about global and national events. In that way, you will learn about the history that forms the background to those events. And you will learn more about current topics in geography, economics, and government.

For additional practice, visit *LiteracyLink* online at
http://www.pbs.org/literacy.

GED Social Studies Test Overview

The GED Social Studies Test assesses your ability to understand, analyze, apply, and evaluate social studies information. You do not need to memorize social studies facts. However, familiarity with important social studies concepts and key events will help you pass the test.

You will have 70 minutes to answer 50 multiple-choice questions. Each question has five possible answers, and you must choose the best one. Questions are based on documents, brief reading passages, and graphics, including charts, tables, graphs, maps, photographs, and editorial cartoons. This workbook will give you practice with these different types of materials.

The questions on the GED Social Studies Test are divided into five main content areas. These correspond to the videos you will see and to the lessons that go with them in this book.

- **U.S. History (25%)**—from the time of Native Americans to the present.
- **World History (15%)**—from ancient times to the present.
- **Economics (20%)**—including basic concepts, such as types of economic systems and supply and demand.
- **Civics and Government (25%)**—including how federal, state, and local governments work and the role of the citizen in the nation.
- **Geography (15%)**—including peoples, regions, and natural resources.

The questions on the GED Social Studies Test can also be described by the reading and thinking skills needed to answer them. These skills will be explained further in the video you are about to see and in this lesson.

- **Comprehension (20%)**—requires that you understand what you read and see in graphics.
- **Application (20%)**—requires that you use information you are given in a new situation.
- **Analysis (40%)**—asks you to figure out relationships among ideas.
- **Evaluation (20%)**—requires that you make judgments about the information you are given.

Finally, this lesson will give you practice in reading and answering questions about the different types of social studies passages and graphics that you will find on the test. These include:

- **Bar graphs**—show and compare quantities.
- **Line graphs**—show changes over time.
- **Maps**—show political divisions, physical features, resources, and other features.
- **Editorial cartoons**—comment on current events and people in the news.

➡ **NOW WATCH PROGRAM 16:**

Try the sample questions and pay close attention to the explanations of the correct answers—these can help you develop strategies to use on test day. As you watch, think about activities in your own life that relate to Social Studies, so you can focus your study on areas with which you're least familiar.

After you watch the program, work on:

PBS LiteracyLink®

- pages 13–24 in this workbook
- Internet activities at http://www.pbs.org/literacy

Key Social Studies Concepts and Skills

The video program presented an overview of the GED Social Studies Test. This workbook lesson will give you the opportunity to learn some of the basic skills and concepts that you will be using on the GED Social Studies Test.

KEY SKILLS

The GED Social Studies Test will assess your knowledge and understanding of social studies topics through the following types of skill questions:

- Comprehension
- Application
- Analysis
- Evaluation
- Interpreting Graphics

Understanding What You Read: Comprehension

About one-fifth of the questions on the GED Social Studies Test are comprehension questions. These questions require you to understand the information in reading passages, graphs, maps, diagrams, or cartoons.

When answering comprehension questions, you may have to:
- summarize the main idea of a passage or graphic
- restate information in other words
- identify ideas that are implied or suggested, but not actually stated, in the passage or graphic

Now try your comprehension skills by reading this passage.

> During the New Stone Age, between 8,000 and 3,500 B.C., some societies mastered agriculture. They learned to cultivate grain and domesticated some animals. The development of agriculture led to permanent settlements. For the first time in human history, food surpluses existed. This meant that farmers could produce enough food to support people who did not farm. A new group arose—people who made goods such as tools and woven cloth in exchange for food.

GED PRACTICE

Based on the information in the passage, which of the following was true of the time <u>before</u> the New Stone Age?

(1) Dogs and cattle had been domesticated.
(2) Barley and other grains had been successfully cultivated.
(3) Human groups moved from place to place to find food.
(4) Specialized toolmakers were an important part of society.
(5) Many small towns were surrounded by farmland.

Using What You Read: Application

One of the purposes of learning about social studies is to use what you have learned. Often you learn a general principle or idea and apply it to a specific situation. For example, arithmetic skills such as addition and subtraction can be applied to balance a checkbook or plan your food budget.

On the GED Social Studies Test, you may be given some general facts, such as those in the following table, and asked to apply them to a new situation.

REQUIREMENTS FOR U.S. OFFICE			
Office	**Citizenship**	**Age**	**Residency**
President and Vice President	Natural (born in the United States)	At least 35	Has lived in the United States for 14 or more years
Senator	U.S. citizen for 9 or more years	At least 30	Lives in state where elected
Representative in Congress	U.S. citizen for 7 or more years	At least 25	Lives in state where elected

Read the following passage about Dwight D. Eisenhower, the 34th President. Then use the table to check his qualifications for the office.

> Dwight D. Eisenhower was born in 1890 in Texas. He attended the U.S. Military Academy at West Point from 1911–1915. He became a professional soldier, and served in the U.S. Army for many years, including World War II. He was elected president on November 4, 1952.

Use this information to see how Eisenhower fulfilled each of the three requirements listed in the row next to *President*.

- *Citizenship*—Eisenhower was a natural citizen because he was born in the United States (in the state of Texas).
- *Age*—He was at least 35 years old—actually 62 when he was elected.
- *Residency*—Even though he was overseas off and on during the 14 years before his election, he had lived in the United States from his birth to his first overseas assignment in 1922 at the age of 32. The 14-year requirement does not need to be consecutive years, nor must the 14 years be those immediately before the election.

Eisenhower met all three requirements for the office of President.

GED PRACTICE

At 25, Carla Mendez was the youngest woman elected to her state legislature. At the age of 32, Ms. Mendez considered a run for U.S. office. Ms. Mendez, who emigrated from Mexico when she was 5 and became a U.S. citizen when she was 20, was eligible to run for which office or offices?

(1) president

(2) vice president

(3) senator only

(4) representative only

(5) senator or representative

Answers and explanations start on page 252.

SOCIAL STUDIES

Thinking About What You Read: Analysis

Identifying Cause and Effect

In social studies, ideas, facts, and events are often linked. One type of linkage is the cause-and-effect relationship. One thing (the cause) results in another (the effect). For example, if you miss your local voter registration deadline (a cause), you will not be able to vote in the next election (an effect).

When you interpret social studies passages or graphics, look for cause-and-effect relationships. Remember that in history, a cause must happen before its effect. Study this timeline and answer the question that follows.

IMPORTANT EVENTS DURING PRESIDENT NIXON'S ADMINISTRATION

1969	1970	1971	1972	1973	1974
Apollo 11 and 12 astronauts land on moon.	Nixon orders the invasion of Cambodia.		Nixon visits U.S.S.R.; signs Strategic Arms Limitation Treaty.	Senate hearings on Watergate scandal begin; Nixon is implicated in cover-up.	Nixon resigns; only president to do so.
Massive protests against the Vietnam War.	Massive protests against the Cambodian invasion.		Nixon becomes first president to visit China.	Vice President Spiro Agnew resigns.	

Which event caused Nixon to resign in 1974?

_____

If you answered **the Watergate scandal,** you are right. Nixon's role in the Watergate scandal led to his resignation. Most of the other events on the timeline did not reflect poorly on his actions as president.

GED PRACTICE

In the years after his resignation, Nixon's reputation for significant foreign policy achievement grew. Which of the following events is most likely to have contributed to this view of Nixon?

    (1)   the first moon landings by Apollo astronauts, in 1969

    (2)   the invasion of Cambodia, in 1970

    (3)   the first visit to China by a U.S. president, in 1972

    (4)   the Senate committee investigation into Watergate, in 1973

    (5)   the resignation of Vice President Spiro Agnew, in 1973

Answers and explanations start on page 252.

Distinguishing Facts from Opinions

When you read and interpret social studies materials, you need to distinguish facts from opinions. Facts are items that can be proven to be true. Opinions cannot be proven true: they are ideas or beliefs about something, and they are based on a person's values and background. For example, it is a fact that the Mississippi River is the longest river in the United States. It is a fact because it can be proven through measurement. However, it is an opinion that the Mississippi is the most beautiful river in the United States. Some may think so, but others may not.

Here is a passage that contains both facts and opinions.

> Brooklyn, Ohio, a suburb of Cleveland, was the first place in the United States to ban drivers from talking on cell phones while driving. People caught disobeying this law face a penalty of $100 plus $45 in court costs. Brooklyn's mayor, John Coyne, believes the ordinance is just common sense. If you are driving, he says, you need to concentrate on the road and keep both hands on the wheel. Cell phones distract from driving, according to the mayor, making accidents more likely.
>
> The Cellular Telecommunications Industry Association, a trade group, opposes Brooklyn's new law. Tom Wheeler, president of the group, says the issue should be the driver, not the phone. Many things can distract a driver, including the kids in the back seat. Wheeler claims that cell phones have made driving safer. Nearly 100,000 cell phone calls a day are made by motorists seeking help, he says.

a. What is Wheeler's opinion of Brooklyn's ban on using cell phones while driving?

_____

b. What facts did he use to support his opinion? _____

_____

To find the answer, reread the second paragraph of the passage.
a. Wheeler thinks that Brooklyn's ban on cell phones is a bad idea.
b. Wheeler claims that 100,000 cell phone calls are made daily by motorists seeking help.

GED PRACTICE

Which of the following statements is an opinion rather than a fact?

    (1)   Brooklyn, Ohio, was the first place in the United States to ban the use of cell phones while driving.

    (2)   Drivers who talk on a cell phone while driving in Brooklyn face a penalty of $100 plus $45 in court costs.

    (3)   The ban on cell phones while driving is simply a matter of common sense.

    (4)   The Cellular Telecommunications Industry Association opposes Brooklyn's new law.

    (5)   A number of different things can distract a person who is driving a car.

Answers and explanations start on page 252.

Comparing and Contrasting

When you compare things, you note how they are alike. When you contrast them, you note how they are different. For example, when you shop for clothes, you may compare similar items to see how they are alike in color, fabric, or style. You also contrast the items to see how they differ in price. Your buying decision is based on comparing and contrasting.

Comparing and contrasting are thinking skills needed to answer some of the questions on the GED Social Studies Test. For example, you may need to compare and contrast

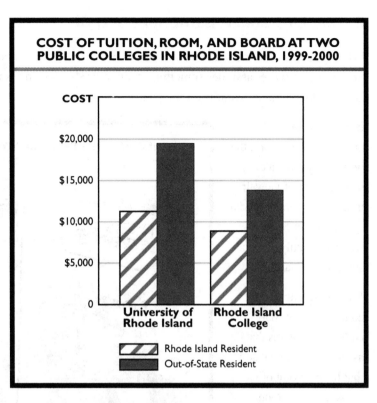

COST OF TUITION, ROOM, AND BOARD AT TWO PUBLIC COLLEGES IN RHODE ISLAND, 1999-2000

data in a graph. The graph above shows the cost of tuition, room, and board for students who are state residents and for out-of-state students at two public colleges in Rhode Island.

What statement could be made about the difference in the cost of tuition, room, and board for Rhode Island College students?

_____

_____

Contrast the height of the bars on the graph. **Out-of-state students are charged more than students who are state residents.**

GED PRACTICE

Which of the following statements is supported by the bar graph?

(1) It is more cost effective to attend an out-of-state college rather than a local college.
(2) The cost of attending the University of Rhode Island is about $8,000 higher for out-of-state students than for Rhode Island residents.
(3) Rhode Island residents who attend Rhode Island College pay about half the amount out-of-state students pay.
(4) Out-of-state residents pay less tuition, room, and board than Rhode Island residents.
(5) Tuition at the University of Rhode Island for out-of-state students is double the cost of tuition for Rhode Island residents.

Answers and explanations start on page 252.

Judging What You Read: Evaluation

Seeing Unstated Assumptions and Bias

When you evaluate social studies materials, you often must go beyond what is directly stated. Sometimes a writer assumes something that he or she does not say. Seeing what is unstated is key to understanding what is on the page.

Beyond his or her unstated assumptions, the writer may have a clear bias or point of view. It is important to understand a writer's point of view when you analyze social studies material.

Editorials, letters to the editor, and editorial cartoons are items that assume a great deal and that have a point of view. Look at this cartoon about the Internal Revenue Service—the agency that collects federal taxes—and a typical taxpayer.

IMPROVING THE TAXPAYER-IRS RELATIONSHIP

[Source: Clay Jones, *Honolulu Star Bulletin*. Reprinted by permission.]

What does the cartoonist assume about the American taxpayer?

_____

_____

Look at the way the cartoonist shows the taxpayer. He is upside down, helpless, being forced to pay every dollar and cent he owes. **The cartoonist assumes that taxpayers are helpless and that they are no match for the IRS.**

GED PRACTICE

What is the cartoonist's point of view of the IRS?

   (1) It does an excellent job of collecting taxes.
   (2) It is an agency of the federal government.
   (3) It cannot force taxpayers to pay their taxes.
   (4) It is not sincerely interested in the taxpayer.
   (5) It treats taxpayers with great respect and care.

Answers and explanations start on page 252.

SOCIAL STUDIES

Evaluating the Role of Values and Beliefs

What you believe and value influences the choices you make in life. For example, if you value honesty, you try not to lie. If you value friendship, you try to be a good friend to others. Similarly, the decisions individuals and societies make reflect the values they hold. As Americans, we reveal our values through the people we elect as our leaders. We also reveal our nation's values through different government spending programs. How we help different nations through our foreign policy and how we use and recycle natural resources are also indications of what we, as Americans, believe and value.

When you read social studies materials, be alert to the role that values and beliefs play. Here is a selection about the U.S. economy and how people make important decisions based on their beliefs about the economy:

> During the late 1990s, the labor market was tighter than at any time during the previous 30 years. The unemployment rate was low, and employers were adding new jobs each month. In fact, workers' confidence was so high that the "quit rate" rose to 14.5 percent. The "quit rate" is the percentage of employees who quit one job before they have found another.

Why do people who have jobs quit them before they find new jobs?

_____

If you answered that **the workers quit because they believe they will be able to find better jobs very easily you are right.** The level of confidence people have in the economy influences their decisions about which job to take, how long to hold it, and how, when, and whether to look for new jobs.

GED PRACTICE

1. What would a decrease in the "quit rate" indicate?

    (1) Employers have confidence in their long-time employees.
    (2) Employers are not trying to hold on to valued employees.
    (3) Workers are more confident in their ability to find better jobs.
    (4) Workers think it is too risky to leave a job without having another.
    (5) The economy is continuing to grow at a record pace.

2. What would employees who quit one job before having another job probably value?

    (1) loyalty
    (2) kindness
    (3) ambition
    (4) helpfulness
    (5) thriftiness

Answers and explanations start on page 252.

Interpreting Social Studies Graphics

Reading Double-Bar Graphs

In social studies, numbers are often presented in a graph, making them easy to read and interpret. Glancing at a graph gives you a quick overview of the meaning of the numbers. Studying a graph gives you the details.

A bar graph is used to show quantities. For example, an economist may want to show how much the U.S. Treasury has taken in (receipts) and paid out (outlays). He or she can present the information in a double-bar graph. A double-bar graph shows sets of information for easy comparison.

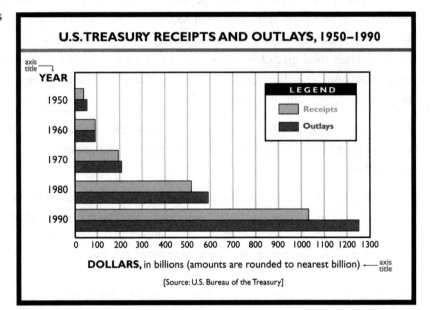

When you read a bar graph, pay particular attention to the following items:

- **Graph Title** The title tells you the topic. This graph shows how much money came into and went out of the U.S. Treasury.
- **Axis Titles** In this case, the vertical axis shows years and the horizontal axis shows dollar amounts in billions.
- **Legend** The legend tells how information is shown. In this case, green bars show money coming in and blue bars show money going out.
- **Bars** The height or length of a bar lines up with one of the axes. It shows you how much. For example, to find receipts for 1980, locate 1980 on the vertical axis. Then look at the green bar for that year. The 1980 receipts were about 520 billion dollars.

How much money left the Treasury in 1950? _____

If you answered **almost 50 billion dollars,** you are right. The blue bar lined up with 1950 shows the Treasury laid out almost 50 billion dollars—halfway between 0 and 100.

GED PRACTICE

Which year had the greatest difference between receipts and outlays?

(1) 1950
(2) 1960
(3) 1970
(4) 1980
(5) 1990

Answers and explanations start on page 252.

Interpreting Line Graphs

In social studies, line graphs are an excellent way to show numeric changes over time. They present historical data in a way that is easy to grasp. For example, a political scientist could show changes in voter turnout in the last 50 years. An economist could show the growth of the gross national product. A geographer could show population growth in a particular nation.

This line graph shows the number of immigrants who arrived in the United States each year. The data cover the years 1835 to 1996.

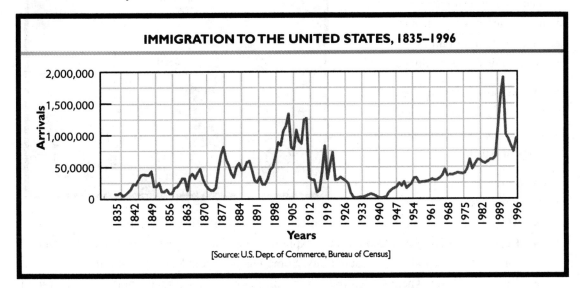

When you read a line graph, pay attention to the following items:

- **Graph Title**   The title states the topic: immigration to the United States from 1835 to 1996.
- **Axis Titles**   Each axis title tells what is shown on the axis. In this case, the vertical axis shows the approximate number of arrivals, and the horizontal axis shows the years.
- **Data Points**   A point on the line gives you the number of arrivals for a particular year. For example, in 1996 about 900,000 people arrived.
- **Trends**   The line itself shows trends. An upward slope shows an increase: from 1947 to 1991, for example. A downward slope shows a decrease.

Look at the graph to answer this question: What year had the most new immigrants?

To find the answer, look for the highest point on the trend line. The year **1991** had the most new immigrants—about 1,800,000.

GED PRACTICE

Immigration usually decreases during periods of economic depression or war. Which of the following changes in the number of immigrants was probably the result of a prolonged depression and/or war?

(1) 1849 to 1856
(2) 1877 to 1884
(3) 1905 to 1912
(4) 1933 to 1947
(5) 1989 to 1995

Interpreting Maps

Maps are an important part of the GED Social Studies Test, so understanding how to read them is an important skill. There are many types of maps showing different aspects of an area. For example, maps can show political boundaries; physical features, such as mountains and rivers; transportation networks; natural resources; population density; and climate.

One of the most common types of maps shows the boundaries of nations and states. This map shows the political divisions of Australia.

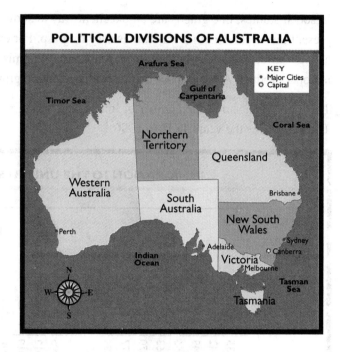

POLITICAL DIVISIONS OF AUSTRALIA

When you read a map, pay attention to the following items:

- **Map Title**   The title gives you the topic of the map: political divisions of Australia.
- **Legend or Key**   The legend, if any, explains symbols. This map uses different symbols for major cities and for the capital city. Some legends include a scale of miles.
- **Compass Rose**   The compass rose shows direction. On most maps, north is at the top of the map, and the other directions are indicated.

Look at the map above. Which city is on the west coast of Australia?

_____

To find the answer, check the compass rose to find which direction is west: to the left. Then locate the city shown on the west coast: **Perth.**

GED PRACTICE

The capital of Australia is located in which state?

(1) Western Australia
(2) Queensland
(3) New South Wales
(4) Victoria
(5) South Australia

Answers and explanations start on page 252.

SOCIAL STUDIES

Looking at Other Common Maps

Another common type of map shows the physical features of an area. Physical features include natural formations, such as lakes, rivers, plains, and mountains. This map shows the physical features of Australia.

Notice how this map of Australia differs from the one on the previous page. It does not show political boundaries or cities. Instead, it shows the major features of the landscape: seas, deserts, rivers, and mountains. The legend or key shows the symbols used for deserts and mountains.

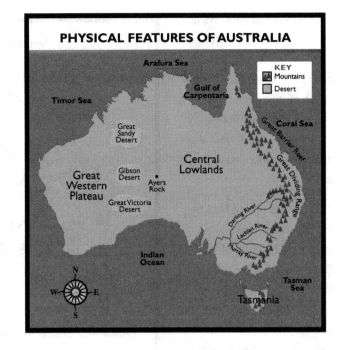

PHYSICAL FEATURES OF AUSTRALIA

In what area is the driest part of Australia located? _____

Since deserts are dry areas, look at the key to see how deserts are shown on the map. They are shaded areas. Now look at the map to find the part of Australia that contains the most deserts (shaded areas). Australia's three deserts are all in one area, **the western part.**

GED PRACTICE

1. In what area are ski resorts most likely to be located?

    (1) Ayers Rock
    (2) Great Western Plateau
    (3) Great Dividing Range
    (4) Darling River valley
    (5) Gulf of Carpentaria

2. An Australian family wants grow apples and pears. In which part of the country are they likely to establish the most successful orchard?

    (1) Ayers Rock
    (2) Great Western Plateau
    (3) Great Dividing Range
    (4) Darling River valley
    (5) Gulf of Carpentaria

Answers and explanations start on page 252.

Interpreting Editorial Cartoons

Opinions about the news are often expressed in editorial cartoons. Editorial cartoons can be found on the editorial pages of newspapers and news magazines. They may express a point of view about an issue or poke fun at people in the news.

The cartoon shown here is about women in the U.S. military. The point of view of this cartoon is that although the number of women in the military has grown in the last 25 years, women still face opposition from many high-ranking male officers.

WOMEN IN THE MILITARY

[Source: Reprinted with permission of North American Syndicate.]

In a cartoon, one person or thing often represents a larger group. For example, in this cartoon the man represents male Army recruiters and trainers. Who does the woman represent?

_____

The woman represents **women in the military.** You can tell because she is wearing a military uniform.

GED PRACTICE

Which of the following statements most closely reflects the cartoonist's point of view about women in the military?

    (1)   Women are tough enough to serve in the armed forces partly because they often deal with opposition from male soldiers.

    (2)   Women should not be allowed to serve in the armed forces.

    (3)   Although women should not serve in the Army, they may serve in the other armed forces.

    (4)   Although women may serve in the Army, they should not serve in combat positions.

    (5)   Most women who enlist in the armed services are not tough enough to get through basic training, much less combat situations.

Answers and explanations start on page 253.

SOCIAL STUDIES

How did diverse cultures come together to create the American nation? An archaeologist at the first permanent British settlement of Jamestown, a college professor who portrays abolitionist Frederick Douglass, and a historian at the Museum of the Cherokee Indian are a few of the people who bring the story of the United States to life in this program.

Themes in U.S. History

OBJECTIVES

1. Explore the multicultural nature of U.S. society.

2. Recognize how technology has changed work and working in the United States.

3. Identify how Americans gained some of their rights and freedoms.

4. Investigate the rise of the United States as a world power during the twentieth century.

You can refer to the U.S. history timelines on pages 29 and 272 as you work through this lesson.

Why do we study history? History gives us a sense of what people and life were like in the past. Studying history allows us to understand why our world is the way it is now and how it became that way. If we understand history, we can better deal with changes we face in our lives today and in our future. We can see how changes in the past affected other Americans and we can learn from them.

Knowing how to identify important events in the history of the United States and how to figure out what they meant will help you succeed on the GED Social Studies Test. In addition, the skills you gain in applying and evaluating social studies information will prove valuable in your study of other subjects, as well as in real life.

On the following pages, you will find a brief exercise called *Sneak Preview*. It introduces you to the topics in the video program and the corresponding lesson. After you complete the exercise and check your answers, turn to the vocabulary on page 28. There you will find terms that will help you better understand the video and the lessons that follow. After reviewing page 28, you will be ready to watch Program 17.

For additional practice, visit *LiteracyLink* online at http://www.pbs.org/literacy.

Sneak Preview

This exercise previews some of the concepts from Program 17. After you answer the questions, use the chart on page 27 to help set your learning goals.

FAMILY LINK: Homer has come home with a history assignment. He asks his grandfather, "What is the most important event that has taken place in your lifetime?" His grandfather thinks for a moment. Then he begins to tell Homer the story of astronaut John Glenn's first orbit around Earth.

A Story That's Out of This World

The story Homer's grandfather told took place on February 20, 1962. On that day, President John F. Kennedy sat silent, watching a television set. Television sets also held the attention of 9,000 people at Grand Central Station in New York City and thousands upon thousands all over the country. At Florida's Cape Canaveral, astronaut John Glenn sat in the spacecraft Friendship 7, waiting for the countdown. An earth-shuddering blastoff started his journey.

In the 4 hours, 55 minutes Glenn was in space that day, he orbited the earth three times. He watched the sun rise and set and rise and set, again and again, as he circled the globe. Then Glenn's spacecraft reentered earth's atmosphere and landed in the Atlantic Ocean. Americans were overjoyed.

John Glenn was not the first person to orbit the earth. However, his successful voyage focused America's attention and technology on developing a space program that would be unrivaled. Only seven years would pass before another American would become the first human to set foot on the moon. Today Americans are working together with people from a number of different nations on an international space station. Americans are considering sending astronauts to our neighbor planet Mars. Since the days of John Glenn's first voyage, space is no longer just a setting for science fiction. It has become the new frontier.

Answer these questions based on the reading above.

1. Before Glenn's 1962 space flight, the Soviet Union had already sent two astronauts into orbit. Why would this motivate the United States to speed up its space efforts in the 1960s?

   (1) The United States targeted itself to be the world's leader in space technology.
   (2) The Soviet Union neglected to do experiments in space.
   (3) The United States was content to be second in the space race.
   (4) The United States wanted to cooperate with the Soviet Union any way it could.
   (5) The Soviets shared their technology secrets with the United States.

2. Space missions are expensive. After multiple U.S. moon landings, many people questioned the value of such landings. As a result, the government cut funding for further missions to the moon. What effect do you think this has had on government scientists planning space missions?

(1) They have decided not to send any more astronauts into space, since Americans don't value this kind of exploration.

(2) They have decided not to send astronauts on long missions, since they don't want people stranded far from Earth if funds get cut.

(3) They have decided to keep their plans for space exploration a secret, so that people cannot question the value of their programs.

(4) They have decided to spend all government funds quickly, because they never know when their funds will be cut.

(5) They have decided to keep costs low and fund programs that people are interested in, so their funds are less likely to be cut.

3. After John Glenn's successful voyage, President Kennedy called outer space "the new ocean." What did Kennedy mean by that?

(1) Space and the ocean are both mysterious.

(2) Space and the ocean are both big and blue.

(3) Soon people will find space travel as easy as ocean travel.

(4) Space separates Earth and other planets just as the ocean separates two continents.

(5) People will explore space as they once explored oceans.

4. Glenn knew that space travel was dangerous. Years later, when asked why he decided to ignore these risks, Glenn said, "While I wasn't rushing to leave this life any more than anyone else, I always felt it was more important how you live your life than how long you live." Which statement best explains what Glenn meant?

(1) A space mission is not a suicide mission.

(2) Space travel is very dangerous.

(3) Some things are important enough to risk death.

(4) The Soviet Union will be superior to the United States if I don't go.

(5) I will do anything for my country.

Feedback

- If you got all of the answers right...   you have the basic skills needed to understand U. S. history.

- If you missed question 1...   you need to develop your ability to identify key concepts important to U.S. history.

- If you missed question 2...   you need to work on connecting past and current events.

- If you missed question 3...   you need to work on understanding the impact the past can have on the future.

- If you missed question 4...   you need to work on identifying values.

Vocabulary for *Themes in U.S. History*

abolitionist	a person who fought to end slavery
amendment	an addition or change, especially to a law or legal document, such as the Constitution
apprentice	a young person who works for a period of years to learn a skill or trade from a craftsperson
colony	a settlement with close political ties to its parent country; colonists live in these settlements
communism	a system of government with a single party and state ownership of almost all property
democracy	a system of government in which people have many political and economic choices
immigrant	a person who leaves his or her homeland for a new life in another country
indentured	legally bound to work for someone for a certain number of years, generally in exchange for passage to a new homeland
industrialize	to replace human labor with machines
labor union	an organization of workers who try to get better wages, benefits, and working conditions
manifest destiny	the belief that it is the nation's future to stretch from ocean to ocean
manufacture	to make or produce goods
progressives	people who worked for the improvement of workers' lives and other reforms
secede	to break away from a nation and form a separate nation
segregation	the separation of groups of people, usually by race
self-sufficient	dependent only on oneself for life's necessities

---

➡ **NOW WATCH PROGRAM 17:**

The program covers American history from the earliest native people through the 20th century and can serve as the starting point for your study of American history. Which eras and events would you like to read more about? Pursue your interests at the library or online.

After you watch the program, work on:

- pages 29–48 in this workbook
- Internet activities at http://www.pbs.org/literacy

Themes in U.S. History

On the following pages, you will learn more about the ideas discussed in the video program and have an opportunity to develop and practice your GED social studies skills.

Key Points to Think About

In the video program, you explored:

- How the rights and freedoms of American citizens evolved over time.
- How the United States became a multicultural nation.
- How the United States assumed its position as world leader.

On the GED Social Studies Test:

- You will identify important events in the history of the United States.
- You should recognize how conflict leads to change.
- You will analyze information presented in charts, graphs, maps, and tables.

As you work through the lesson for Program 17:

- Keep in mind during what time period the events happened.
- Identify the kinds of information presented in illustrations.
- Be aware of current events that tie back to events in America's past.

U.S. HISTORY TIMELINE

more than 12,000 years ago
Humans first arrive in the Americas

1400s–1600s
European immigrants come to America

1776
American colonies declare independence from Britain

early 1800s
The United States joins the Industrial Revolution

1861–1865
Civil War fought and slavery is abolished

1917–1945
Two World Wars and the Great Depression

1945–present
The United States becomes a world power

You can refer to the United States map on page 271 as you work through this lesson.

A Multicultural Nation

The Beginning of a Nation

An **immigrant** is a person who leaves his or her homeland for a new life in a new place. The United States has been called a nation of immigrants. As LaDonna pointed out, everyone who lives here either is an immigrant or is descended from immigrants. Even Native Americans, who were the only people on this continent for thousands of years, were immigrants.

Scientists believe that Native Americans first came to this country from Asia. More than 12,000 years ago, a land bridge formed between Asia and North America at the Bering Strait, off the west coast of Alaska. Asians followed the animals they hunted across the Bering Strait land bridge to North America. Slowly they spread over the continent, settling North America and eventually South America.

The first Europeans in America were explorers. Some crossed the Atlantic Ocean around 1000. More began arriving in the late 1400s. For the next 300 years, the number of European immigrants grew and grew. Some Europeans brought Africans to America to work as servants or slaves.

The European immigrants formed colonies along North America's eastern coast. A **colony** is a settlement with political ties to the parent country. Britain controlled most of these colonies. In time, the colonists rebelled against British rule. In 1776, thirteen colonies declared independence and fought the Revolutionary War to break away from Britain. They won the war and organized their own government, forming the United States.

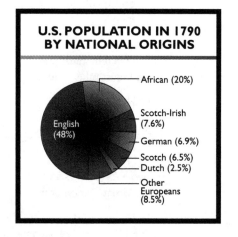

U.S. POPULATION IN 1790 BY NATIONAL ORIGINS

- English (48%)
- African (20%)
- Scotch-Irish (7.6%)
- German (6.9%)
- Scotch (6.5%)
- Dutch (2.5%)
- Other Europeans (8.5%)

SKILL PRACTICE

Use the reading and circle graph above to answer these questions.

1. Why could the first Native Americans be considered immigrants?

    _____

2. Based on the graph of the U.S. population in 1790, from which two places did more than two-thirds of Americans come? _____

3. Which was the largest group of immigrants in the colonies? Give one possible reason why.

    _____

4. Compare the information in the reading and the graph. Which group of Americans is not included in the graph? _____

Answers and explanations start on page 253.

SOCIAL STUDIES

Reasons for Immigrating

During the 1800s, the United States was called the Land of Opportunity. Some immigrants came for religious or political freedom; others came to earn a living. Often it was not just opportunity pulling immigrants to the United States. What was happening in their own nations often pushed them out. For example, in the 1800s Ireland was under British rule, and laws in Ireland would not allow Catholics to buy land. Over the years, Catholic farmers parceled off parts of their farm to their children. By the 1840s almost half of Ireland's farms were less than five acres. With such small plots, Irish farmers grew potatoes as the main crop since one and a half acres of potatoes could feed a family for a year.

Then, in 1845, disaster struck. A fungus infected Ireland's potatoes. For the next four years, the fungus turned Ireland's potato crops into black, uneatable pulp. A million people in Ireland starved to death. Those who could, left. Over the next decade, 1.3 million Irish immigrants entered the United States. The cartoons below show Irish immigrants on both sides of the Atlantic.

IRISHMAN CONSIDERING SAILING TO THE UNITED STATES

Reprinted by permission of the New York Historical Society Collection

IRISHMAN CONSIDERING SAILING BACK TO IRELAND

The Metropolitan Museum of Art, The Edward W. C. Arnold Collection of New York. Prints, Maps, and Pictures, Bequest of Edward W. C. Arnold, 1954. (54.90.227). Photographic Services, The Metropolitan Museum of Art, New York, NY 10028.

SKILL PRACTICE

Use the reading and cartoons above to answer these questions.

1. Why did many Irish immigrate to the United States in the 1840s? _____

   _____

2. Compare the cartoons above. What do these cartoons tell you about the fate of many Irish immigrants who came to the United States? _____

   _____

3. According to the cartoon on the right, what was the hope of many Irish immigrants?

   _____

Immigrants Yesterday and Today

Even after 200 years, people continue to move to the United States. Despite the growing number of immigrants, Vicki decided to write a letter against limiting immigration. She believes that immigrants worked hard to build the United States and that they continue to work hard today.

Most immigrants face difficulties trying to come to the United States. The journey here is often expensive and sometimes dangerous. Most immigrants have to leave behind people they love. However, this often motivates them once they get here. One Cambodian immigrant who came to the United States in the 1980s discussed why she works so hard in her new homeland:

> Another reason that I work and try to save money is to be able to sponsor my cousin and her family from Cambodia. . . . I would like for them to be here with us. . . . That's one of the main reasons I want to have this donut shop and try to keep it open. There're three reasons: for my children, for my cousin's family, and for the little house that I dream of.

The dreams of immigrants have remained similar throughout U.S. history. What has changed is the starting point of present-day immigrants. For example, most of the immigrants who first settled the colonies came from Europe. For much of the twentieth century, however, many immigrants have come from Asia, Mexico, Central America, and the Caribbean. Like the immigrants who came before them, some were pulled by opportunities in the United States. War or political pressure pushed others out of their own lands, as shown in the table below.

MAJOR IMMIGRATION GROUPS, 1910–1990			
COUNTRY OF ORIGIN	Periods of Greatest Migration	Number of Immigrants	Major Reasons
MEXICO	1910s–1920s 1950s–1990s	700,000 5 million	1910 Mexican Revolution, poverty, unemployment
CUBA	1960s–1970s	700,000	1959 Revolution, poverty, unemployment
DOMINICAN REPUBLIC, HAITI, JAMAICA	1970s–1980s	900,000	poverty, unemployment
VIETNAM	1970s–1980s	500,000	Vietnam War, move to communism

SKILL PRACTICE

Write *True* if the statement is true, *False* if it is false.

_____ 1. Most of the immigrants who settled the colonies were Asian.

_____ 2. Many immigrants come to the United States to escape political pressure.

_____ 3. People today immigrate for very different reasons from the immigrants of 100 years ago.

Answers and explanations start on page 253.

■ Apply What You Learn

Read the following article about the two sides of the issue of limiting immigration.
Then answer the questions that follow.

Setting Limits on Immigration: Yes or No?

In the history of the United States, one issue Americans have always debated is limits on immigration. Some Americans say immigrants take jobs away from U.S. citizens. They worry that the growing numbers of immigrants will use up the country's resources. These Americans want to limit immigration. Other Americans argue in favor of open immigration. They say that immigrants contribute to the nation's economic well-being. They maintain that many immigrants take jobs Americans do not want to do. They point to many immigrants' contributions to the United States. For example, Andrew Carnegie, who helped make steel a big business, came here from Scotland in 1847, when he was 12 years old. Irving Berlin, who wrote the song "God Bless America," came to the United States from Russia in the 1890s. Albert Einstein, the great German-born scientist, became a U.S. citizen in 1940.

SKILL PRACTICE

Answer the questions based on the information above.

1. Give two reasons people have for wanting to limit the number of immigrants coming to the United States. _____

    _____

2. Give two reasons people have for wanting to avoid limiting immigration. _____

    _____

3. Which side do you think has the strongest argument? Explain. _____

    _____

    _____

MATH Connection

On this table are 1994 immigration numbers from certain countries.

Immigrants to the United States, by Country of Birth (in thousands)
All Countries 804.4
  Dominican Republic 51.2
  El Salvador 17.6
  Mexico 111.4
  Philippines 53.5
  Vietnam 41.3

Use a calculator to divide each country number by the total number of immigrants.
This will tell you the percentage of immigration each country represents. For example, for the Dominican Republic, divide 51.2 by 804.4 to get .0636, rounded to 6.4%.

Work and Working

WORKPLACE LINK: Steven is happy because his boss just told him he can start working at home. He no longer has to fight traffic to get to the office every day. Right now, few people have the opportunity to work at home, although this number is growing. But Steven knows that in the early days of this country, many people worked at home.

A Self-Sufficient America

Steven was recalling times in early American history. Then, the colonists had to make almost everything they needed to live. They fed their families the crops grown on their farms. They fashioned many of their own tools. They built their houses from logs they cut from the trees around them. They **manufactured,** or made, their clothing, candles, and soap. They were, for the most part, **self-sufficient.** Children rarely went to school, so they could help with the work. During these times, Americans depended on themselves, their family, and their neighbors for life's necessities.

In time, craftspeople became more common. Soon many colonial towns had cabinetmakers, shoemakers, tailors, and printers. These specialists usually worked in their homes or in small shops, where they labored alongside their apprentices. An **apprentice** was a young person who made a promise to work for a master craftsperson for, usually, a term of seven years. During that time, the young person would learn the skills of the trade.

Other Americans had helpers who were **indentured,** or legally bound, to work for them for two to seven years. Their work was in exchange for their paid passage from Europe. After their indenture was up, they were free to start a farm or work in a craft or business of their own.

America of the 1700s was not quick to **industrialize,** or replace human muscle with power-driven machines. One reason for this was that Great Britain discouraged industrialization in the colonies. Without industrialization, the colonists would pay well for British machine-made goods. The British kept the plans for building industrial machines a closely guarded secret.

SKILL PRACTICE

Check all of the statements that are true. There may be more than one true statement.

_____ 1. America's early colonists depended on themselves for their needs.

_____ 2. In early America, apprentices often moved from job to job.

_____ 3. By the end of the 1700s, most Americans worked in factories.

_____ 4. Great Britain discouraged the building of factories in America.

Answers and explanations start on page 253.

The Factory System

As Americans busily worked in their homes and shops in the late 1700s, a revolution was going on in Great Britain. This was not a warlike form of revolution. Instead, it was a revolutionary change in how and where people worked, called the Industrial Revolution. The Industrial Revolution came about because of the invention of many large, labor-saving machines. These machines replaced hand-tools. With the Industrial Revolution, small craft shops were replaced by large factories in many parts of Great Britain.

By the early 1800s, the territory of the United States was vast—about two thirds of its present size. Despite the steady stream of immigrants coming to the United States, there were not enough people to do everything, such as clearing land for farms and manufacturing things people needed. Some Americans realized that the inventions of Europe's Industrial Revolution could help the United States grow more quickly. They memorized plans for labor-saving machines they saw in Great Britain and came back home to build them. In this way, the United States joined the Industrial Revolution.

The Industrial Revolution changed the lives of many Americans. In cities across the land, factories sprang up. Some factories manufactured cloth. Others produced clocks and tools. Factories could house many machines and employ many people in one place. Beginning in the 1800s, many people left their homes and shops to work in the new factories. Factory-created jobs also encouraged new immigrants to settle in the nation's cities.

Other inventions of the Industrial Revolution changed farming. New machines made farm work go more easily and more quickly. No longer did the whole family have to pitch in with the work. During this time, many young people left family farms to take jobs in factories.

PERCENTAGE OF AMERICANS EMPLOYED IN THE CHIEF OCCUPATIONS		
Occupations	**1820**	**1860**
Agriculture	71.88	59.70
Manufacturing	12.15	18.35
Other	15.97	21.95

SKILL PRACTICE

Answer the questions based on the above information.

1. What was the Industrial Revolution, and where did it begin?

    _____

2. In the 1800s, why did many new immigrants to the United States settle in cities?

    _____

3. Summarize the trends in American agriculture and industry up to 1860. Use information from the table to back up your answer.

    _____

    _____

Answers and explanations start on page 253.

Industries Grow, Work Changes

During the mid- and late 1800s, new inventions continued to change both the farm and the factory. Machines that could seed, reap, bind, and thresh increased farm output. Industrial machinery, too, was improved. For example, machines, such as the lathe and the plane, quickly fashioned wood products. There were even machines to make other machines! All these inventions helped industries grow rapidly in the United States.

Americans moving westward also spurred industrial growth. Settlement there brought both new sources of raw materials and new markets for factory goods. Newly built railroads soon crisscrossed the nation. The railroads made moving materials and goods easier, faster, and cheaper.

The growth of industry did not necessarily improve life for factory workers. Before the Industrial Revolution, for example, an apprentice could hope to become his own boss someday. In factories, however, most employees would always be employees. Even worse, factory owners found that they could increase production by giving each worker a single task. The worker would have to do the same thing again and again, all day long, just like Claudio. Many workers grew to hate their jobs, but they needed them to survive. Factory work had physical dangers, too. Unsafe machinery and unsafe working conditions could cripple—or even kill—workers.

Finally, factory wages were often very low. To make a living, whole families, including children as young as six, sometimes had to take factory jobs. In fact, many employers preferred to hire children, because children were paid lower wages than adults. By 1890, almost 20 percent of the nation's children worked full-time.

In the early 1900s, social and political reformers called **progressives** began working toward improving the lives of workers. With their encouragement, many states passed laws to protect workers. Some states also lowered the number of hours people had to work every day and set minimum wages.

SKILL PRACTICE

Write *F* if the statement is a fact, *O* if it is an opinion.

_____ 1. New machines of the mid-1800s made farms more productive.

_____ 2. Jobs in which a worker repeated the same task all day were boring.

_____ 3. Children who worked in factories received lower pay than adults.

_____ 4. As industries grew in the 1800s, workers' lives became more grim.

_____ 5. Without the help of progressives, factory workers still would have to put in 10-hour days.

■ Apply What You Learn

Read the following article. Then answer the questions below.

Business Goes Global

The early 1900s saw the rise of **labor unions,** groups of workers who banded together to demand better working conditions. Their first goals were to get higher wages and shorter workdays. The chart lists some successes labor unions have had. Unions have also fought for and won other benefits, such as health insurance and retirement plans.

But workers' benefits cost employers money. This is one reason many businesses, including Heinz, Ford, and PepsiCo, began in the 1960s to open factories in foreign lands. These businesses realized that labor and other costs were cheaper in other countries than they were in the United States. In time, many U.S. companies set up international production sites.

Nike, Inc., is one example of these international companies. Nike is the world's largest sneaker company. It began making sneakers outside the United States 35 years ago, hiring workers in Japan. When the Japanese demanded higher pay, Nike moved its factories where labor was still cheap. Today Nike has 500,000 workers in Indonesia, China, and Vietnam. In these countries, the minimum wage is only a fraction of the U.S. minimum wage. In 1999, the minimum wage in the United States was $5.15 an hour. In Indonesia, for example, it was $2.50 *a day!*

LABOR MOVEMENT SUCCESS		
	1880	**Today**
Workday	10 hours	8 hours or less
Workweek	6–7 days	5 days
Overtime Pay	almost none	$1\frac{1}{2}$ times normal pay
Vacation	almost none	2–4 weeks/year

SKILL PRACTICE

Answer the questions based on the above information.

1. What were the goals of the first labor unions? _____

2. Why have U.S. businesses been moving jobs to foreign countries?

   _____

3. What do you think living and working conditions in Indonesia are like compared with those in the United States?

   _____

TECHNOLOGY Connection

In recent years, many jobs require workers to perform repetitive motions. **Use the Internet to research health hazards related to computer work.** Search under keywords *dry eye* or *carpal tunnel syndrome.* Read three articles and list ways to prevent computer-related health problems.

Answers and explanations start on page 254.

Rights and Freedoms of Americans

COMMUNITY LINK: Eugene and his friends want to start a group to raise money and get volunteers for a local shelter. Rivka suggests that they write a constitution to spell out the group's goals. Eugene gets a copy of the U.S. Constitution to see what it is like.

Protecting Citizens' Rights

Americans did not always have the rights and freedoms we enjoy today. In fact, Americans fought the Revolutionary War against Great Britain because they wanted a government that protected their rights.

After the Revolutionary War, Americans made a plan for their government called the Constitution. However, some people refused to ratify, or approve, the Constitution as it was presented. They opposed the Constitution, because it did not list the individual rights of U.S. citizens. Like Eugene and Rivka, they wanted to put such important issues in writing. To win approval, the people in favor of the Constitution promised to add a bill, or list, of rights. This Bill of Rights became the first ten **amendments,** or additions, to the Constitution. The Bill of Rights protects our rights and freedoms.

SUMMARY OF THE BILL OF RIGHTS TO THE U.S. CONSTITUTION

Amendment 1	Guarantees freedom of religion, freedom of speech, freedom of the press, the right to assemble, the right to petition the government
Amendment 2	Guarantees the right to keep and bear arms
Amendment 3	Prohibits forced quartering of soldiers in peacetime
Amendment 4	Prohibits unreasonable searches and seizures
Amendment 5	Guarantees that people cannot be: forced to speak against themselves in a trial; be tried twice for the same crime; lose life, liberty, or property without due process of law
Amendment 6	Guarantees those accused of crimes the right to a speedy, public trial by jury; to get legal representation, and to call and question witnesses
Amendment 7	Guarantees a jury trial in civil cases
Amendment 8	Protects people from unusually high bail and fines; forbids cruel and unusual punishment
Amendment 9	Gives rights not mentioned in the Constitution to the people
Amendment 10	All powers not given to the national government nor denied to the states are reserved for either the states or for the people

SKILL PRACTICE

Match the cause to its effect.

Cause

_____ 1. Great Britain did not protect Americans' rights.

_____ 2. The Constitution did not list rights.

_____ 3. Americans wanted the right to a speedy, public trial.

_____ 4. Americans wanted freedom to practice any religion they chose.

Effect

a. The Revolutionary War was fought.

b. The Bill of Rights was added to the Constitution.

c. Amendment 1 was written.

d. Amendment 6 was written.

Answers and explanations start on page 254.

The Right to Be Free

The Constitution and its amendments were written to protect Americans. But in practice, not everyone's rights were protected. For example, beginning in the 1600s, thousands of Africans were kidnapped and brought in crowded ships to America. Most were enslaved to work on farms and plantations in the South. Most lived and died without ever gaining freedom or individual rights.

Americans in favor of slavery claimed it was the law of nature for the "strong" to rule the "weak." People against slavery, called **abolitionists,** argued that slavery was unnatural and wrong. By the 1800s, American abolitionists organized to convince others to work to outlaw slavery. Some of the most dynamic and persuasive abolitionists, including Frederick Douglass and Harriet Tubman, had once been enslaved.

The Republican Party was started by people who were against the expansion of slavery into America's western territories. In 1860, the Republican candidate, Abraham Lincoln, won the presidential election. Southern states were afraid Lincoln would try to end slavery and thereby devastate the southern economy. Eleven southern states decided to **secede** from, or leave, the United States and form their own country, called the Confederate States of America, or the Confederacy. This signaled the start of the Civil War. The North was fighting to keep all the states together. The South was fighting to be independent. The Civil War lasted from 1861 to 1865, causing the death of more than 600,000 people. The North finally won this bloody war, and slavery was abolished.

To make sure that African Americans enjoyed the same rights as other U.S. citizens, three amendments—Amendments 13, 14, and 15—were added to the Constitution. The Thirteenth Amendment formally outlawed slavery in the United States. This guaranteed African Americans one of the most basic rights—freedom. The Fourteenth Amendment made sure that no state could make laws that took away individual rights from any American. And, the Fifteenth Amendment gave freed African American men the vote.

SKILL PRACTICE

Fill in each blank with a word or phrase that correctly completes the sentence.

1. People who spoke out against slavery were called _____.

2. After Abraham Lincoln became president, eleven southern states seceded because _____.

3. The main reason the North fought the Civil War was _____.

4. One important result of the Civil War was _____.

5. Amendments 13, 14, and 15 help protect _____.

Answers and explanations start on page 254.

The Right to Vote

African Americans were not the only people in the United States who did not enjoy all the rights and freedoms guaranteed by the Constitution. For example, in 1840 women had few of the rights enjoyed by men. American colleges educated only men. Married women could work for money but the money they made belonged to their husbands. In most states, men were even allowed to beat their wives!

Many women realized that, to claim the rights enjoyed by other American citizens for themselves and for their daughters, they needed to be able to vote. Some states had actually given women the right to vote. But many men of the time felt it was not natural for women to vote. Voting, they thought, should be left to men. In 1848, Lucretia Mott and Elizabeth Cady Stanton began to work for women's rights. Beginning in 1869, Susan B. Anthony devoted her life to gaining women the right to vote. It would be decades and into the next century, to 1920, before the Nineteenth Amendment to the Constitution guaranteed women the right to vote.

THE RIGHT TO VOTE

1860	1870	1920	1930	1940	1950	1960	1970	1980
	1870 15th Amendment prohibits denying the right to vote based on race	**1920** 19th Amendment guarantees women the right to vote			**1948** Native Americans can vote in all states	**1961** Residents of Washington, D.C. permitted to vote in presidential elections	**1971** 26th Amendment grants 18 to 20-year-olds the right to vote	

SKILL PRACTICE

Use the reading and timeline above to answer these questions.

1. Why does Helene think her daughter should vote? _____

2. Before 1870, which was the only group of Americans allowed to vote? _____

3. Which amendment would Susan B. Anthony have been proud to see passed?

    _____

4. Which group most recently gained the right to vote? _____

Answers and explanations start on page 254.

■ Apply What You Learn

Read the following article. Then answer the questions that follow.

"A Right Lost to One Is Lost to All"

What happens when the Constitution is not enough to guarantee a person's rights? Where can Americans turn when they find themselves forgotten by the government? How can the government be forced to right a wrong?

One way to answer these questions is to contact the American Civil Liberties Union (ACLU). The goal of this organization is, in its own words, "to assure that the Bill of Rights—amendments to the Constitution that guard against unwarranted governmental control—are preserved for each new generation."

In the 70 years since its beginning, the ACLU has addressed the concerns of many Americans. For example, it fought the relocation of 110,000 Japanese Americans. The U.S. government forced them out of their homes and into prison-like camps after the start of World War II. The ACLU supported African Americans by fighting against **segregation**—the separation of people by race—and took part in the 1960s civil rights movement.

The ACLU sometimes takes a stand that is unpopular. For example, the ACLU has defended the rights of groups, such as the American Nazis and the Ku Klux Klan. However, the ACLU does not defend the views of those groups. It defends the right of any group to *express* its views, however controversial those views might be.

SKILL PRACTICE

Answer the questions based on the above information.

1. The title of this article is "A Right Lost to One Is Lost to All." What does that mean?

   _____

2. What is the purpose of the American Civil Liberties Union? _____

   _____

3. How has the ACLU defended the rights of African Americans? _____

   _____

WRITING Connection

The ACLU lists on their Internet home page (http://www.aclu.org) these issues: criminal justice, free speech, police practices, immigration rights, drug policies, students' rights, religious liberty, and workplace rights.

Watch the national or local news on television for three days. As you watch, keep a list of all the cases and events in which you think the ACLU might have interest.

Answers and explanations start on page 254.

A World Power Emerges

COMMUNITY LINK: For Chin's entire life, Hawaii has been the nation's 50th state. But Chin's father remembers when Hawaii was not a state.

America's Manifest Destiny

Chin's father remembers a time when the United States did not have 50 states. In fact, at the end of the Revolutionary War, the United States only had 13 states. However, the government had already claimed the land bounded by the Atlantic Ocean, Canada, the Mississippi River, and Florida.

Over time, people explored the vast area that lay between the settled states and the Pacific Ocean. What they found—rich, sparsely settled land—inspired other Americans to follow them. These Americans cut down forests, plowed land for farms, and built towns and cities as they went West.

Many Americans believed it was the nation's **manifest destiny** to claim all this land. That is, they were certain that it was the United States' future to stretch from ocean to ocean. Although the land was already occupied by groups of Native Americans, the U.S. government took control of the land, one region at a time. For example, in 1803 the United States got much of the area between the Mississippi River and the Rocky Mountains by paying the French $15 million. This territory was called the Louisiana Purchase.

Other land was added to the United States through agreements with other nations. In 1819, for example, Spain agreed to give Florida to the United States. Still more land became part of the United States through war. California, Nevada, and the rest of the Southwest were added to the United States in 1848, at the end of the Mexican War. By 1853, the United States stretched from coast to coast. The United States later bought Alaska from Russia in 1867.

Eventually, the United States became interested in the Hawaiian Islands when it expanded its trade with Asia. Hawaii broke the vast distance that ships traveled across the sea. Ships were able to restock there. The United States also recognized the importance of the location of Hawaii and other Pacific islands for national defense. If another power claimed the islands, it could pose a threat to U.S. trade—or even to the nation itself.

SKILL PRACTICE

Write *True* if the statement is true, *False* if it is false.

_____ 1. All the land of the United States was added peacefully.

_____ 2. Many Americans believed in manifest destiny.

_____ 3. Before the United States bought the Louisiana Purchase, no one lived west of the Mississippi River.

_____ 4. The United States got Florida from Spain.

_____ 5. The United States wanted the Pacific islands for national defense.

Answers and explanations start on page 254.

Two Wars Make the United States a World Power

The addition of all that land made the United States one of the giant nations of the world. But the United States was not very interested in the rest of the world, except as trade partners. Even when World War I started in Europe in 1914, most Americans hoped to remain neutral, or uninvolved.

By 1917, however, German boats were regularly sinking American ships. These and other attacks by Germany pulled the United States into the war. Two million American soldiers crossed the Atlantic Ocean to support the countries fighting against Germany. The presence of U.S. troops turned the tide of the war. In 1918, Germany surrendered.

After World War I ended, the United States continued to play an important role in world affairs. Its economy boomed, and it kept growing until its stock market crashed in 1929. That year signaled the start of the Great Depression. The economic downturn affected the economies of other nations, as well. Many European industries, trying to recover from World War I, had borrowed money from Americans. When the stock market crashed, Americans could no longer loan money to the Europeans.

The demand in Europe for war goods and weapons during World War II brought the United States out of the Great Depression. When the war started in 1939, the United States again hoped to stay neutral. But on December 7, 1941, Japan bombed the U.S. naval base at Pearl Harbor in Hawaii. One day later, the United States declared war against Japan. Three days after that, it declared war on Germany and Italy.

World War II ended with the United States firmly established as a world power. It had helped lead the defeat of Germany and Italy. And it had defeated Japan soon after the fighting had ended in Europe. At this point, the United States embraced its position as a superpower.

1910	1920	1930	1940	1950
1914 World War I begins	**1918** World War I ends	**1929** Great Depression begins	**1941** U.S. enters war	**1945** World War II ends
1917 U.S. enters war		**1939** World War II begins		

SKILL PRACTICE

Write *F* if the statement is a fact, *O* if it is an opinion.

_____ 1. The United States should have stayed neutral during World War I.

_____ 2. The United States entered World War II after Japan bombed Pearl Harbor.

_____ 3. Germany and Italy lost World War II.

_____ 4. At the end of World War II, the United States should not have embraced the role of superpower.

Answers and explanations start on page 254.

FAMILY LINK: The president has ordered U.S. troops into a European trouble spot. Miguel is among the soldiers called up. For his father, it is hard to watch Miguel go to a country that does not pose a direct threat to the United States. Miguel's father would have felt better if his son had been called to fight a clear enemy, such as the Soviet Union during the Cold War.

The Cold War

During World War II, the United States and the Soviet Union fought together against Nazi Germany. But after the war, these two nations became enemies. To preserve and strengthen its country, the Soviet Union took control of nearby nations in Eastern Europe. It helped communist governments gain or keep control there. **Communism** is a system of government with a single political party and state ownership of almost all property. In a communist country, people generally have little voice in government and little economic freedom. The United States is a **democracy**—a government in which people have many political and economic choices. The United States did not want communism to spread to other countries. The hostility that developed between the United States and the Soviet Union was called the Cold War. The war was "cold" because, although there were conflicts, there was never actual combat.

Cold War tensions were high in 1961, when John F. Kennedy became president. One reason was that the nation of Cuba, only 90 miles from the Florida coast, had recently become communist. Cuba welcomed Soviet ships with missiles and other weapons. They aimed some of these weapons at the United States.

President Kennedy sent ships to blockade, or isolate, Cuba and to stop more Soviet arms from reaching the island. He threatened to attack if the missiles aimed at the United States were not taken down. The Soviets responded by removing the weapons.

Over the years, Cold War tensions gradually lessened due to increased political and economic cooperation. In 1989, the Soviet Union dissolved into independent countries, each with their own government. Today only a few countries, including China and Cuba, remain communist.

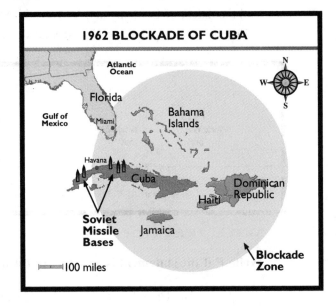

1962 BLOCKADE OF CUBA

Atlantic Ocean
Florida
Gulf of Mexico
Miami
Bahama Islands
Havana
Cuba
Dominican Republic
Haiti
Soviet Missile Bases
Jamaica
Blockade Zone
100 miles

SKILL PRACTICE

Match the effect to its cause.

Cause	Effect
_____ 1. The Soviet Union helps communists in Eastern Europe gain or keep control of their governments.	a. Kennedy blockades Cuba.
	b. The Cold War begins.
_____ 2. The Soviet Union helps Cuba aim missiles at the United States.	c. The Cold War ends.
_____ 3. The Soviet Union dissolves.	

 Answers and explanations start on page 254.

■ Apply What You Learn

Read the following article, which illustrates one role the United States took as a world leader. Then answer the questions that follow.

Peace in the Middle East?

The nation of Israel became a homeland for Jews in 1948. Its borders were carved out of British-occupied Palestine. This land had been a Jewish homeland in ancient times and a homeland to Palestinians for centuries. From Israel's start, neighboring Arab nations bitterly opposed a Jewish state in the region. Decades of conflict followed, including several wars between the Jews of Israel and the Arabs of Egypt, Iraq, Lebanon, and other Middle East nations.

In 1978 the United States tried to help establish peace between Israel and Egypt. U.S. president Jimmy Carter invited Israel's prime minister Menachem Begin and Egypt's president Anwar Sadat to the United States. All three worked together to forge a treaty between these two enemies.

In the 1990s another U.S. president was involved in trying to bring peace to Israel and its neighbors. In 1993 President Bill Clinton witnessed the signing of an agreement between the Israeli prime minister Yitzhak Rabin and leader of the Palestinians Yasir Arafat. This led to increasing Palestinian control in certain parts of the region, such as the Gaza Strip. In 1994 Clinton promoted peace between Israel and Jordan. And in 1999 he met again with Israeli and Palestinian leaders to continue the peace process.

SKILL PRACTICE

Check all of the statements that are true. There may be more than one true statement.

_____ 1. The United States showed itself as a world leader when it became involved in helping other nations make policies.

_____ 2. Arab nations were against the formation of Israel.

_____ 3. No Arab nation in the Middle East wants peace with Israel.

_____ 4. The West Bank is occupied by Israel.

SCIENCE Connection

One of the reasons Soviet missiles in Cuba caused so much concern in the United States was that they were nuclear missiles. Scientists did not learn how to release nuclear energy until 1942. Its first use was for destruction—the United States dropped atomic bombs on the Japanese cities of Hiroshima and Nagasaki in 1945, resulting in horrific damage.

Go to the local library and look up "nuclear energy" in an encyclopedia. Write down all the peaceful uses for nuclear energy.

DIRECTIONS: Choose the one best answer to each question.
Questions 1 through 4 refer to the passage and bar graph.

The Industrial Revolution prompted the great migration from America's farms to its cities. Many of the machines invented during that time helped factories increase production. However, other inventions made farms more productive. For example, on prairies, farmers found rich soil that was difficult to plow. The heavy, root-tangled mud clung like glue to iron-tipped wooden plows. Then, in 1837, John Deere invented a steel plow. Steel made the soil fall away from the plow, dramatically increasing the number of acres one farmer could plant in a day. Because steel was light, horses, rather than oxen, could pull the plow. Inventions like the steel plow meant that it took fewer farmers to meet the food needs of America's growing population.

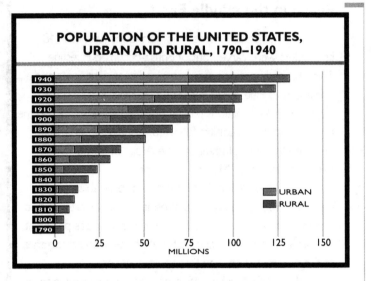

POPULATION OF THE UNITED STATES, URBAN AND RURAL, 1790–1940

1. The steel plow helped make farms more productive. Which of the following do you think had a similar effect?
   (1) a turbine that generates electricity using steam power
   (2) a machine that sews together the tops and bottoms of shoes and boots
   (3) an outdoor electric light bulb powered by its own generator
   (4) a windmill that pumps water for irrigation
   (5) refrigerated train cars that transport harvested fruits and vegetables

2. Which statement is supported by the information in the graph?
   (1) The population in 1790 was under 1 million people.
   (2) The population rose then fell.
   (3) The population fell then rose.
   (4) The population rose steadily.
   (5) The population in 1940 was higher than it is today.

3. In which year was the number of rural residents about equal to the number of urban residents?
   (1) 1940
   (2) 1920
   (3) 1900
   (4) 1880
   (5) 1790

4. Which of these generalizations cannot be made based on the graph?
   (1) In its first century, the United States was primarily a nation of farmers.
   (2) After 1870, the urban population of the United States grew more quickly than the rural population.
   (3) The United States gradually moved from an economy based on farming to an economy based on manufacturing.
   (4) The actual number of American farmers declined from 1790 to 1940.
   (5) The number of people living in urban areas has increased steadily since 1800.

Questions 5 through 8 refer to the passage and maps.

In the early 1800s, Americans built railroads to connect cities in the East. The first transcontinental railroad line was completed in 1869.

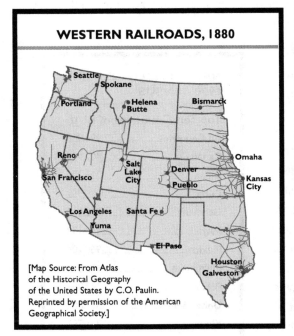

WESTERN RAILROADS, 1880

[Map Source: From Atlas of the Historical Geography of the United States by C.O. Paulin. Reprinted by permission of the American Geographical Society.]

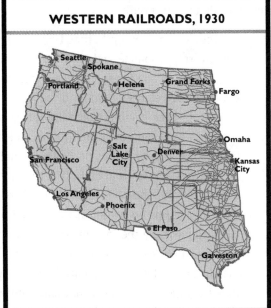

WESTERN RAILROADS, 1930

5. Which best describes what these two maps together illustrate?
   (1) settlement patterns in the American West
   (2) railroads of the eastern United States
   (3) the growth of western railroads between 1880 and 1930
   (4) railroad development around the world at the turn of the century
   (5) railroad development in 1880

6. What generalization can you make about the cities that became hubs, or centers, for railroad traffic by 1930?
   (1) Most were located in the central part of the region on the map.
   (2) Most were located in the southwestern part of the region on the map.
   (3) They were evenly distributed throughout the region on the map.
   (4) Most were located along the eastern edge of the region on the map.
   (5) Most were located where there were no rail lines in 1880.

7. According to the map dated 1880, from which West Coast city did the earliest eastward railroad expansion probably occur?
   (1) Seattle
   (2) Portland
   (3) San Francisco
   (4) Los Angeles
   (5) Yuma

8. From the information on the maps, what can you conclude?
   (1) Railroads were not important to America's westward expansion.
   (2) Railroad lines greatly increased in the 1800s and early 1900s.
   (3) Railroad growth in the United States stopped in 1930.
   (4) Most rail lines ended in the Northwest.
   (5) Most rail lines ended in the Southwest.

Questions 9 through 12 refer to the passage and table.

In 1990 there were about 20 million foreign-born people living in the United States. The table below shows some of the main countries that they came from. Many of these immigrants eventually become citizens in a process called naturalization. To become a naturalized citizen, immigrants take this oath:

I hereby declare, on oath, that I absolutely and entirely renounce and abjure all allegiance and fidelity to any foreign prince, potentate, state, or sovereignty of whom or which I have heretofore been a subject or citizen; that I will support and defend the Constitution and the laws of the United States of America against all enemies, foreign and domestic; that I will bear true faith and allegiance to the same; that I will bear arms on behalf of the United States when required by the law; or that I will perform noncombatant service in the armed forces of the United States when required by the law; or that I will perform work of national importance under civilian direction when required by the law; and that I take this obligation freely without any mental reservation or purpose of evasion; so help me God.

NATURALIZED CITIZENS, 1990 CENSUS

Top Ten Countries of Birth

All Countries	7,996,998
Canada	402,954
China	233,399
Cuba	375,952
Germany	512,018
Italy	440,143
Mexico	969,704
Philippines	492,214
Poland	242,294
United Kingdom	317,803
Vietnam	231,799

[Source: U.S. Immigration and Naturalization Service]

9. Which of the following is not part of the oath of citizenship?
   (1) promising to support the Constitution
   (2) promising to serve in the armed forces, if called
   (3) renouncing any enemy of the United States
   (4) renouncing any allegiance to another country
   (5) renouncing any allegiance to another leader

10. Of the countries of birth listed in the table, which three produced the largest numbers of naturalized U.S. citizens?
   (1) Canada, Germany, and Mexico
   (2) Canada, Cuba, and Mexico
   (3) Cuba, Germany, and Mexico
   (4) Germany, Mexico, and Vietnam
   (5) Germany, Mexico, and the Philippines

11. Based on the text and table, what fraction of America's foreign-born were naturalized citizens in 1990?
   (1) approximately one-tenth
   (2) approximately one-quarter
   (3) approximately one-half
   (4) approximately three-quarters
   (5) approximately nine-tenths

12. According to the oath of citizenship, what are some values people taking the oath should have?
   (1) love of the United States and love of the country where they were born
   (2) loyalty to the country where they were born and a willingness to work hard
   (3) loyalty to the United States and willingness to obey U.S. laws
   (4) loyalty to the United States and to the country where they were born
   (5) a willingness to work hard and to follow the U.S. laws

Answers and explanations start on page 255.

How did irrigation, the printing press, and gunpowder change history? Find out in this program exploring the events, inventions and ideas that have shaped the world from Ancient Egypt and the Great Wall of China to the modern Middle East.

Themes in World History

OBJECTIVES

1. Understand the impact of the Industrial Revolution on the world.

2. Analyze the relationship between nationalism and nation building.

3. Evaluate the trend toward more democracy among the peoples of the world.

You can refer to the world history timeline on pages 53 and 273 as you work through this lesson.

Why do we study world history? We study it because it is the story of humanity. Understanding world history gives us a perspective on the history of our own nation and helps us identify the events and innovations that link Americans with the rest of the world.

Having a firm grasp of world history will help you succeed on the GED Social Studies Test. In addition, it will help you understand in what ways world events continue to have a profound influence on our lives. Each year we develop deeper connections to other parts of the world—the foods we eat, the clothes we wear, even the alphabet and language we use—all are examples of ways in which we interact with the world.

On the following pages, you will find a brief exercise called *Sneak Preview*. It introduces you to the topics in the video program and the corresponding lesson. After you complete the exercise and check your answers, turn to the vocabulary on page 52. There you will find terms that will help you better understand the video and the lesson that follow. After reviewing page 52, you will be ready to watch Program 18.

For additional practice, visit *LiteracyLink* online at http://www.pbs.org/literacy.

Sneak Preview

This exercise previews some of the concepts from Program 18. After you answer the questions, use the chart on page 51 to help set your learning goals.

COMMUNITY LINK: Henry is walking slowly through a museum, observing all sorts of tremendous inventions on display there. He thinks about how many mechanical devices have now advanced to computerized, electronic, or miniaturized forms.

A Great Exhibition

The British started the Industrial Revolution. They pioneered the technology for weaving cloth on mechanized looms and for mass-producing shoes. They also improved farming techniques and invented new medicines. Many of the inventions that impressed Henry originated in Great Britain.

The British were proud of their technological achievements during the Industrial Revolution. In 1849, Great Britain's Prince Albert, Queen Victoria's husband, began plans for an exhibition to showcase all kinds of new technologies. He hoped the exhibition would highlight the achievements of different nations and inspire people to keep inventing and creating. He invited the whole world to attend.

THE CRYSTAL PALACE, HOME OF THE GREAT EXHIBITION

Corbis/Bettman

Prince Albert's Great Exhibition of 1851 opened in the specially constructed Crystal Palace in London. The palace itself was an industrial miracle, a vast glass-and-iron hall, housing exhibits from nations around the world. Even the picture of the Crystal Palace shown here is a symbol of the industrial advancements of the time, since photography was a new invention.

British exhibits took up about half of the Crystal Palace. They displayed examples of the nation's industry and art from clocks to chemicals to musical instruments. The other half contained the art and industrial achievements of more than a dozen nations, including the United States, which brought, among other inventions, Cyrus McCormick's reaper for grain.

Answer these questions based on the reading above.

1. One visitor described Great Britain's exhibits at the Crystal Palace as "England's arms of conquest . . . the trophies of her bloodless war." What did the visitor mean?

   (1) Technology that improves daily life can conquer the world as surely as guns can.
   (2) Many of England's inventions were guns, tanks, and other weapons.
   (3) The Great Exhibition of 1851 was a way for industrialized nations to show their military strength.
   (4) England's military might was superior to the might of other nations.
   (5) England had experienced conquest and war in its past.

2. What was Prince Albert's primary goal in creating the Great Exhibition of 1851?

    (1) He wanted to show Great Britain's industrial superiority to the world.
    (2) He hoped to reveal Germany's backward ways.
    (3) He wanted to bring nations together to share information and further industrial development among nations.
    (4) He wished to bring honor to the queen of Great Britain.
    (5) He planned to steal the exhibitors' best ideas to better Great Britain's industrial position.

3. What kind of technology would not be exhibited in 1851 but would be prominent in an industrial exhibition today?

    (1) steel making
    (2) agricultural technology
    (3) computer technology
    (4) textile manufacturing
    (5) weapons

4. Reread the description of the Crystal Palace and look at the picture on page 50. Which statement does not describe the Crystal Palace?

    (1) It matched the technological achievements of the time.
    (2) It recorded how far Great Britain had come in industrial development.
    (3) It represented Great Britain's leadership in the Industrial Revolution.
    (4) It was made mainly from a new kind of brick.
    (5) Its structure impressed people as much as its exhibits.

Feedback

- If you got all of the answers right...   you have a grasp of the forces that have shaped world history.

- If you missed question 1...   you need to study the impact of the Industrial Revolution on the world.

- If you missed question 2...   you need to work on understanding the relationship between nationalism and international cooperation.

- If you missed question 3...   you need to develop your ability to link information about the past and present together.

- If you missed question 4...   you need to think about the role values play in events in world history.

ANSWERS FOR SNEAK PREVIEW:

1. Choice (1)   2. Choice (3)   3. Choice (3)   4. Choice (4)

Vocabulary for *Themes in World History*

city-state	a city and its surrounding territory
dictatorship	a government in which its leader holds absolute power
ethnic	relating to a person's race or place of origin
fallow	the state of farmland purposely left idle during the growing season
feudal	concerning the relationship between a lord and his land tenants, called vassals
imperialism	the practice of taking control over nations for their raw materials
irrigate	to water farmland artificially
monarchy	a government led by a hereditary ruler, either a king or a queen
nation	a community of people who control a specific territory under a government; a country
nationalism	loyalty and devotion to a nation rather than to a local ruler or government
ostracism	in ancient Greece, the act of voting to force a dangerous leader to leave his city-state for a period of ten years
patrician	in ancient Rome, a member of one of the oldest and richest families
republic	a government in which citizens elect officials to represent them
revolt	to rise up in protest
silt	fine particles of fertile soil, sometimes deposited by rivers

➤ NOW WATCH PROGRAM 18:

Take note of the chronology of world events covered—what happened when. Although you don't need to memorize dates, having a general sense of the major periods in world history will help prepare you to answer questions on the GED Social Studies Test.

After you watch the program, work on:

- pages 53–68 in this workbook
- Internet activities at http://www.pbs.org/literacy

SOCIAL STUDIES

Themes in World History

On the following pages, you will learn more about the ideas discussed in the video program and have an opportunity to develop and practice your GED social studies skills.

Key Points to Think About

In the video program, you explored:
- how technology transformed the world.
- how the world's nations evolved.
- how democracy took seed and continues to grow.

On the GED Social Studies Test:
- You will be expected to identify important events that have shaped the world.
- You will analyze the impact of the Industrial Revolution on world history.
- You will need to draw conclusions about the links between the world and the United States.

As you work through the lesson for Program 18:
- Keep in mind parallel developments and events in world and U.S. history.
- Compare the impact of the Industrial Revolution in Europe with its impact in the United States.
- Be aware of ways in which world events continue to influence our nation.

WORLD HISTORY TIMELINE

around 3000 B.C.
Egypt irrigates its desert

around 500 B.C.
Rome creates a republic; Athens becomes a democracy

1500s–1600s
First national governments are formed in Europe

1776
American colonies declare their independence from Great Britain and form the United States of America

1800s
To get more raw materials for growing industries, Europeans set up colonies in Africa and Asia.

1989–2000
Many formerly Communist countries in Europe test or adopt democratic ways

Technology and Development

WORKPLACE LINK: Omar's friends thought he was crazy when he bought acres of dry land to farm. But Omar knows he can have a good harvest, just as long as he can get water to the soil.

Irrigation in Early Civilizations

Omar will probably use a form of technology employed by ancient Egyptians, who also lived on arid land. The Egyptians made use of a reliable water source—the Nile River. This great river runs through the Sahara desert to the Mediterranean Sea. Its dependable annual floods covered the riverbanks with a layer of rich **silt.** These deposits of fertile soil encouraged people to settle along the river. The Nile also offered a convenient means of transportation.

Technological developments helped the people of ancient Egypt direct the waters of the Nile where they were needed. For example, farmers **irrigated,** or watered, the land using a system of catch basins and canals. These irrigation systems allowed farmers to bring water to their crops even after the floodwaters dried up and the season they called "drought" began.

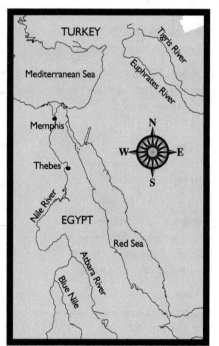

Irrigation improved harvests and, as a result, Egypt's early population grew. Irrigation also allowed Egypt—with its pharaohs and pyramids, its tombs and its treasures—to become one of the richest civilizations the world would ever see.

Other early civilizations used technology to lessen flooding. In Mesopotamia people built canals and dikes to control the Tigris and Euphrates Rivers. In China irrigation techniques and flood-control systems helped harness the river Huang He. In all these places, irrigation led to increased food production, which caused populations to grow and civilizations to flourish.

SKILL PRACTICE

Answer the questions based on the above information.

1. One early traveler called Egypt "the gift of the Nile." What might he have meant by that?

   _____

2. Why was irrigation important to the growth of Egypt? _____

3. What other early civilizations used technology for flood control?_____

4. How did irrigation affect the development of civilization?_____

   _____

Answers and explanations start on page 255.

SOCIAL STUDIES

The Agricultural Revolution

You have already read about how technology changed the lives of early farmers. As the centuries went by, technology continued to improve farmers' lives. The 1700s brought so many improvements, especially in Great Britain, that this period is called the Agricultural Revolution.

Some changes of the Agricultural Revolution involved breeding bigger, stronger animals. Other changes came from new inventions, such as Jethro Tull's seed drill. Still others involved improved farming methods. One improvement was in the yearly crop rotation. Generally, farmers of the time followed the centuries-old practice of three-field rotation. One field of three was left **fallow,** or unplanted, every year, while farmers sowed crops in the other two fields. The kind of crops changed with each growing season. The practice of crop rotation helped keep plants from using up the soil's nutrients.

In the early 1700s, British farmer Viscount Townshend discovered that a four-field rotation system with turnips as the fourth crop and grains and legumes as the other crops made it unnecessary to leave fields fallow. This was because each of the crops took different nutrients from the soil and replenished the soil with other nutrients. With four-field rotation, farmers could plant all their land every year, dramatically increasing Great Britain's harvest.

In addition, "Turnip" Townshend's system provided turnips and clover (a legume) as feed for livestock. Before this system, farmers were not able to grow enough food to feed their herds through the winter. That meant animals were slaughtered in the fall, with the meat preserved for the lean winter months. Thanks to Townshend's rotation system, farmers no longer had to slaughter most of their animals all at once. They could have fresh meat, both to eat and to sell, year-round.

CAUSES AND EFFECTS OF THE AGRICULTURAL REVOLUTION

Cause	Effect
new ways of growing crops	greater food production
new ways of breeding animals	greater food production
new farm equipment	greater food production
greater food production	less infant mortality; increased population
increased population	greater demand for manufactured goods
greater demand for manufactured goods	the Industrial Revolution

SKILL PRACTICE

Answer the questions based on the above information and chart.

1. What was the Agricultural Revolution, and when did it start?

    _____

2. Compare the British crop rotation system before and after the Agricultural Revolution.

    _____

3. List two ways the Agricultural Revolution affected the raising of farm animals.

    _____

Industrialization Encourages Imperialism

This happened to Paula last week, but she could have had the same experience if she had lived during the Agricultural Revolution. She could have been one of many people whose lives changed during that time. Then, when she lost her work on the farm, she could have joined thousands of others who became factory workers during the Industrial Revolution.

But the Industrial Revolution required more than just factory workers. With the growth in industry came a need for raw materials from all over the world. For example, businesses in Europe needed copper and uranium from the Congo in Africa. They got tin and rubber from Sumatra, an island in Indonesia.

The growing demand for raw materials caused industrialized countries in Europe, such as Great Britain, France, and Germany, to send explorers and merchants to Africa, Asia, and Australia. There they gained control of nations, which they then set up as colonies. This practice of taking control over other nations is called **imperialism.** The imperialistic nations then sent raw materials from their colonies to help industrialization back home.

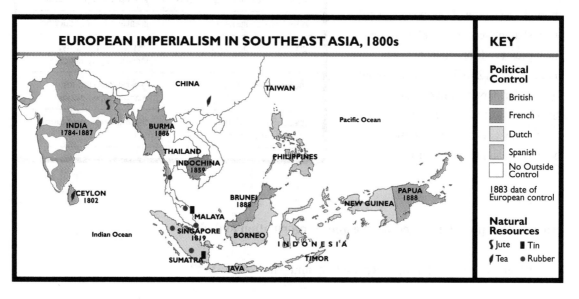

EUROPEAN IMPERIALISM IN SOUTHEAST ASIA, 1800s

KEY

Political Control
- British
- French
- Dutch
- Spanish
- No Outside Control

1883 date of European control

Natural Resources
- Jute
- Tin
- Tea
- Rubber

SKILL PRACTICE

Write *True* if the statement is true, *False* if it is false.

_____ 1. France took control of Indochina in 1895.

_____ 2. Industrialization encouraged European imperialism.

_____ 3. In the 1800s the Netherlands had colonies in Asia.

_____ 4. During the 1800s Great Britain controlled much of India.

Answers and explanations start on page 255.

■ Apply What You Learn

Read this interview of Matthew Crabtree, conducted during an 1832 investigation of conditions in Great Britain's textile factories. Then answer the questions that follow.

Have you ever been employed in a factory?

    Yes.

At what age did you first go to work in one?

    Eight.

How long did you continue in that occupation?

    Four years.

Will you state the hours of labour at the period when you first went to the factory, in ordinary times?

    From 6 in the morning to 8 at night.

Fourteen hours?

    Yes. . . .

During those long hours of labour . . . how did you awake?

    I seldom did awake spontaneously; I was most generously awoke or lifted out of bed, sometimes asleep, by my parents.

Were you always on time?

    No.

What was the consequence if you had been too late?

    I was most commonly beaten.

Severely?

    Very severely, I thought.

In those mills is chastisement [punishment] towards the latter part of the day going on perpetually?

    Perpetually.

So that you can hardly be in a mill without hearing constant crying?

    Never an hour, I believe.

SKILL PRACTICE

Write *F* if the statement is a fact, *O* if it is an opinion.

_____ **1.** Laws failed to protect children from working in early factories.

_____ **2.** Millwork was the most miserable work in all of Great Britain.

_____ **3.** Children should have been happy to work in the mills.

READING Connection

Sometimes it is possible to figure out the meaning of a word by the words around it. For example, find the sentence in the interview above that uses the word *spontaneously*. From the rest of that sentence, you can guess that the word *spontaneously* means "automatically" or "without prompting." The sentence states that the child's parents woke him or lifted him out of bed.

Reread the last five lines of the interview. Then write a definition for the word *perpetually*. Look in the dictionary to see if your definition is accurate.

Nation Building and Nationalism

COMMUNITY LINK: Darlene is having coffee in an outdoor restaurant in Paris. The person at the next table speaks to her. "Where are you from?" she asks. Darlene answers, " I'm from the United States."

A Time Before Nations

We all have an answer to the question Darlene was asked. We all call one nation home. But it wasn't like that for people in ancient times. Many of them lived in small kingdoms. Others lived in **city-states**—cities and their surrounding territories. Frequently outsiders conquered them, and they became part of great empires. Consequently, empires contained people of many **ethnic** backgrounds and cultures. The Persian Empire was one example. The Roman Empire was another.

The first group to populate the area that is now Rome used the word "Latin" for both their name and their language. They settled in farming villages in the hills above the Tiber River. Eventually, the villages banded together, and the city of Rome was born. Also living near the Tiber were Etruscans, who conquered the Latins, or Romans, in about 600 B.C.

In 509 B.C., the Romans rose up against the Etruscans. The newly independent Rome created a **republic**—a government in which citizens elect representatives. This republic lasted for almost five centuries. It ended when Rome's first emperor came to power in 44 B.C.

The republic Rome created had a senate and an assembly, where people made decisions about matters of public interest and law. At first, **patricians,** or members of Rome's richest and oldest families, dominated both groups. Other citizens had very little say in government. Then the other citizens banded together and formed their own assembly. Eventually, they had as much say in government as the patricians did.

Throughout the time of the republic and into the time of the empire, the Roman army marched across northern Africa, Europe, and the Middle East. It conquered the people in its path and set up the great Roman Empire. Roman laws held the vast empire together. But, eventually it got so big that the Roman government could not rule it well. The empire fell in A.D. 476 after invaders marched down from northern Europe and took control of Rome.

SKILL PRACTICE

Check all of the statements that are true. There may be more than one correct answer.

_____ 1. The Roman Empire included all of Europe, Asia, and Africa.

_____ 2. Other Romans were glad to let patricians dominate the assembly.

_____ 3. Persia and Rome both built early empires.

_____ 4. Latin was the language of the early Romans.

Answers and explanations start on page 256.

Europe's First Nations

With the end of the Roman Empire, Europe again was split into many small, independent political units that were governed locally. It would be more than 500 years before the first **nations,** or countries, would be formed.

The first modern nations developed in Europe, when people who shared a common culture and ethnic heritage began to unite. Spaniards, unified by their Catholic faith and their desire to be free of their Muslim Moor rulers, solidified their nation by about A.D. 1500. Similarly, a common religion and ethnic heritage helped form the modern state of France by about 1600.

One of the later modern nations to arise out of Europe was Italy. Since Rome's fall, the region that would become Italy had broken into numerous unstable kingdoms, small provinces, and city-states, which were often controlled by foreign rulers. In 1860, Sicilian peasants, armed with ancient weapons, pitchforks, and pruning hooks, **revolted,** or rose up in protest, against their king, who was of Spanish descent. A series of revolutions spread quickly across the peninsula, to rid the land of its foreign rulers.

In 1861, the goal of a united Italy was realized when Victor Emmanuel became the first king of the new Kingdom of Italy. By 1870, the Italian king had taken control of the whole peninsula.

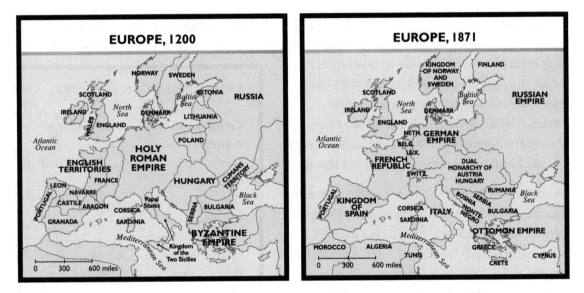

SKILL PRACTICE

Answer the questions based on the above information and maps.

1. After the fall of the Roman Empire, how was Europe organized politically?

    _____

2. List some factors that inspired groups of Europeans to unite and form nations.

    _____

3. Compare the two maps. Name three nations that were absorbed into the Russian Empire between 1200 and 1871.

    _____

FAMILY LINK: Fredericko knows his grandparents are Portuguese and his parents are Portuguese. But Fredericko never lived in Portugal. He was born in Brazil, and if someone asked him, he'd say that Brazil was his homeland.

The Drive Toward Nationalism

Portugal also was one of the first nations in Europe. It became a nation after its people decided to separate from Spain, the country to the east. They had feelings of **nationalism,** or loyalty and devotion to a nation rather than a local ruler or government. Once they had secured nationhood, the Portuguese worked to increase their power and wealth by sailing the oceans and setting up colonies. On April 22, 1500, they claimed the area in South America that is now eastern Brazil.

For the next 300 years, thousands of Portuguese settlers colonized Brazil. They and the native people they enslaved created giant sugarcane plantations, whose sweet export product made Portugal rich. Brazilians also exported cotton, beef, gold, and diamonds back to Portugal.

During those centuries of settlement, the descendants of the early Portuguese colonists, such as Fredericko, began to shift their feelings of nationalism from Portugal to Brazil. The colonists watched with interest as thirteen colonies in North America broke away from Great Britain to form the United States of America. Following the new nation's example, Brazil declared its independence from Portugal on September 7, 1822. Portugal let the colony go, and Brazil was established without bloodshed.

Brazil was not the only colony in South America. In fact, the entire continent was colonized by Europeans. Most of the colonies were Spanish, but the French and the Dutch also laid claims to parts of the region. By the end of the 1800s, however, most colonies were gone. Colonists fought for their freedom. New, independent nations developed, free of European rule.

SOUTH AMERICAN NATIONS	
Country	**Date of Independence**
Argentina	1816
Bolivia	1825
Brazil	1822
Chile	1818
Columbia	1819
Ecuador	1830
Falkland Islands	British Colony
French Guiana	French Colony
Guyana	1966
Paraguay	1811
Peru	1821
Suriname	1975
Uruguay	1828
Venezuela	1830

SKILL PRACTICE

Check all of the statements that are true.
There may be more than one correct answer.

_____ 1. Most of the colonies in South America were Portuguese.

_____ 2. Paraguay was the first South American nation to achieve independence.

_____ 3. Most South American nations were independent by the end of the 1800s.

_____ 4. Feelings of nationalism encouraged Brazilians to declare their independence.

_____ 5. Colonists in British North America were inspired by Brazilians to declare their independence.

Answers and explanations start on page 256.

■ Apply What You Learn

Read the following article about the effects of nationalism on the African continent. Then answer the questions that follow.

Trouble in Africa

Nationalism has a different face in Africa, where the people are divided into more than 800 ethnic groups, each with its own language, religion, and culture. In the late 1800s, the British, French, Germans, Belgians, Italians, and Spanish carved Africa into colonies. They generally were ignorant of the different African ethnic groups, so the political lines they drew often cut across the traditional ethnic boundaries. The colonies sometimes split tribal groups; other times, people who were historically enemies found themselves joined together under the same colonial flag.

By the 1970s, most African nations had achieved independence from their colonial rulers. For some African nations, however, independence has not brought peace. During the 1990s, for example, Liberia, Angola, Sierra Leone, and the Democratic Republic of the Congo were rocked by civil war. Many conflicts in African nations today are a consequence of the artificial colonial boundaries established more than a century ago.

SKILL PRACTICE

Answer the questions based on the above information.

1. How did today's African nations come into existence?

   _____

2. In what way are the political boundaries of African nations different from, for example, the political boundaries of Europe's countries?

   _____

3. Why are some nations of Africa politically unstable today?

   _____

MATH Connection

When the Roman Empire finally crumbled, it left its mark on the lands it used to rule. For example, many of the languages of Europe developed from Latin, the language of Rome. In addition, the legal systems of many western European nations were based on Roman law. The world also still uses Rome's number system—Roman numerals. Roman numerals include seven symbols: I (1), V (5), X (10), L (50), C (100), D (500), and M (1,000). For example, 2000 in Roman numerals is MM.

Use books, magazines, movies, and television to find two examples of Roman numerals. For each example, write down the Roman numerals. Try to figure out what the corresponding Arabic numbers (1, 2, 3) would be.

Answers and explanations start on page 256.

The Democratic Impulse

COMMUNITY LINK: José has left Cuba in a little boat and headed across the waters to the United States. José is afraid, but he does not like living in Cuba. He wants to have more say in his government. He wants to live in a democracy.

The World's First Democracy

Most early people were ruled by tribal chiefs or kings. Some rulers claimed to be connected to God. Ancient China's emperors, for example, ruled by the Mandate of Heaven. Egypt's pharaohs represented themselves as god-kings.

However, about 2,500 years ago, the Greek city-state of Athens developed a unique form of government. They called their government a democracy. The word *democracy* comes from two Greek words: *demos* for people and *kratos* for rule. In a democracy, the people make decisions about their government by voting.

The democracy Athens created allowed all Athenian citizens to take part in the Assembly. This was the group that made new laws and discussed matters of government. In addition, government officials, including judges, were chosen by lot from the names of all Athens' citizens. This ensured that each citizen had equal opportunity to hold office.

However, in Athens citizenship was granted only to free, native-born males over the age of 18. This meant that only about one out of every 16 residents was a citizen.

One interesting practice of Athenian democracy was the practice of **ostracism,** or banishment. Once each year, each citizen could write down the name of a political leader he felt was dangerous to the community. Any person receiving 6,000 or more votes was banished from Athens, without trial, for ten years.

SKILL PRACTICE

Answer the questions based on the above information.

1. Who qualified as a citizen of Athens? _____

2. Why were government officials chosen by lot? _____

3. How did ostracism help protect Athens' democratic government? _____

   _____

4. Why would José have liked the government of ancient Athens? _____

Answers and explanations start on page 256.

The Age of Revolution

For hundreds of years after Athens' democracy ended, the world would see only a few attempts at government by the people. However, during that time, many people worked to limit the power of their kings and to ensure their own rights as citizens. For example, in 1688, the British king was forced to sign a Bill of Rights. This document listed the rights and freedoms of the British people. It stated that, in a **monarchy,** hereditary rulers would share power with the people's elected representatives. It also said that only elected representatives could tax the British people.

Britain's Bill of Rights indirectly led to the American Revolution. This is because British colonists in America had no elected representatives in the British government. And yet, the colonists paid taxes as British citizens. "Taxation without representation is tyranny (unjust)!" was the cry of the American rebels. When the revolution ended, America no longer belonged to Britain. It now was a democracy, the United States.

Not long after the American Revolution, the French also revolted. Many people protested against France's **feudal,** or lord-vassal, system. This social and economic system had created three classes— the clergy, the nobles (or lords), and everyone else. "Everyone else" paid most of the taxes.

In 1789, the newly formed French National Assembly, which included representatives from all three classes, adopted the Declaration of the Rights of Man. This document listed the basic rights all people should enjoy, such as the right to freedom and security. France's king refused to approve it. This fueled the revolution and eventually led to the end of the French monarchy. The revolution ended in 1799. However, the results were not the hoped-for republic but a **dictatorship,** or one-person rule, with Napoleon Bonaparte at its head, holding absolute power.

The United States and France were not the only regions in which people rose up in a quest for independence. The table identifies other revolts during the Age of Revolution.

THE WORLD REVOLTS	
1775	American colonists begin revolution against Great Britain, which ends in the formation of the United States of America in 1783.
1787	Belgium revolts against the Netherlands, resulting in the establishment of the Republic of the United Belgium Province in 1790.
1789	France revolts against its monarchy; the revolution ends in 1799 when Napoleon seizes control.
1790	Hungary unsuccessfully fights for greater independence within the Habsburg Empire.
1791	Haiti begins fight for independence, which it achieves in 1804.
1798	Ireland unsuccessfully seeks independence from England.
1810	Revolutionary activities begin in Argentina and soon spread throughout South America with result that many South American nations gain independence.

SKILL PRACTICE

Write *F* if the statement is a fact, *O* if it is an opinion.

_____ 1. The feudal system in French politics was unfair to most of the people who lived in France.

_____ 2. The French Revolution replaced France's monarchy with a dictatorship.

_____ 3. The French were better off when France was a monarchy.

_____ 4. The revolts that marked the Age of Revolution were not limited to Europe.

Answers and explanations start on page 256.

The Movement Toward Democracy Continues

Even after the Age of Revolution ended, the world's move toward democracy has continued. The fall of communism showed how people still yearn for the rights and freedoms democracy promises.

In a communist government, the country owns all property and businesses. Communism began with the Russian Revolution in the early 1900s. During the revolution, the Bolsheviks replaced the monarchy with a communist government, which promised equality for people of all socioeconomic classes. By the late 1940s, communism had spread from the Soviet Union, as communist Russia and surrounding regions was called, into eastern Europe and China.

In the 1950s and 1960s, people found they had very few rights and freedoms under communism. The Soviet-controlled communist governments in such countries as Poland, Hungary, and Czechoslovakia, fought off democratic uprisings. The governments made poor economic decisions, so many people did not have jobs. By the late 1980s, communism began to lose its hold. Soviet-controlled countries slowly opened their borders. Some began introducing democratic practices. As a result, the republics in the Soviet Union broke away from the union. Today, only China, Sun-ye's homeland, remains as a major communist presence in the world.

COMMUNIST NATIONS BY CONTINENT, 1989	
Africa	None
Asia	Afghanistan, China, Kampuchea (Cambodia), Laos, Mongolia, North Korea, Vietnam
Australia	None
Europe	Albania, Bulgaria, Czechoslovakia, East Germany, Hungary, Poland, Rumania, Soviet Union, Yugoslavia
North America	Cuba
South America	None

SKILL PRACTICE

Answer the questions based on the above information.

1. In 1989 which two continents had the most communist countries?

_____

2. By the end of which decade did most communist countries adopt this form of government?

_____

3. Why did communism begin to fail?

_____

Answers and explanations start on page 256.

SOCIAL STUDIES

■ Apply What You Learn

Read the following article about the price people will pay for the principles of democracy. Then answer the questions that follow.

The 1989 Revolt in China

"I am a student at Qinghua University. I am twenty years old. I spent last night sitting on the steps [at Tiananmen Square]. I witnessed from start to finish the shooting and suppression by the army of students and citizens.

. . . The [Students'] Union told everyone in the Square that the situation was extremely grave, that bloodshed seemed inevitable, and that they wanted students and citizens to leave the Square. But there were still 40,000 to 50,000 students and about 100,000 citizens determined not to go. I, too, decided not to go.

The mood was extraordinarily tense. This was the first time we'd ever experienced such danger. I'd be lying if I said we weren't afraid, but everyone was psychologically braced and tempered. . . . In a word, we were imbued with a lofty sense of mission. We were prepared to sacrifice ourselves for China's democracy and progress.

. . . At four o'clock sharp, just before daybreak, the lights in the Square suddenly went out. The loudspeakers broadcast another order to 'clear the Square.' I suddenly had a tight feeling in my stomach. There was only one thought in my head: the time has come, the time has come.

. . . [As troops fired upon the crowds] I was running and weeping. I saw a second batch of students running off under machine-gun fire. I saw lots of people lying on their stomachs on the road.

. . . Then a large crowd of citizens came pouring out of the Front Gate. They clashed violently with these troops. They protected us while we escaped in the direction of Beijing railway station. The troops pursued us. It was five o'clock. Dawn was breaking."

SKILL PRACTICE

Write *True* if the sentence is true, *False* if it is false.

_____ 1. Chinese troops refused to fire upon Chinese protesters.

_____ 2. Chinese citizens saved some of the student protesters.

_____ 3. There is a movement in China favoring democracy.

WRITING Connection

Many people have been willing to die for the principles of freedom and democracy. In the American Revolution, about 7,200 Americans died for those principles. At Tiananmen Square, about 2,500 people were killed.

Imagine you are a student in Tiananmen Square in 1989. Write a letter home explaining why you chose to risk your life for democracy.

Answers and explanations start on page 256.

DIRECTIONS: Choose the one best answer to each question.
Questions 1 through 4 refer to the table.

INVENTORS OF THE INDUSTRIAL REVOLUTION		
When	**Who**	**Contribution**
about 1710	Abraham Darby	succeeds in using **coke,** which is made from coal, to **smelt,** or refine, iron
1760s	James Hargreaves	invents the **spinning jenny,** which makes it possible for one spinning wheel to operate eight spindles instead of just one
1769	James Watt	develops a workable **steam engine,** which could replace horses and water wheels as a power source
1793	Eli Whitney	introduces the idea of **interchangeable parts**
early 1800s	John Loudon McAdam	originates the **macadam road,** made of layers of crushed rocks, resulting in faster, smoother travel
1804	Richard Trevithick	constructs the first **steam locomotive**
1844	Samuel B. Morse	constructs the first **telegraph line,** which opens communication between Washington and Baltimore
1856	Henry Bessemer	creates the **Bessemer converter,** which dramatically lowers the cost of producing steel
1866	Cyrus W. Field	crosses the Atlantic Ocean with a **telegraph cable** that allows messages to travel between the U.S. and Europe

1. For which of the following reasons was James Watt's invention important?
   (1) It improved hand-weaving techniques in home-based textile industries.
   (2) It introduced the idea of interchangeable parts.
   (3) More new inventions could rely on the steam engine as a power source.
   (4) It opened new lines of communication.
   (5) Agricultural output was increased.

2. The British traditionally used charcoal, made by burning hardwoods, to refine iron. By the 1600s, overuse caused a shortage of trees. Which inventor solved this crisis?
   (1) Abraham Darby
   (2) Cyrus W. Field
   (3) Samuel B. Morse
   (4) Henry Bessemer
   (5) Eli Whitney

3. In which two centuries did the Industrial Revolution occur?
   (1) the fourteenth and sixteenth
   (2) the sixteenth and seventeenth
   (3) the seventeenth and eighteenth
   (4) the seventeenth and nineteenth
   (5) the eighteenth and nineteenth

4. Which generalization tells the impact of invention on the Industrial Revolution?
   (1) The Industrial Revolution included new inventions for the textile industry alone.
   (2) The Industrial Revolution was a time of change in world agriculture.
   (3) The Industrial Revolution echoed the principles of democracy.
   (4) Inventions and the Industrial Revolution happened coincidentally at the same time.
   (5) New inventions were one of the main causes of the Industrial Revolution.

During the nation-building times, from 1500 to 1800, the people who lived in the British Isles formed several political unions. In 1536, Wales became a part of England. In 1707, Scotland and England joined together to form the United Kingdom of Great Britain. During the 1700s, England, Wales, and Scotland were commonly called Great Britain.

In 1801, Ireland reluctantly joined the United Kingdom. Because most Irish were Catholic, they resented the Protestant-led Britain. Throughout the 1800s, many Irish resisted British rule, often through violence. In 1922, the British divided Ireland. Northern Ireland stayed a part of the United Kingdom but southern Ireland became independent. Today it is called the Republic of Ireland. Throughout the 1900s, many Irish Catholics in Northern Ireland fought for a unified Irish nation.

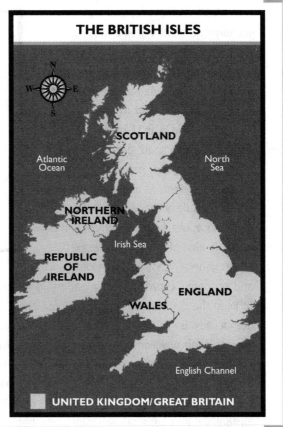

THE BRITISH ISLES

SCOTLAND

Atlantic Ocean

North Sea

NORTHERN IRELAND

Irish Sea

REPUBLIC OF IRELAND

ENGLAND

WALES

English Channel

■ UNITED KINGDOM/GREAT BRITAIN

5. Today the United Kingdom consists of England, Wales, Scotland, and Northern Ireland. As these neighbors united in an ever larger political unit, they all had things in common. Based on the information in the passage, what was one thing they shared?
(1) Most of the people were Protestants.
(2) Most of the people worked in factories.
(3) They all spoke English.
(4) They all wanted independence.
(5) They were all on the same island.

6. Suppose the number of representatives in the United Kingdom's legislature were determined by land area. Which member of the United Kingdom would have the fewest representatives?
(1) England
(2) Northern Ireland
(3) Republic of Ireland
(4) Scotland
(5) Wales

7. Throughout the 1900s, Ireland was beset with violence. Which statement does not describe a cause of this conflict?
(1) Groups in Northern Ireland differed about the country's relationship with Great Britain.
(2) Some Irish wanted one government for everyone on their island.
(3) Northern Ireland had closer political ties to Great Britain than to southern Ireland.
(4) The Irish Republic wanted to become a part of the United Kingdom.
(5) Irish Protestants and Irish Catholics clashed on political issues.

8. Which conflict is similar to the conflict the Irish experienced during the 1800s?
(1) the American Revolution
(2) the Civil War
(3) World War I
(4) World War II
(5) the Cold War

Historically, democracy and a strong economy go hand in hand. Most of Europe, Australia, and the Americas have democratic governments and stable economies, but these have been slower to develop in Asia and Africa.

After World War II, much of East Asia and Africa south of the Sahara formed independent nations. Most nations set up one-person or one-party rule rather than democracy. East Asian and African nations, however, differed on how well this kind of government worked.

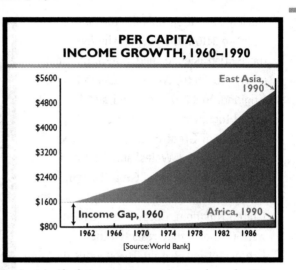

In general, East Asian leaders during the last half of the 1900s emphasized production and economic growth. Strong leaders in Japan and Singapore built their economies, trying to keep the government out of business practices as much as possible. Japan has a strong democracy. By 2000, with balanced economies, South Koreans and the Taiwanese also pressed their governments toward greater democracy.

In contrast, the leaders of many African nations came and went as civil wars erupted among groups. The economies of these nations suffered. With frequent droughts, food supplies grew scarce, and Africans died of hunger or disease. By 2000, many African nations were in political, economic, and health crises.

9. By which percentage did the per capita income in East Asia increase from 1960 to 1990?
   (1) about 30 percent
   (2) about 50 percent
   (3) about 100 percent
   (4) about 150 percent
   (5) about 200 percent

10. Which of the following predictions about the era of the 2000s is best supported by the information above?
   (1) The income gap between East Asia and Africa will decrease significantly.
   (2) Some East Asian nations will resist democracy.
   (3) East Asian nations will experience economic instability.
   (4) More nations in Asia will adopt democracy than will those in Africa.
   (5) More governments in Africa will achieve stability.

11. Which assumption is most likely about East Asian governments during the decades after World War II?
   (1) Many adopted democracy.
   (2) Most gained economic stability.
   (3) Most fought in civil wars.
   (4) Most failed.
   (5) Many interfered with business.

12. China, the world's most populated country, has a one-party government and a rapidly growing economy. Which prediction for the 2000s would be supported by the information above?
   (1) East Asian governments will play a bigger role in business practices.
   (2) China will limit their foreign trade.
   (3) The Chinese will adopt democracy.
   (4) The Chinese government will crush protesters.
   (5) China's population will reach 2 billion.

Answers and explanations start on page 256.

SOCIAL STUDIES

What does the global economy have to do with you—and with pizza? Find out, as businesspeople and economics teachers explain basic concepts such as scarcity, supply and demand, and GNP.

Economics

OBJECTIVES

1. Examine the roles the U.S. government plays in the economy.

2. Identify factors that influence the job market and wages.

3. Evaluate the roles that individuals play in the U.S. economy.

Where do you work? What groceries do you buy? Where do you shop, and how much do you spend? Every day, both as workers and as **consumers,** we make many decisions that affect the economy. Our decisions influence what is produced, how much is produced, what it will cost, and how the products reach us in the marketplace. The more we know about the economy, the better decisions we make.

Understanding economics is important to your success on the GED Social Studies Test. It also is important to real life. Every time you discuss taxes, job prospects, unemployment, credit cards, and budget expenses, you are discussing the economy.

On the following pages, you will find a brief exercise called *Sneak Preview.* It is designed to introduce you to the topics in the video program and the corresponding lesson. After you complete the exercise and check your answers, turn to the vocabulary on page 72. There you will find terms that will help you better understand the video and the lesson that follow. After reviewing page 72, you will be ready to watch Program 19.

For additional practice, visit *LiteracyLink* **online at http://www.pbs.org/literacy.**

Sneak Preview

This exercise previews some of the concepts from Program 19. After you answer the questions, use the chart on page 71 to help set your learning goals.

WORKPLACE LINK: Sophia wants to open a gift shop. But she finds that there are many rules and regulations to follow. It will cost Sophia money to follow all the laws the government has set for stores. "How can I make a living?" she complains.

The Government Learns a Lesson in Economics

If Sophia had lived in the 1920s, she would have had a very different experience. Up to that time, the government of the United States passed few laws regulating how people ran their businesses.

Then in 1929, the stock market crashed. The **stock market** is where people invest in major corporations. It was—and is today—a symbol of the rich and powerful U.S. economy. This crash signaled the beginning of the Great Depression. The country had survived depressions before, but this depression was more severe. It lasted longer than 12 years and put millions out of work.

The government, led by President Herbert Hoover, did little at first, waiting for the economy to improve on its own as it had in the past. But it did not. Banks failed, companies closed, and 25 percent of workers lost their jobs. The U.S. economy had actually weakened during the 1920s, but contrasting signals had misled Americans. Industry was rapidly growing, producing varied goods for the marketplace. Yet 42 percent of consumers made poverty-level incomes and bought only what they needed to live. And, more than 7,000 banks failed even before the 1929 crash. These were just two factors that prevented the U.S. economy from bouncing back.

Then in 1932, most Americans voted against Hoover and for Franklin D. Roosevelt for president. Roosevelt promised to use the government to help the economy recover. Under his leadership, Congress passed laws and set up agencies to help the poor, provide jobs, and support business. The goal was to create economic stability so Americans would never again live through such hard economic times. The Great Depression ended in 1942 during World War II. Today, government policies still provide an economic safety net.

Answer these questions based on the reading above.

1. What was the U.S. government's involvement in the nation's economy before the Great Depression?

   (1) It controlled business through laws and regulatory agencies.
   (2) It passed relatively few laws regulating businesses.
   (3) It helped the economies of other countries through trade.
   (4) It made sure people would never suffer economically.
   (5) It entered World War I.

2. Which statement is a fact that is supported by the reading?

   (1) The jobless rate climbed steadily during the seven years of the Great Depression.
   (2) The 1929 stock market crash led to high levels of unemployment.
   (3) President Roosevelt helped the economy by cutting government jobs.
   (4) World War II made it even harder for people to find jobs.
   (5) President Roosevelt was the American worker's best friend.

3. If today's government leaders stopped setting policies that help people find jobs and support unemployed workers, which effect would be least likely?

   (1) The number of unemployed workers who are highly skilled and highly educated would drop.
   (2) Employers would set wages at low levels.
   (3) Business owners would send their manufacturing work to other countries where workers work for less money.
   (4) The stock market would suddenly crash.
   (5) The unemployed would face economic hard times.

4. How did individuals positively influence the economy during the Great Depression?

   (1) They elected Franklin D. Roosevelt.
   (2) They stopped buying luxury items.
   (3) They earned poverty-level incomes.
   (4) They defaulted on loan payments.
   (5) They panicked as banks failed.

Feedback

- If you got all of the answers right...

  you have a firm understanding of how the government affects the nation's economy.

- If you missed question 1...

  you need to think about how the government's involvement in the economy has changed over time.

- If you missed question 2...

  you need to analyze different influences on jobs in the United States.

- If you missed question 3...

  you need to think about the pros and cons of government involvement in the economy.

- If you missed question 4...

  you need to read about the many ways in which each of us influences the economy.

Vocabulary for *Economics*

consumer	one who buys a product or service from someone else
credit	money available to borrow with the promise of repayment
debit card	a card that subtracts money directly from a checking account
demand	what consumers or businesses will buy of a particular good or service at a given price
export	to sell goods produced in one's own country to those in another country
gross domestic product	the value of a nation's production of goods and services during a particular year
import	to bring to one's own country goods from another country
inflation	a period during which prices of many items rise sharply and continually
interest rate	the amount of money a loan will cost, usually given in a percentage of the borrowed money that will be paid back every year
monopoly	a business that is the only one providing a certain good or service
producer	one who makes a product for others to buy
stock market	a place where investors buy and sell shares of stock in major corporations
strike	a work stoppage intended to force an employer to respond to workers' demands
supply	what producers will provide of a particular good or service for sale at a given price
tariff	a tax on imported goods
trust	relating to economics, a combination of companies that are under one organization's control

➡ **NOW WATCH PROGRAM 19:**

You'll see plenty of charts and graphs in this program. Keep in mind that knowing how to read and use the information from graphics will help you answer questions on the GED Social Studies Test.

After you watch the program, work on:

- pages 73–88 in this workbook
- Internet activities at http://www.pbs.org/literacy

Economics

On the following pages, you will learn more about the ideas discussed in the video program and have an opportunity to develop and practice your GED social studies skills.

Key Points to Think About

In the video program, you explored:
- The government's role in the economy.
- What factors influence jobs and wages.
- How individuals influence the economy.

On the GED Social Studies Test:
- You will be expected to know key economic concepts affecting American society.
- You will identify ways in which government policies and regulations influence the economy.
- You will learn to recognize factors that affect a worker's employment opportunities and earning power.

As you work through the lesson for Program 19:
- Be aware of ways in which you influence the economy and ways the economy influences you every day.
- Watch the news for ways in which government continues to affect the economy.
- Evaluate how Americans' working, spending, saving, and voting behaviors affect the economy.

GED TIPS

When taking the GED Test, you should:

- Read the test directions carefully to make sure you understand how to answer the questions.

- Have a strategy for answering questions. Some people read the passage, then read the questions, while others skim the questions before reading the passage.

- Check each answer by looking back at the reading and illustrations. Don't rely on your memory of what you have just read or seen.

Government's Role in the Economy

COMMUNITY LINK: The government drops the interest rate. Now Henri can afford a loan to buy a car. The salesperson who sells Henri the car uses the money he makes to purchase a lawnmower.

Government Policies Influence the Economy

Henri provides a good example of how, since the Great Depression, the government has remained involved in controlling the nation's economic health. A tool it uses to prevent bad economic times is its monetary policy—its decisions on managing money. It was the government's monetary policy that influenced Henri's decision to buy a car. Congress created an agency called the Federal Reserve System (nicknamed the Fed). It manages the nation's money supply. It lowers the interest rate to pep up a sluggish economy. The **interest rate** is the fee a borrower pays for a loan, which is based on a percentage of the loan amount. A lower interest rate encourages Henri and millions of others to borrow on credit and spend money. This new spending stimulates the economy, because it increases demand for goods and services. **Demand** is what consumers or businesses will buy of a particular good or service at a given price.

If the supply of a good or product is not enough to meet the demand for it, its price goes up. **Supply** is generally what **producers** will provide of a particular good or service.

If prices of many goods rise sharply and continually, the country enters a period of **inflation.** With inflation, each dollar buys less than it used to. Sometimes prices can rise so high that many people no longer can afford the product. They stop buying, so companies stop manufacturing, and people lose their jobs. In times of inflation or to hold off inflation, the Fed might decide to tighten the money supply. It raises interest rates on loans to discourage spending on credit. This lowers the demand for products and services. Now it is easier for supply to meet demand, and prices should drop.

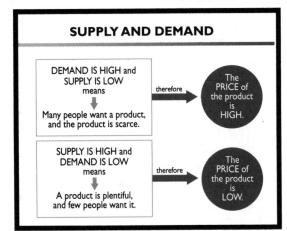

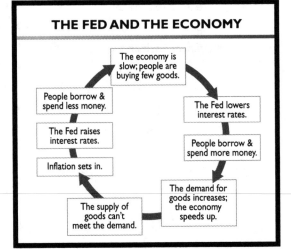

SKILL PRACTICE

Match the effect to its cause.

Cause

_____ 1. The economy is healthy.

_____ 2. The economy is sluggish.

_____ 3. Inflation is high.

Effect

a. The government lowers interest rates.

b. Government continues its monetary policy.

c. Many people have to cut their spending.

Answers and explanations start on page 257.

SOCIAL STUDIES

Foreign Policies Influence the Economy

The government uses domestic—national—policies relating to our own country, such as its monetary policy, to help control the economy. It also uses foreign policy to protect the economic well-being of its citizens.

In general, U.S. foreign policy encourages good relations with other countries. To this end, the U.S. government often provides aid to various governments. Such aid might promote the political stability and economic development of other nations. There are economic reasons why good foreign relations benefit Americans. One is that the United States needs materials from other countries to produce certain goods. For example, about three-fourths of the potash U.S. farmers need to fertilize their fields is **imported,** or brought to the United States from other countries. In addition, many U.S. businesses depend on sales to foreign markets. In 1996, for example, U.S. car manufacturers **exported,** or sold to those in other countries, more than a million cars and trucks.

In many other countries, workers' wages and other production costs are lower than they are in the United States. This means that imported goods from these countries can often be sold more cheaply here than American-made goods can. In addition, the U.S. government has agreements with many nations to promote trade that is free of **tariffs,** or taxes on imported goods. This policy also keeps the cost of imported goods low for Americans.

Some U.S. companies have suffered from the low costs of imported goods. To remain competitive, many companies have lowered their costs by moving production overseas, resulting in fewer manufacturing jobs in the United States.

MATERIALS FULLY IMPORTED TO THE UNITED STATES (1996)		
Mineral	**Major Sources (1992–1995)**	**Major Uses**
Arsenic	China, Chile, Mexico	Wood preservatives, glass mfg;, agricultural chemicals
Bauxite & alumina	Australia, Jamaica, Guinea, Brazil	Aluminum production, abrasives, chemicals, refractories
Columbium	Brazil, Canada, Germany	Steelmaking, superalloys
Manganese	South Africa, Gabon, Australia, Brazil	Steelmaking
[Source: U.S. Department of the Interior]		

SKILL PRACTICE

Answer the questions using the passage and table above.

1. Why have many American companies been moving their operations overseas?

    _____

2. What industry would be affected if the United States stopped trading with Brazil? Explain.

    _____

3. Explain why a nation that exports a product has an advantage if another nation needs to import all it uses of that product. _____

Regulations Influence the Economy

The government makes laws and regulations that influence how businesses operate. Most government regulations protect the public when large and powerful companies decide on a course of action that might not be in society's best interests. In the late 1800s, for example, the nation saw a rise in monopolies. A **monopoly** occurs when one business or a small group of businesses takes over an industry. Monopolies affect the economy because there is no competition to keep prices reasonable and to ensure product quality.

Many of these monopolies were created by trusts. A **trust** is a combination of several companies controlled by one organization. These companies then work together to set prices within an industry, eliminate competition, and control the supply of the product or service produced.

The government responded to the threat of trusts in the railroad, tobacco, oil, and other industries by passing several antitrust laws, starting in 1890 with the Sherman Antitrust Act. It also created the Federal Trade Commission, with the authority to investigate businesses suspected of breaking antitrust laws. Other government regulations are aimed at protecting the environment. Still others are concerned with workers' health and safety. Companies such as Adeline's employer often find that meeting all these regulations costs them money, but they generally pass such expenses on to **consumers**—people who buy products or services—by increasing prices.

THE CONSUMER'S FINAL BILL

"Good evening, sir. As you may know, the soaring costs of recent environmental-protection legislation have forced us to pass part of this burden along to the consumer. Your share comes to $171,947.65."

SKILL PRACTICE

Check all of the statements that are true. There may be more than one true statement.

_____ 1. Government regulations of businesses have little effect on Americans.

_____ 2. Government regulations often cost companies money.

_____ 3. The government passed laws and established commissions to stop trusts.

_____ 4. As a result of following government regulations, businesses usually lower the prices they charge consumers.

■ Apply What You Learn

Read the following article about welfare changes. Then answer the questions that follow.

A Change in Government Policy Changes the Economy

In 1996, President Clinton signed the Personal Responsibility & Work Opportunity Reconciliation Act. This act dramatically changed the federal government's policy on welfare. Welfare refers to government programs that help people who do not have enough money to survive financially. The welfare system provides a safety net for the nation's poor. With the 1996 law, however, responsibility for welfare programs fell to the states, which would receive some federal money. In exchange for the money, the states had to figure out how to get half their welfare recipients back to work by the year 2002. If they failed to lower the number on the welfare rolls by a certain percentage each year until then, they would receive fewer federal dollars.

Both the state and local governments leaped into action. Many states began to offer tax credits or payroll supplements to businesses that hired people receiving aid. Some states began to offer help with child-care services, which traditionally kept welfare parents from working. Local governments set up transportation programs. Atlanta and Philadelphia, for example, changed bus routes to accommodate people entering the workforce, and vans in Gary, Indiana, deliver people to work.

SKILL PRACTICE

Answer the questions based on the information above.

1. Why do you think child-care concerns can make it hard for some welfare recipients to take jobs? _____

    _____

2. How are some businesses benefiting from changes in the government's welfare policy?

    _____

3. In what way do you predict that this change in welfare policy will benefit the U.S. economy? _____

    _____

TECHNOLOGY Connection

Almost every state has now put into place a welfare-to-work program to help reach the goals of the new welfare policy.

Use the local library's Internet connection to find your state's home page: www.your state.gov. Look for information on how your state is handling this policy change. Use keyword: *welfare-to-work*. Write down any programs and policies you find there.

Answers and explanations start on page 257.

Factors Influencing Jobs and Wages

WORKPLACE LINK: Margaret worked at a travel agency for ten years. Lately, however, people have been using the Internet to make their own travel arrangements. Margaret was laid off, and since many travel agencies have closed, she can't find another travel job.

SOCIAL STUDIES

Supply and Demand Affects Jobs and Wages

Margaret has just become a victim of supply and demand. That is, the demand for travel agents is lower than the supply of travel agents, so Margaret is having a hard time finding a job. On the other hand, if Margaret were a computer programmer, she probably would find employment quickly, for the demand for computer programmers is higher than the supply of people skilled in that field.

In addition to jobs, wages also depend on supply and demand. In general, wages are higher if the demand for certain workers is great and the supply of those workers is low. This is because employers use higher wages to draw in the few people who can fill the job openings. Sometimes, a supply of certain workers is low because the job requires a great deal of education. As a result, often the more education someone gets, the more that person earns. Generally, that is because demand for that person's skills is high.

Consumer demand also influences wages. Wages generally are higher if demand for a product is high. Booming sales make it likely that the manufacturer is making a profit, which may be passed on to the workers through higher wages.

EDUCATION AND ANNUAL EARNINGS, 1995

	annual averages per person, 18 and over
Not a High School Graduate	$14,013
High School Graduate	$21,431
Some College or Associate Degree	$23,862
Bachelor's Degree	$36,980
Advanced Degree	$56,667

0   10   20   30   40   50   60

[Source: U.S. Bureau of the Census, Department of Commerce]

SKILL PRACTICE

Answer the questions based on the information above.

1. Explain how, in looking for a new job, Margaret was a victim of supply and demand.

_____

2. According to the graph, which group of people makes the most money?

_____

3. How are wages tied to supply and demand? To education?

_____

Answers and explanations start on page 257.

Other Influences on Wages and Jobs

Many people join labor unions in an attempt to even out the impact of supply and demand on wages. Through unions, workers attempt to improve their wages and benefits by negotiating with their employer as a group rather than as individuals. Teachers, machinists, nurses, letter carriers, musicians, and mine workers are among the occupations that have unions.

To protect the income of those who are not union members, the national government guarantees that workers receive at least a minimum wage. The first national minimum wage law was passed in 1938. It set the minimum wage for workers at 25 cents per hour. Over the years, the minimum wage has increased. By 1998, the minimum wage was $5.15 per hour. But during those 60 years, the cost of goods and services has also gone up. The graph below shows the buying power of the minimum wage over time. Rather than showing the exact minimum wage for that year, the chart shows the value of products and services that one hour's wage could buy.

Although wage increases are good for workers in the short term, higher wages create high U.S. labor costs overall. Some people argue that high labor costs have made American companies less able to compete in world markets. They say that this, in turn, leads to fewer jobs in this nation.

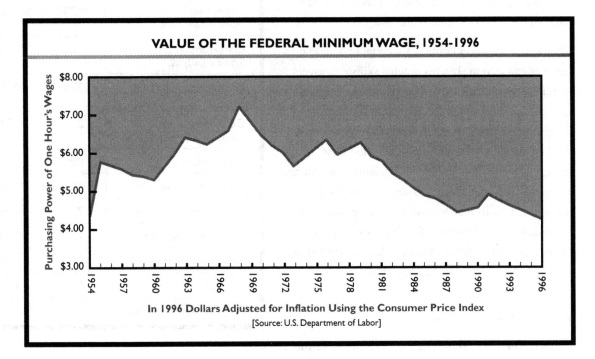

VALUE OF THE FEDERAL MINIMUM WAGE, 1954-1996

In 1996 Dollars Adjusted for Inflation Using the Consumer Price Index
[Source: U.S. Department of Labor]

SKILL PRACTICE

Check all of the statements that are true. There may be more than one true statement.

_____ 1. Labor unions make it hard for their workers to get wage increases or better benefits.

_____ 2. The purpose of the minimum wage law was to guarantee at least a certain hourly wage for every worker.

_____ 3. Although the minimum wage has gone up over the years, its buying power has gone down since the mid-1960s.

_____ 4. Higher wages usually result in more jobs.

Answers and explanations start on page 257.

Investing in Your Economic Future

Labor union membership is one way in which people try to ensure that they can make a good living. Another way is for workers to invest in themselves, by acquiring new knowledge and skills or upgrading skills they already have.

Just like businesses, workers compete with one another to sell their product. In this case, their product is their labor. In the U.S. marketplace, workers who possess skills that are in demand are more likely to be hired and can also expect to earn higher wages.

Changes in consumer demand for certain goods and services can lead to changes in what skills employers demand from workers. In addition, just like machines in a factory, workers' skills can become outdated. To be competitive in such an economic environment, workers must invest their time—and often their money as well—in education and training. As Abraham realizes, this commitment to better one's skills or acquire new skills may involve sacrificing short-term wants and needs. However, the choices workers make about education, training, and skill development greatly influence the money they will earn in their lifetimes.

TOP TEN FASTEST-GROWING OCCUPATIONS, 1994–2005

	Percent Change	Number Change
Homemaker/ Home-health aides	107%	640,000
Computer scientists and Systems analysts	91%	755,000
Physical therapy assistants and aides	83%	64,000
Occupational therapy assistants and aides	82%	13,000
Physical therapists	80%	81,000
Human service workers	75%	125,000
Service sales representatives	72%	441,000
Occupational therapists	72%	39,000
Medical assistants	59%	121,000
Paralegals	58%	64,000

[Source: U.S. Department of Labor]

SKILL PRACTICE

Answer the questions based on the information above.

1. What product do workers offer for sale? _____

2. Based on the chart, what generalization can you make about the future of the field of physical therapy?

   _____

3. By working through this book's lessons, what might you have in common with Abraham? How does this relate to your job-finding potential?

   _____

Answers and explanations start on page 257.

■ Apply What You Learn

Read the following article about the kinds of training available to American workers. Then answer the questions that follow.

More Training Equals Higher Wages

The graph on page 78 is proof that more education often leads to higher wages. In fact, those who go on after high school to get additional training make an average of $150 a week more than those who don't.

There are many ways to gain more marketable skills. One way is through vocational training. Workers entering the job market as nursing aides, orderlies, licensed practical nurses, and bookkeepers need vocational training. In many programs, students may be eligible for financial aid from the government.

Community colleges offer another advantage to those wishing to increase their skill levels and wages. These colleges can quickly change their courses to reflect changes in business. For example, in the late 1990s, an explosion in computer use created a demand for information technology specialists. These people design and maintain websites, write computer programs, and provide support or customer service for computer users. Soon information technology programs became available at many community colleges. Demand was so great that some students were hired before they had completed the program!

SKILL PRACTICE

Write *F* if the statement is a fact, *O* if it is an opinion.

_____ 1. Vocational programs are a fantastic way of ensuring you get a job.

_____ 2. An increase in computer use created a demand for information technology specialists.

_____ 3. People with technical skills are better workers than people with other skills.

_____ 4. Community colleges can change their programs to meet the shifting demand for workers with different kinds of training.

MATH Connection

The bar graph on page 78 shows how more training can lead to more money. Not allowing for raises or inflation, what would a worker's lifetime earnings be? For example, most people earn a bachelor's degree at age 22. Assuming they retire at age 65, they will earn an average of $36,980 annually for 43 years. Lifetime earnings would be at least $1,590,140, or $1.6 million.

Look at the data in the graph on page 78. Calculate the lifetime earnings of a person with a high school diploma, or the GED equivalent (age 18), and a person with an associate's degree (age 21) to age 65.

Answers and explanations start on page 258.

The Roles of Individuals in the Economy

WORKPLACE LINK: It is 5:00 P.M. Friday. Lydia has worked hard all week in the bakery, and now she looks forward to being paid for her labor. She will use part of the money she gets today to buy a birthday present for her son.

Worker = Producer + Consumer

Lydia has influenced the economy in two ways. First, she has been a producer, making a product for others to buy. Then she has been a consumer, using her earnings to buy a product from someone else. So there are two ways in which workers influence the economy—as producers and as consumers.

Producers have many things to think about as they make their economic decisions. For example, producers must first make sure that consumers want the goods and services they offer. They also must make sure that consumers are willing to pay the price they set for the goods and services. Producers who can provide wanted goods and services at attractive prices ensure their sales. Steady or increasing sales lead to profits for sellers, continued employment for workers, and a stable economy for the nation.

Consumers also influence the economy as they buy goods and services. Like producers, consumers have to answer many questions when making economic choices. Is the item they are thinking of buying high on their list of wants and needs? How much can they afford to pay for the item? How do different brands of the item compare to each other in price and quality? What store is offering the best price on the item today?

Neither producers nor consumers are completely free in the economic decisions they make. For example, government regulations try to prevent producers from making inferior products. However, these same regulations limit consumer decisions by removing inferior, but perhaps cheaper, products from the market.

SKILL PRACTICE

Check all the statements that are true. There may be more than one true statement.

_____ 1. The words *producer* and *consumer* both describe the American worker.

_____ 2. Only consumers can make economic decisions with complete freedom.

_____ 3. Consumers must think of many things to make wise economic choices.

_____ 4. Price is a major concern in producers' and consumers' decisions.

_____ 5. Consumers and producers have little influence on each other.

Answers and explanations start on page 258.

Americans as Money Managers

The money American consumers spend on goods and services promotes the employment of the workers who produce those goods and services. But spending money is not all Americans do. Americans also save and invest money to protect their financial future. Banks use the money Americans save and invest by loaning funds to businesses. Business owners then use the money to expand or improve their businesses. Such business expansion is good for the economy.

Businesses are not the only elements in the economy to take out loans. Individuals also sometimes borrow money when they cannot meet their needs with the earnings and savings they have. This borrowed money can be a personal loan, or it may be in the form of charge accounts and credit cards.

The availability of **credit**—money to borrow—in the 1990s encouraged Americans to go into debt. By 1998, American consumers had borrowed over $1 trillion! There are signs, however, that this borrowing has reached a turning point. For example, in 1998, over a third of all credit card users said they canceled at least one credit card in the last year to help control their borrowing. And many consumers claim to have drastically cut their impulse buys—those spur-of-the-moment purchases like dinners out and magazines in the grocery lines. In addition, some people are replacing credit cards with **debit cards.** Although these cards look like credit cards, they allow the bank to immediately transfer money, subtracting it directly from a checking account.

Sometimes people borrow too much on credit and find they have trouble paying back their debt. When this happens, groups like the National Foundation for Consumer Credit (www.nfcc.org) can help them reach a better balance between spending and saving.

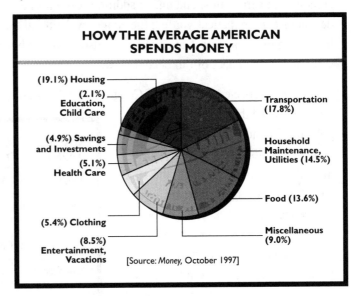

HOW THE AVERAGE AMERICAN SPENDS MONEY

(19.1%) Housing
(2.1%) Education, Child Care
(4.9%) Savings and Investments
(5.1%) Health Care
(5.4%) Clothing
(8.5%) Entertainment, Vacations

Transportation (17.8%)
Household Maintenance, Utilities (14.5%)
Food (13.6%)
Miscellaneous (9.0%)

[Source: *Money*, October 1997]

SKILL PRACTICE

Answer the questions based on the information above.

1. Why do businesses and individuals borrow money? _____

   _____

2. On what do Americans spend the greatest percentage of their income? What percentage of income do they save and invest? _____

   _____

3. If Americans increased their savings, what might be one effect on the economy?

   _____

Answers and explanations start on page 258.

COMMUNITY LINK: Marianne is preparing to vote in the upcoming election. One issue on the ballot is a tax increase to hire more teachers for the school district. Marianne doesn't want to pay more taxes. But, she also realizes that everyone benefits from a strong school system.

SOCIAL STUDIES

Voters Influence the Economy

Ordinary citizens influence the economy as producers, consumers, savers, investors, and credit users. But people can also have an impact on the nation's economy with their votes. In this case, Marianne's vote will have a direct effect on the economy. But the other votes she casts on Election Day also will have an economic impact.

Under the U.S. Constitution, Congress and the president make economic policy. The House of Representatives and the Senate handle most of the nation's money matters. They both must authorize government spending. In addition, Congress oversees many regulatory agencies, whose decisions can dramatically affect the economy. With all this power, Congress can have a big impact on the economy. The president is also involved because it usually takes the president's signature for a budget bill to become law.

American voters elect members of Congress and the president. This means that the voters determine who will make the nation's economic policies. Candidates campaign based on their position about certain issues—including economic issues. In the 1992 and 1996 presidential elections, one independent candidate, Ross Perot, built his whole campaign around economic issues—support for a balanced budget and a simplified tax code. As you can see from the chart, the Democratic and Republican candidates campaigned on a wide variety of issues, including economic ones.

CANDIDATES' STANDS IN 1996 PRESIDENTIAL ELECTION

Issue	Republican Robert Dole	Democrat Bill Clinton
Federal Budget	favored a constitutional amendment requiring a balanced budget; favored balancing the budget by 2002	favored balancing the budget by 2002
Gun Control	supported instant background checks	supported a 5-day waiting period to buy guns; favored banning assault weapons
Taxes	supported 15 percent cut in income tax; supported cutting top tax rate in half	supported reform in the tax process; supported tax cut for middle class; supported tax credits for college

SKILL PRACTICE

Write *F* if the statement is a fact, *O* if it is an opinion.

_____ 1. Voters influence the economy by choosing candidates based on their economic beliefs.

_____ 2. The instant background check on gun buyers, supported by 1996 presidential candidate Dole, would cost too much to enforce.

_____ 3. An amendment requiring the federal government to balance its budget should be added to the Constitution.

_____ 4. Some candidates campaign for office on economic issues alone.

Answers and explanations start on page 258.

■ Apply What You Learn

Read the following article. Then answer the questions that follow.

The Effect of Advertising on Consumers

Whether they use their earnings or they use credit, consumers spend money to take care of their wants and needs. But consumers have only a certain amount of money to spend. As a result, producers work hard to influence how consumers spend their money.

One way in which producers persuade consumers is through advertising. In 1998, U.S. advertisers spent $201.6 billion, on radio, television, direct mail, magazine, Internet, outdoor billboard, and Yellow Pages ads. These advertising dollars encouraged consumers to eat certain brands of foods, drive certain makes of cars, take vacations to certain cities, and buy certain brands of sports equipment.

Some people think producers spend too much money on advertising. Advertising raises the prices of goods and services because the ads are a part of production costs. Others say that although the goal of the advertiser is to sway consumers' opinions, advertising also serves to supply people with information. For example, when Volvo advertised side air bags, consumers learned about a new safety feature. Now, consumers can make a more informed decision about safety features when it comes time to buy a car, even if the car they choose is not a Volvo.

SKILL PRACTICE

Answer the questions based on the information above.

1. Why do producers advertise? _____

_____

2. Why do some people believe advertising helps consumers? _____

_____

3. How can advertisers affect the nation's economy? _____

_____

MATH Connection

Advertising is big business. Of the $201.6 billion spent in 1998, the top three spending categories for advertising were:

- Television $47.4 billion
- Newspaper $44.3 billion
- Direct mail $39.7 billion

Use a calculator to find the percent of total advertising dollars spent on each category. For example, $15.1 billion was spent on radio advertising. Divide that amount by the total: $15.1 ÷ $201.6 = 0.0749007. Round to the thousands place, and change to a percent: 0.075 = 7.5%.

DIRECTIONS: Choose the one best answer to each question.
Questions 1 through 4 refer to the passage and graph.

Part of the government's job is to evaluate the health of the economy. The government uses several measures to do this. One is the gross domestic product, which measures how much was produced inside the nation's borders for a particular year. Often you will find two figures for the GDP. One is the actual dollar amount of production. However, the dollars in this figure may not show that inflation has affected the buying power of each dollar. So the government also may give GDP figures in constant dollars, or dollars adjusted for inflation. A second measure of the nation's economy is unemployment. This tells how many people were out of work for a specific time period. The third measure on which the government depends is the consumer price index. This tells how inflation has caused the prices of a certain group of items to change from year to year.

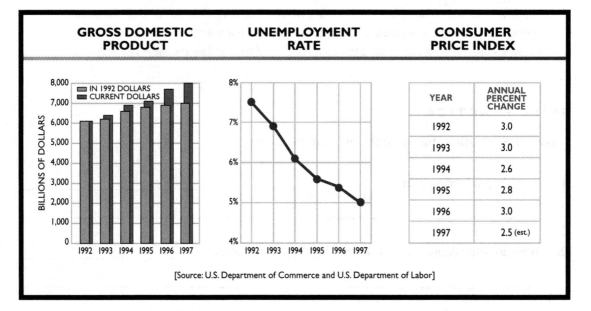

[Source: U.S. Department of Commerce and U.S. Department of Labor]

1. Which is not a measure of economic health?
   (1) the consumer price index
   (2) the rate of inflation
   (3) unemployment statistics
   (4) the number of high school graduates
   (5) the gross domestic product

2. Look at the unemployment chart on this page. Then predict what likely happened to unemployment by 2000.
   (1) The rate rose slowly.
   (2) The rate fell slowly.
   (3) The rate rose to almost 8 percent.
   (4) The rate fell to around 2 percent.
   (5) The rate matched the consumer price index.

3. Which statement best describes inflation?
   (1) It rarely affects the nation's economy.
   (2) It measures price decreases.
   (3) It affects the value of a dollar.
   (4) It varies depending on sales in different parts of the country.
   (5) It is never the same from year to year.

4. Based on the data in the graphs, what conclusion can you draw about the U.S. economy between 1992 and 1997?
   (1) Prices were stagnant.
   (2) The data shows a failing economy.
   (3) Inflation increased.
   (4) Unemployment rose.
   (5) Growth was slow but steady.

Labor unions work for higher wages, better working conditions, and increased benefits for their members. In 1997 the average union member made $640 in a 40-hour, 5-day workweek. In contrast, the average nonunion worker made $478 for the same time work period.

One of the main tactics unions use to influence employers is the strike, or work stoppage. Strikes mean immediate losses of profits for business owners. However, workers also lose income during a strike. The table gives information about strikes between 1950 and 1997. Despite the potential benefits of belonging to a union, union membership has fallen steadily since its peak in 1954. Then, one out of every three U.S. workers was a union member.

UNION STRIKES, 1950–97

Year	Number of Strikes	Workers Involved (thousands)	Number of Days Idle (thousands)
1950	424	1,698	30,390
1960	222	1,381	60,850
1970	381	2,468	52,761
1980	187	795	20,844
1990	44	185	5,926
1997	29	339	4,497

[Source: U.S. Department of Labor]

5. What has been the general trend in union membership since the mid-1950s?
   (1) It has risen steadily.
   (2) It has dropped steadily.
   (3) It rose and then dropped.
   (4) It dropped and then rose.
   (5) It has remained stable throughout the period.

6. Why would strikes be effective means for workers to get higher wages?
   (1) Strikes make employers angry; they want to fire striking employees.
   (2) Strikes can cause economic slowdowns, which effectively cause the value of the dollar to rise.
   (3) Because of the loss of profits business owners experience during a strike, they sometimes will give in to worker demands to get them back on the job.
   (4) Because of the loss of profits business owners experience during a strike, owners let the government subsidize a pay hike for workers.
   (5) Business owners know that the costs of increased wages and benefits won by strikes can be added to the costs of products.

7. How could you figure out the total number of work hours lost in 1960 due to workers out on strike?
   (1) Add the number of days idle in the last column.
   (2) Multiply 1,381,000 workers by 60,850,000 days idle, then by 8 hours in a workday.
   (3) Multiply the 60,850,000 days idle by 8 hours in a workday.
   (4) Multiply the 222 strikes by the 1,381,000 workers by 8 hours in a workday.
   (5) Not enough information is given.

8. What effect could a drop in union membership have on the U.S. economy?
   (1) Wages might go up, causing businesses to move production to countries where wages are lower.
   (2) Wages might go down, causing businesses to remain or move back to the United States.
   (3) People might refuse to work a full work week, and so production would drop.
   (4) People might be willing to work harder, so production would go up.
   (5) Workers would receive better benefits and thus be willing to spend more money.

The Environmental Protection Agency (EPA), established in 1970, protects human health and the environment. To carry out its mission, the EPA regulates air and water quality, as well as the management of waste, poisons, and pesticides. The line graph shows levels of these pollutants during the first 24 years of the EPA's existence. The graph also gives information about the economy that can help you interpret the other data.

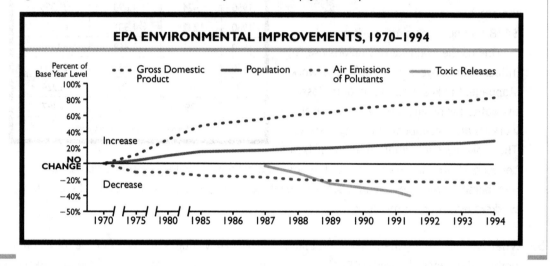

9. Which of the following is illustrated by the line graph?
   (1) levels of pollutants considered safe
   (2) the effectiveness of the EPA's work
   (3) the amount of certain pollutants
   (4) how the EPA's budget works
   (5) the harm of pollutants

10. Why is it important to know what the population growth is during this period?
   (1) Without regulations, a higher population would cause an increase in pollution.
   (2) Trying to control pollution in the United States is now even harder.
   (3) The population experienced a dramatic decrease since 1985.
   (4) Government regulations on pollution levels affect population growth.
   (5) Population growth affects economic stability.

11. Over the 24 years shown on the graph, in what area has the EPA had its <u>most dramatic</u> environmental improvement?
   (1) Improvement was greatest in air emissions.
   (2) Improvement was greatest in toxic releases.
   (3) Improvement was greatest in clean water.
   (4) No improvement was recorded.
   (5) Improvement was equal in all areas.

12. The gross domestic product (GDP) is a measure of our nation's manufacturing of goods. Why would the EPA place the nation's GDP on this graph?
   (1) To identify the causes of pollution.
   (2) To show the relationship between higher production and higher pollution levels.
   (3) To show that the EPA has been effective despite continued increases in manufacturing.
   (4) To illustrate a strong economy.
   (5) To show that more people produced more goods.

Answers and explanations start on page 258.

BEFORE YOU WATCH

20

Civics and Government

OBJECTIVES

1. Understand the purposes and functions of the U.S. constitutional system of government.

2. Describe the structure of the federal and state levels of government in the United States.

3. Identify some of the rights and responsibilities of U.S. citizens.

Every day students go to school. Every day workers ride buses or travel highways. Every day people call 911 for help, and every day citizens pay taxes and obey the laws. In all of these everyday situations, Americans are interacting with their **government.** Knowing that government touches our daily lives is one reason to study both civics and government. These two subjects are often thought of together, and they have a lot in common. Both describe the ways government works to meet the needs of citizens. Civics, however, also focuses on how citizens can be involved in their own governing.

An understanding of government is important to passing the GED Social Studies Test. Understanding how government works and how we can participate in it is very important in the United States, because our democracy is a government by *all* the people.

On the following pages, you will find a brief exercise called *Sneak Preview.* It is designed to introduce you to the topics in the video program and in the corresponding lesson. After you complete the exercise and check your answers, turn to the vocabulary on page 92. There you will find terms that will help you better understand the video and the lesson that follow. After reviewing page 92, you will be ready to watch Program 20.

For additional practice, visit *LiteracyLink* **online at http://www.pbs.org/literacy.**

Sneak Preview

This exercise previews some of the concepts from Program 20. After you answer the questions, use the chart on page 91 to help set your learning goals.

COMMUNITY LINK: Sheila wants to empty a local pond because its standing water could cause disease. Her neighbor Bob feels the pond adds to the beauty of the area and should be left alone. Sheila and Bob decide to take the matter before their local government.

Why Do We Have Government?

Sheila and Bob looked to the government to help resolve their disagreement. People, however, did not always have governments. Prehistoric people mostly hunted and farmed and lived in small groups. These groups had no need for a formal, central government.

Time passed, and people began to form larger, more complex groups. With increased size came more conflict—disagreements that individuals could no longer resolve without structure. People found they needed a system. It would serve several purposes—to keep order, maintain the group's culture, and set group goals. It would also protect members' lives, freedom, and property from other members and from other groups. They called this system a government.

Governments developed in different ways. Some governments came about through force as one strong person or group claimed control of a people or region. Today this kind of government is called a dictatorship. Other governments developed when one person claimed a divine right, or a right given by God, to rule. Today this kind of government is called a monarchy.

Some governments, however, were created when a group's members decided to make a contract with each other. The people would give up some of their freedoms for the good of the group. Their leaders would promise to work for goals common to all the people, rather than for goals set by just a few people. This is the basis of government in the United States, as well as in other democracies.

Answer these questions based on the reading above.

1. Which of the following is <u>not</u> implied within the reading as a reason why people established governments?

   (1) to resolve conflict
   (2) to solve land disputes
   (3) to punish thieves and murderers
   (4) to sustain culture
   (5) to form even larger, more complex groups

2. Which reason <u>best</u> explains why the government of the United States developed into a democracy?

    (1) The founders were not successful in handling disputes.
    (2) The founders could not find a single forceful leader.
    (3) The founders rejected the British monarchy.
    (4) There was no common culture to maintain.
    (5) All were willing to give up their individual freedoms.

3. Which is <u>not</u> an example of how government in the United States maintains the nation's unique culture?

    (1) promoting Fourth of July fireworks
    (2) maintaining the United Nation's headquarters
    (3) putting on a Thanksgiving Day parade
    (4) establishing the Presidents' Day holiday
    (5) teaching students the Pledge of Allegiance

4. Which of the following actions is an example of a U.S. citizen's responsibilities to ensure government by the people?

    (1) voting in government elections
    (2) contributing money to a political candidate
    (3) watching political debates
    (4) reading the editorial section of the local newspaper
    (5) buying U.S.-made products only

Feedback

- If you got all of the answers right...   you have a firm understanding of why governments were created and why they continue to exist.

- If you missed question 1...   you need to learn about the functions of government.

- If you missed question 2...   you need to learn more about the basic form and structure of the U.S. government.

- If you missed question 3...   you need to think about how governments meet specific needs of the groups they govern, including maintaining cultural identity.

- If you missed question 4...   you need to learn more about some of the rights and responsibilities of U.S. citizens.

ANSWERS FOR SNEAK PREVIEW:
1. Choice (5)   2. Choice (3)   3. Choice (2)   4. Choice (1)

Vocabulary for *Civics and Government*

bill	a proposed law
checks and balances	a system by which each branch of government can limit the powers of other branches
federalism	a government system in which the national government and the state governments share power
government	a system a group adopts to keep order, maintain its culture, and set its goals
House of Representatives	the house of the national legislature in which states are represented according to their population
interest group	an organization of people who share a common interest and who work to influence government policies
legislature	a lawmaking body
municipality	an urban area, such as a city or a village
override	to overturn; to cancel
political party	a group of citizens with similar opinions on public issues who work together to influence public policy, win elections, and control the government
Preamble	the introduction to the Constitution
ratification	the process of approving the Constitution
Senate	the house of the national legislature in which states are represented equally
separation of powers	a system by which government power is separated among the branches of government
veto	to reject a bill passed by Congress
volunteer	someone who contributes time and skills for no money

---

➡ NOW WATCH PROGRAM 20:

Think about how the topics introduced in the program—such as the Constitution, Supreme Court decisions, jury duty, and voting—affect people's daily lives. What do you think are the most important responsibilities of being a U.S. citizen?

After you watch the program, work on:

- pages 93–108 in this workbook
- Internet activities at http://www.pbs.org/literacy

AFTER YOU WATCH

20

Civics and Government

On the following pages, you will learn more about the ideas discussed in the video program and have an opportunity to develop and practice your GED social studies skills.

Key Points to Think About

In the video program, you explored:

- How government influences people in their daily lives.
- How governments at all levels work to achieve their goals.
- How citizen involvement protects a democracy.

On the GED Social Studies Test:

- You will be expected to recognize the importance of the Constitution to the government of the United States.
- You will identify the different levels of government in the United States.
- You should know the rights and responsibilities of citizens that are protected by the United States' government structure.

As you work through the lesson for Program 20:

- Be aware of ways in which you interact with the government on a daily basis.
- Compare similarities and differences in the structure of the U.S. government at different levels.
- Evaluate ways in which citizens can influence a democratic government.

GED TIPS

When taking the GED Test, you should:

- Arrive 15 to 20 minutes before the test is scheduled to start, to make sure you can find the room and get situated.
- Know the time limit for each test.
- Use deep breathing and stretching to remain relaxed during the test.

A Constitutional System

A Written Constitution

Jesse was right. The Constitution does guarantee his right to meet. In fact, the Constitution was written to protect the rights and freedoms of all U.S. citizens. It also was written to spell out how the new nation would be run.

After the colonies won their independence, they realized that they needed to unite as one nation, the United States. In 1787, state representatives met in Philadelphia to write a new **plan** for government. It replaced the Articles of Confederation, the new nation's first try at self-government.

The states came to the Constitutional Convention with various concerns and plans. Yet they shared common goals. These goals included the desire to form a more perfect union, to establish justice, and to ensure peace at home. They also had the goals of defending the new nation, promoting the country's well-being, and preserving the rights and freedoms of U.S. citizens. The goals were so important that they became part of the Constitution's **Preamble,** or introduction.

How could 13 different states agree on one document? They reached agreement because of their ability to compromise. For example, the larger states wanted population to determine how many people represented each state. But smaller states wanted equal status with larger states. A compromise created a national **legislature,** or lawmaking body, with two houses. In the **Senate,** each state had the same number of representatives. In the **House of Representatives,** the number of representatives from each state varied according to its population.

After months of debate and compromise, the finished Constitution went to the states for **ratification,** or approval, which it received in 1788. By 1789, the government structure created by the Constitution was in place. Under the Constitution, George Washington became the nation's first president.

SKILL PRACTICE

Answer the questions based on the information above.

1. Why did the colonists feel the need to write a constitution? _____

2. What role did compromise play in ratification of the Constitution? _____

3. In what ways did the workings of the Constitutional Convention show democracy in action?

   _____

Answers and explanations start on page 259.

A Changing Constitution

The writers of the Constitution wanted a government that could adapt to the changing times. They built an amendment process into the Constitution.

The Constitution's amendment process guarantees that the government's power comes from the people. However, the steps that must be followed to amend the Constitution also ensure that major changes in the U.S. government will not result from changing public whims or from one powerful group's efforts. In more than 200 years, the Constitution has been amended only 27 times.

The amendments are listed in the chart.

The Constitution also can change by the ways we interpret what it says. For example, the Constitution gives Congress the right to make all laws that are necessary for the government to carry out its duties. Congress interpreted this to mean that it could make laws to create a federal court system and set up the Postal Service. The Supreme Court determines whether the government has interpreted the words of the Constitution correctly.

AMENDMENTS TO THE CONSTITUTION		
Amendment 1–10	1791	Bill of Rights
Amendment 11	1798	limits lawsuits that can be brought against a state
Amendment 12	1804	changes election methods for president and vice-president
Amendment 13	1865	abolishes slavery in the United States
Amendment 14	1868	forbids states to deny a citizen due process of law or equal protection under the law; defines "citizen"
Amendment 15	1870	guarantees the right to vote regardless of race
Amendment 16	1913	allows Congress to collect income taxes
Amendment 17	1913	requires Senators be elected by the people
Amendment 18	1919	bars manufacture, sale, and transportation of alcoholic beverages
Amendment 19	1920	gives women the right to vote
Amendment 20	1933	changes the start of congressional and presidential terms
Amendment 21	1933	voids the Eighteenth Amendment
Amendment 22	1951	limits the presidency to two terms
Amendment 23	1961	allows electoral votes for Washington, D.C., residents
Amendment 24	1964	abolishes collecting taxes in order to vote
Amendment 25	1967	lists who will take control if the president becomes ill or dies
Amendment 26	1971	gives the right to vote to 18 year olds
Amendment 27	1992	bars Congress from voting itself midterm pay raises

SKILL PRACTICE

Study the chart and the information above. Then check all of the statements that are true. There may be more than one true statement.

_____ 1. The Constitution can be changed by amendments and interpretation.

_____ 2. Only one amendment voided an earlier amendment.

_____ 3. Originally, the people did not elect Senators.

_____ 4. Only the original ten amendments deal with citizens' rights.

_____ 5. Most of the amendments were added in the nineteenth century.

Answers and explanations start on page 259.

The Constitution Limits Power

The Constitution's amendment process allows people to change their government. However, no amendment can go against the Constitution's basic principles.

One of the principles underlying the Constitution is **separation of powers.** According to it, government power is divided to ensure that no one person or group gets too much power. This principle is so important that the Constitution devotes its first three parts to explaining it. Article I describes the legislative branch, with its Senate and House of Representatives, and its power to make laws. That is why Sarah suggested that Rick write Congress instead of the president. Article II outlines the executive branch, with the president at its head, and its power to enforce the laws. And Article III details the judicial branch, made up of the Supreme Court and other courts, and its power to interpret the laws.

In addition, the Constitution uses a system of **checks and balances** to limit the power of any one branch of the government. This system provides each branch with ways to influence—or even undo—the actions of the other branches. For example, the system of checks and balances allows the president to veto, or reject, a bill passed by Congress. (A **bill** is a proposed law.) However, Congress can, with enough votes, **override,** or cancel, a veto.

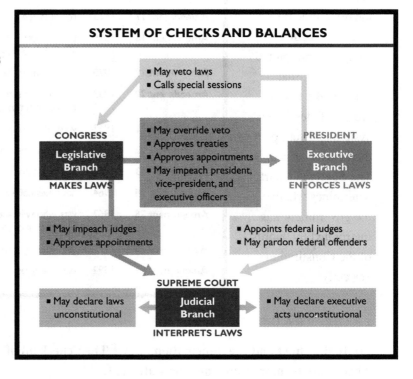

SYSTEM OF CHECKS AND BALANCES

- May veto laws
- Calls special sessions

CONGRESS
Legislative Branch
MAKES LAWS

- May override veto
- Approves treaties
- Approves appointments
- May impeach president, vice-president, and executive officers

PRESIDENT
Executive Branch
ENFORCES LAWS

- May impeach judges
- Approves appointments

- Appoints federal judges
- May pardon federal offenders

SUPREME COURT
Judicial Branch
INTERPRETS LAWS

- May declare laws unconstitutional
- May declare executive acts unconstitutional

SKILL PRACTICE

Write *True* if the sentence is true, *False* if it is false.

_____ 1. The Constitution limits the power that each branch of government has.

_____ 2. Congress can impeach judges.

_____ 3. No bill can become law unless it has the support of both Congress and the president.

_____ 4. The Supreme Court approves treaties.

Answers and explanations start on page 259.

■ Apply What You Learn

Read the following article. Then answer the questions that follow.

When to Amend

One way the Constitution limits the power of the government is by making it hard to change the Constitution itself. Note that 11,000 changes to the Constitution have been suggested but only 27 have passed! This article is about the process that one recently proposed amendment is following.

In 1989 the Supreme Court struck down a Texas law against flag burning. The Court said flag burning was protected under the free speech guarantee of the First Amendment. Congress responded to this decision by proposing an amendment that would outlaw flag burning.

Those supporting the flag-burning amendment say that the flag should be protected because it is a symbol of our nation. Those against the amendment worry that it limits rights of expression guaranteed to all U.S. citizens by the Constitution. They argue that the First Amendment also protects free speech that is ugly and hateful to us. They also point out that there have only been 45 reported flag burnings in our history.

In 1995 the amendment passed in the House and failed in the Senate. It was reintroduced in the House again in 1997, and again received approval. In 2000 the Senate debated and voted on the flag-burning amendment. The amendment received only 63 votes, 4 votes short of a two-thirds majority. If two-thirds of the senators had approved it, the amendment would have been sent to the states for approval. The Constitution requires that three-fourths of the states ratify an amendment before it becomes part of the Constitution.

SKILL PRACTICE

Write *F* if the statement is a fact, *O* if it is an opinion.

_____ 1. The flag-burning amendment will never pass.

_____ 2. The amendment process was designed to be difficult to complete.

_____ 3. Those against the flag-burning amendment are unpatriotic.

_____ 4. For a proposed amendment to become part of the Constitution, it must be ratified by three-fourths of the states.

_____ 5. Out of 11,000 proposed amendments, only 27 have passed into law.

WRITING Connection

The Nineteenth Amendment to the Constitution was passed in 1920. This amendment granted women the right to vote. Before the amendment was passed, no women could vote in any national election.

In a sentence, write one reason why you think supporters wanted the amendment. In another sentence write one reason why other people opposed it. Finally, write one sentence giving an example of the difference it has made for women to have the right to vote.

Answers and explanations start on page 259.

Federal and State Governments

WORKPLACE LINK: It is tax time, and George is frustrated and worried. "Gee," he thinks, "I pay taxes to the national government. I pay taxes to the state. I even pay city taxes. Why can't there just be one tax that covers everything?"

The Constitution Divides Government Powers

Before the Constitution was ratified, under the Articles of Confederation, the nation was a loose league of states. Each state governed itself almost independently. The central government itself held little power.

The Constitution changed this, making the central government much stronger. However, the writers of the Constitution built in limits on the powers of the central government by creating **federalism.** In a federal system, one national government and many state governments share power. The Constitution further restricts the national government's power by listing its powers. All other powers, according to the Constitution, are reserved for the states or the people.

The Constitution gives the national government responsibility for maintaining the general welfare of the nation and its citizens. Therefore, the national government protects national security and manages trade relations with other nations. In the interest of maintaining a strong national economy, the Constitution permits the national government to maintain a national monetary system and to regulate trade among states.

Many day-to-day government functions are reserved for the states. These include providing education, licensing drivers, issuing marriage licenses, and establishing city and county governments and courts.

The national government and the states also share certain powers. Among these shared powers are the power to collect taxes (as George noticed), the power to borrow money, and the power to enforce the laws.

SKILL PRACTICE

Answer the questions based on the information above.

1. What kinds of powers are granted to the national government? _____

2. Why is the power to collect taxes shared by the national government and the states?

    _____

3. How would having a single tax collected by one level of government cause problems for the part of the government that could not collect taxes?

    _____

Answers and explanations start on page 259.

SOCIAL STUDIES

The Structure of State Government

According to the U.S. Constitution, every state has responsibilities to its people. To carry out these responsibilities, each of the 50 states has created a government structure much like the structure of the national government. For example, each state has a constitution. Like the U.S. Constitution, state constitutions describe the structure of the governments they create.

Like the national government, each state government also has three branches—a legislative, an executive, and a judicial branch. In 49 of the 50 states, the legislature has two houses. Nebraska, with its one-house legislature, is the exception. In every state, the legislature is responsible for passing laws and deciding how money collected by the state will be spent.

Each state executive branch is headed by a governor, who is elected by the state's citizens. The job of the governor is to make sure the state's laws are enforced. Other state executive officers help the governor do this work. So do various departments and agencies that also report to the governor.

The responsibility of the state judicial branch is to interpret the laws. State courts deal with both criminal cases, in which someone breaks the law, and civil cases, in which there is a dispute between citizens or groups. In every state, a state supreme court tops the court hierarchy.

Together the state government branches, with the guidance of their constitutions, provide many services. They offer education, administer public welfare programs, protect the environment, and help maintain the highway system. In addition, states are involved in regulating banks and public utilities. They also safeguard citizen health by establishing standards for things ranging from restaurant cleanliness to water purity.

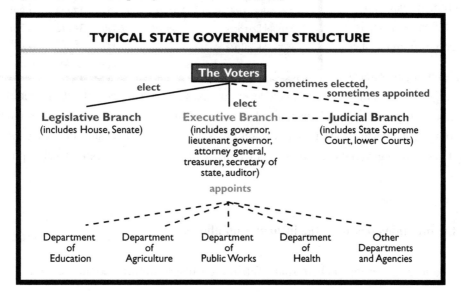

SKILL PRACTICE

Write *F* if the statement is a fact, *O* if it is an opinion.

_____ 1. All state governments have three branches.

_____ 2. It is unnecessary for states to have constitutions.

_____ 3. A state's most important responsibility is to provide education.

_____ 4. States provide many different kinds of services for citizens.

_____ 5. The job of a state governor is similar to the job of the U.S. president.

COMMUNITY LINK: It is snowing heavily outside. Sergio is depending on the local government to make sure he will be able to get to work in the morning. He's not worried, because he knows that his county does a good job of snow removal.

States Create Local Governments

One very important power states have is the power to create local governments. These local governments help the state meet the needs of its citizens. Each state decides what local governments it will use and what responsibilities they have. Counties, **municipalities**—urban areas such as cities and villages—school districts, and townships and towns all are examples of local governments. Other local governments are called special districts, because they are created to provide a specific service, such as overseeing the county's environment.

The relationship between a state and its local governments is not the same as the relationship between a state and the national government. That is because local governments have no authority of their own. Their authority comes from the state.

LEVELS OF GOVERNMENT

	1942	1952	1962	1972	1982	1992
Total	155,116	116,807	91,237	78,269	81,831	85,006
U.S. Government	1	1	1	1	1	1
State Governments	48	50	50	50	50	50
Local Governments	155,067	116,756	91,186	78,218	81,780	84,955
County	3,050	3,052	3,043	3,044	3,041	3,043
Municipality	16,220	16,807	18,000	18,517	19,076	19,279
Townships and Towns	18,919	17,202	17,142	16,991	16,734	16,656
School Districts	108,579	67,355	34,678	15,781	14,851	14,422
Special Districts	8,299	12,340	18,323	23,885	28,078	31,555

[Source: Statistical Abstract of the United States, 1997]

The local level of government provides Sergio's snow removal. It is also the level that fixes potholes in most streets, provides public transportation, puts police on patrol, maintains local libraries, and lights up streets. It keeps records of births, marriages, and deaths, collects and disposes of garbage, and offers health services to its residents. In fact, local governments probably affect daily life more than any other level of government.

SKILL PRACTICE

Answer the questions based on the information above.

1. How do local governments help states fulfill their responsibilities to their citizens?

    _____

2. Use the table to explain how the number of counties and the number of school districts have changed over time. _____

3. What are four services provided by local governments that you use?

    _____

Answers and explanations start on page 259.

■ Apply What You Learn

Read the following article. Then answer the questions that follow.

Government Power Shifts

You know that the Constitution carefully divides powers among the national and the state and local governments. But recently there has been a trend toward concentrating power and responsibility at the national level of government. Here is an example of how that can happen.

Providing education is the responsibility of the states. But the cost of education is high. For example, many people agree that in order to provide a solid education, U.S. schools and libraries must be connected to the Internet. But the expense of equipment, telephone lines, wiring, and Internet access is more than many local and state governments can afford.

That's where the national government stepped in. President Bill Clinton signed into law the Telecommunications Act of 1996. It set up a fund to help schools and libraries buy Internet-related products and services at a specially discounted education rate, nicknamed the E-rate.

Some representatives tried to place limits on the fund. They wanted to pass a law that would deny the E-rate to any school or library that did not use filtering software. Filtering software limits what can be accessed on the Internet. However, librarians and others argued that policies about filtering were best left to the local governments, such as library boards and school districts. Eventually, the government officials dropped the filtering idea.

SKILL PRACTICE

Check all of the statements that are true. There may be more than one true statement.

_____ 1. The responsibilities of the national government and the states never overlap.

_____ 2. Sometimes the national government tries to influence state and local government through rules for funding specific projects.

_____ 3. The issue over the E-rate shows that the national government always gets its way when it clashes with local governments.

READING Connection

In the front section of a recent newspaper were these stories—the major state highway running through the city will soon be repaved, and someone tampered with a neighborhood's roadside mailboxes.

Look in the telephone book to find which national and state offices or government departments represent your area. Then determine from their names which office or department at either government level would probably be involved in each story.

Answers and explanations start on page 259.

Rights and Responsibilities

The Rights of U.S. Citizens

American citizens are guaranteed many rights. Some rights are protected by the U.S. Constitution. For example, Article I prohibits punishment without a court trial. As you know, some amendments also identify and protect rights of U.S. citizens. In fact, it was the purpose of the Bill of Rights— the first ten amendments—to protect Americans' rights and freedoms. The Ninth Amendment goes even further, extending this constitutional protection to rights not listed in the Constitution and its amendments. Freedoms that fall into this category include the freedom to travel anywhere in the United States, freedom to work, freedom to choose to marry, and freedom to get involved in the political process.

In the United States, some laws also protect citizens' rights. For example, a 1974 law passed by Congress defined the constitutional right to a "speedy trial" as the right to have a trial within 100 days of an arrest. In addition, court rulings define and expand the rights of citizens. In 1963, for example, the Supreme Court ruled that everyone accused of a crime had a right to legal counsel.

However, as Megan discovered, the rights of American citizens are not absolute. This is because the rights of many outweigh the rights of one. So the First Amendment's guarantee of freedom of speech does not mean that someone can yell "Fire!" in a crowded movie theater, which could result in panic and injury. Similarly, the right to bear arms, guaranteed by the Second Amendment, does not give Americans the right to go target shooting on a crowded street.

SKILL PRACTICE

Write *F* if the statement is fact, *O* if it is an opinion.

_____ 1. All U.S. citizens have the right to become involved in the political process.

_____ 2. There are too many restrictions on First Amendment rights.

_____ 3. The rights guaranteed to U.S. citizens makes the United States the best country in which to live.

_____ 4. The Bill of Rights is the greatest document ever written.

_____ 5. The Ninth Amendment extends protections to certain rights not listed in the Constitution.

Answers and explanations start on page 260.

SOCIAL STUDIES

Responsibilities of Citizenship

You have seen that the people of the United States enjoy many government-protected rights. However, with those rights come responsibilities. As a democracy, the United States is governed by the people. Therefore, for the government to succeed, citizens must be involved and responsible.

Some of the responsibilities of U.S. citizens are duties they must perform by law. For example, the law requires citizens to defend the nation if defense becomes necessary. Also, the law states that citizens called as jurors or witnesses must go to court and fulfill that duty.

Another legally bound duty is paying taxes. The government uses the taxes Americans pay to support government functions and services. When Americans look for ways to avoid taxes, they ultimately rob the American public of the full use of government services. Perhaps this income loss shows up in fewer police officers on the streets. Or it might result in less funding for government-sponsored health research. Americans who shirk this responsibility can find themselves in jail.

Other responsibilities are voluntary. For example, voting is a right guaranteed by the Constitution. Although U.S. citizens are not legally bound to vote, with the right comes serious responsibility. This is because high citizen participation in elections ensures that candidates who are elected truly represent the wishes and will of the majority of the people.

Sometimes voting is linked to another responsibility—the duty to serve on a jury. Citizens sometimes do not exercise their right to vote because, in some states, courts use lists of registered voters to call people for jury duty. The people who don't vote to evade jury duty consider serving on a jury an unwanted interference in their lives. However, Americans are guaranteed the right to a jury of their equals. This means that other Americans must be willing to take on this responsibility to ensure that this right is secure for all.

SKILL PRACTICE

Answer the questions based on the information above.

1. What is the relationship between Americans' rights and Americans' responsibilities?

   _____

2. What are two reasons citizens might have trouble at times carrying out the responsibility to vote?

   _____

3. What are three duties of American citizens required by law?

   _____

Answers and explanations start on page 260.

COMMUNITY LINK: Indira is concerned about the installation of metal detectors at her son's school. She talks to teachers, administrators, and students to learn more about the issues surrounding this decision. She is not satisfied with the answers she gets, so she decides to run for election to the school board.

Getting Involved in Government

Fulfilling the responsibilities of citizenship automatically involves people in their government. By voting on Election Day, for example, people directly influence who their leaders will be.

People find many other ways in which they can get involved in the government. Thousands of responsible citizens, like Indira, become active in local governments. They might serve on a park board, sit on a county planning group, or participate in a neighborhood watch association.

Thousands also find that becoming involved in a political party is an effective way to influence government. A **political party** is a group of citizens with similar opinions on public issues who work together to influence public policy, win elections, and control the government. In the United States, there are two main political parties—Democrats and Republicans. However, there have been times in our nation's history when a third party has emerged. Often this third party is focused on one issue or one candidate. For example, the Prohibition Party (created in 1872) sought to prevent the manufacture and distribution of alcoholic beverages in the nation. And the Progressive "Bull Moose" Party supported Theodore Roosevelt's 1912 run for the presidency.

Many Americans contribute money to political parties. Many also give their time, doing what the party needs done to ensure its continued strength. Some are paid for the work they do for political parties. But most participants in political parties are **volunteers**—people who contribute their time and their skills for no money.

POLITICAL PARTY IDENTIFICATION, 1994

Republican (43%) Democrat (47%) Other (10%)

[Source: Statistical Abstract of the United States, 1997]

SKILL PRACTICE

Write *Agree* if the author of this article would agree with the sentence, *Disagree* if the author would not agree with the sentence.

_____ 1. Participating in the political process of a democracy is important.

_____ 2. Political parties are bad for the government.

_____ 3. Citizens' communicating their views to their elected officials is one way to show responsibility.

_____ 4. Third-party candidates often focus on a wider range of issues than candidates in either the Democratic or Republican party.

_____ 5. In terms of numbers of people identifying with each party, the Republicans have a slight edge over the Democrats.

   Answers and explanations start on page 260.

■ Apply What You Learn

Read the following article. Then answer the questions that follow.

Interest Groups Influence Government

There are many ways in which Americans exert their influence on government. One way is to join an interest group. An **interest group** is an organization of people who share a common interest. It is different from a political party, because parties want to win elections, while interest groups want to influence government policy.

Some interest groups, such as labor unions, work to influence the government's economic policies. Other interest groups work for the benefit of a specific population. For example, the National Association for the Advancement of Colored People (NAACP) works for African Americans; the Easter Seal Society represents Americans with disabilities.

A third type of interest group promotes specific causes. Some interest groups work to protect the environment (the National Wildlife Federation), while others work to protect consumers (Common Cause).

In 1980, the events in Candy Lightner's life inspired her to become involved in trying to influence government policy. That year a drunk driver killed her daughter. To try to prevent such tragedy from happening to others, Lightner created an interest group to promote policies that would discourage drinking and driving. The group she created was called Mothers Against Drunk Driving, or MADD. Today MADD has almost three million members working together to stop drunk driving.

SKILL PRACTICE

Answer the questions based on the above information.

1. How is an interest group different from a political party?

   _____

2. Name a way that interest groups contribute to American government or society.

   _____

3. Write one reason why you think interest groups are controversial.

   _____

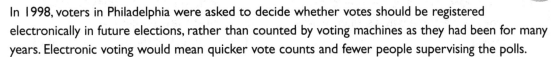

TECHNOLOGY Connection

In 1998, voters in Philadelphia were asked to decide whether votes should be registered electronically in future elections, rather than counted by voting machines as they had been for many years. Electronic voting would mean quicker vote counts and fewer people supervising the polls.

Decide whether you are for or against applying technology to vote counting. Write a paragraph supporting your position.

Answers and explanations start on page 260.

PROGRAM 20: Civics and Government

DIRECTIONS: Choose the <u>one best answer</u> to each question.
<u>Questions 1 through 4</u> refer to the passage and diagram.

The law-making process starts when a person or group has an idea for a new law. They then must take the idea to a senator or a representative, for only people in these two positions can introduce a bill into Congress. The law-making process, as spelled out in the Constitution, is difficult and complex. This prevents Congress from making many unnecessary laws. The diagram illustrates the steps a bill must go through to become a law.

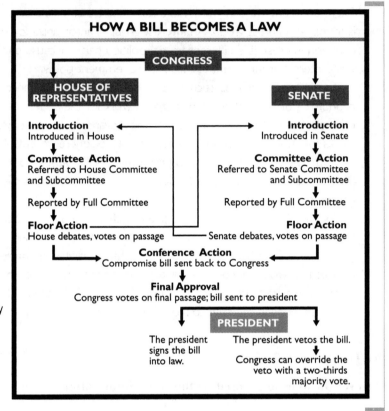

HOW A BILL BECOMES A LAW

CONGRESS

HOUSE OF REPRESENTATIVES | SENATE

Introduction
Introduced in House

Introduction
Introduced in Senate

Committee Action
Referred to House Committee and Subcommittee

Committee Action
Referred to Senate Committee and Subcommittee

Reported by Full Committee

Reported by Full Committee

Floor Action
House debates, votes on passage

Floor Action
Senate debates, votes on passage

Conference Action
Compromise bill sent back to Congress

Final Approval
Congress votes on final passage; bill sent to president

PRESIDENT

The president signs the bill into law.

The president vetos the bill.
Congress can override the veto with a two-thirds majority vote.

1. Who can introduce a bill in Congress?
   (1) the president
   (2) the American people
   (3) a member of Congress
   (4) a judge
   (5) a congressional committee

2. Which statement is true?
   (1) Senate members rarely see a bill introduced in the House.
   (2) Congress does little of its bill work in committees.
   (3) A bill rarely reaches the president worded the same way as when it was introduced.
   (4) The legislative branch is the only branch of government involved in making national laws.
   (5) There is little room for debate in the bill-to-law process.

3. When can a bill become a law?
   (1) after the states approve it
   (2) after it makes its way through the House
   (3) after it makes its way through the Senate
   (4) after the president signs it
   (5) when local governments enforce it

4. Which statement <u>best</u> summarizes the information in the passage and diagram?
   (1) Congress's ability to pass laws is limited by the complexity of the bill-to-law process.
   (2) Congress is the most powerful of the national government branches.
   (3) Separation of powers ensures that no one branch becomes too powerful.
   (4) Congress established the steps a bill must take to become a law.
   (5) The Supreme Court is not involved in making laws.

Questions 5 through 8 refer to the passage and chart.

The president was never meant to run the government's executive branch alone. Early in U.S. history, executive departments were formed to help set government policy. Today, there are 13 executive branches. The heads of these branches meet regularly with the president in a group called the President's Cabinet, advising the president on many important matters.

In addition, hundreds of independent agencies help carry out the work of the executive branch. Some of these agencies deal with specific government policies. For example, the Veteran's Administration carries out policies dealing with people in the armed forces. Other independent agencies were set up to regulate some part of the nation's economic policies. The Interstate Commerce Commission, which regulates people and property moving across state lines, is a regulatory agency. Still other agencies, called government corporations, are responsible for the government's business activities. The United States Postal Service is a government corporation in charge of distributing the nation's mail.

DEPARTMENTS OF THE EXECUTIVE BRANCH

Executive Departments	Year Established	Responsibilities
State	1789	advises president on foreign relations
Treasury	1789	advises president on financial matters
Interior	1849	responsible for the environment
Justice	1870	responsible for enforcing the laws
Agriculture	1889	works to improve farming and foods
Commerce	1913	deals with national and international trade
Labor	1913	works for the welfare of workers
Defense	1947	provides military forces to protect the country
Health & Human Services	1953	promotes citizens' health and welfare
Housing & Urban Development	1963	concerned with housing needs
Transportation	1966	establishes transportation policies
Energy	1977	directs energy policies
Education	1979	works to improve education

5. What is the main purpose of the executive departments and independent agencies?
   (1) to give advice on Supreme Court cases
   (2) to help the president carry out the duties of the executive branch
   (3) to keep Congress abreast of new issues
   (4) to alert the American people to changes in government
   (5) to maintain the separation of power of government branches

6. Which executive departments are most likely to handle the relationships the United States has with other nations?
   (1) Interior and Justice
   (2) Transportation and Energy
   (3) State, Defense, and Commerce
   (4) Treasury, Justice, and Commerce
   (5) Agriculture and Labor

7. When would advice from the Department of the Treasury be especially important?
   (1) during conflicts among different states
   (2) in times of technological development
   (3) in times of famine
   (4) during an economic depression
   (5) in times of international conflict

8. What does the chart show about trends in the executive branch over the years?
   (1) The executive branch has grown in size and responsibilities.
   (2) The executive branch has shrunk in size and limited its responsibilities.
   (3) The executive branch has stayed the same size and kept the same responsibilities.
   (4) More departments have been added, but department staffs have been cut.
   (5) More departments have been added, and the department staffs have grown.

Questions 9 through 12 refer to the following circle graphs.

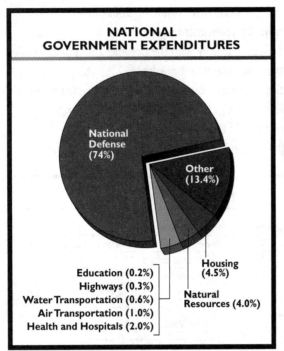

NATIONAL GOVERNMENT EXPENDITURES

National Defense (74%)

Other (13.4%)

Education (0.2%)
Highways (0.3%)
Water Transportation (0.6%)
Air Transportation (1.0%)
Health and Hospitals (2.0%)

Natural Resources (4.0%)

Housing (4.5%)

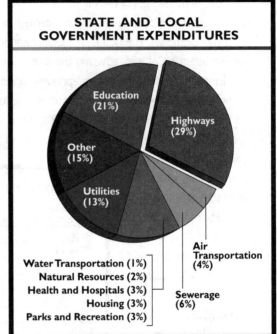

STATE AND LOCAL GOVERNMENT EXPENDITURES

Education (21%)

Highways (29%)

Other (15%)

Utilities (13%)

Water Transportation (1%)
Natural Resources (2%)
Health and Hospitals (3%)
Housing (3%)
Parks and Recreation (3%)

Sewerage (6%)

Air Transportation (4%)

9. On which two areas does the national government spend similar amounts of money?
   (1) education and housing
   (2) education and highways
   (3) natural resources and national defense
   (4) natural resources and utilities
   (5) highways and air transportation

10. Which statement can be inferred from the graphs?
   (1) The national government spends more money in total than do the state and local governments.
   (2) The states hold most of the responsibility for education.
   (3) For both the national government and the state and local governments, health and hospitals take a lower priority than housing.
   (4) Property taxes provide most of the money governments spend.
   (5) Too little money is spent on transportation in this country.

11. What do the graphs tell you about state and local government spending?
   (1) Utilities are the responsibility of the state and local governments.
   (2) Utilities include water, electric, and gas.
   (3) Education includes only elementary schools.
   (4) Each state contributes a different amount to the totals illustrated here.
   (5) Spending at the state and local levels has increased in the last 50 years.

12. Which statement is best illustrated by the data in both graphs?
   (1) Government in the United States is based on federalism.
   (2) Both the national government and the states have the power to borrow money.
   (3) The Constitution is the Supreme Law of the Land.
   (4) States do not contribute to citizen health.
   (5) States are sometimes unwilling to carry out their responsibilities.

Answers and explanations start on page 260.

In this program, geography is called "the mother of all sciences," and you'll understand why after watching. Explore man's impact on the Florida Everglades, learn how maps helped cure cholera, and find out why a California woman went in search of a confluence (the point where longitude and latitude meet).

BEFORE YOU WATCH

21

Geography

OBJECTIVES

1. Understand how places and regions help define our world.
2. Identify geographic factors that shape people's activities and interactions.
3. Examine the relationship between human development and the environment.

Does the weather interest you? Do you like to watch television programs about the ocean or about earthquakes? Are you concerned about how oil spills affect seals and sea birds? Are you curious about wedding customs in faraway places? If you answered yes to any of these questions, then you are interested in geography.

Geography is the study of physical surroundings and their impact upon the people who live in them. The study of geography is especially important since transportation and communication technology have improved, bringing people from all corners of the world in closer contact. Studying geography can help us understand the many different ways people live. It also can help us determine how we can adjust our surroundings for better social and economic development.

On the following pages, you will find a brief exercise called *Sneak Preview.* It introduces you to the topics in the video program and the corresponding lesson. After you complete the exercise and check your answers, turn to the vocabulary on page 112. There you will find terms that will help you better understand the video and the lesson that follows. After reviewing page 112, you will be ready to watch Program 21.

For additional practice, visit *LiteracyLink* online at http://www.pbs.org/literacy.

Sneak Preview

This exercise previews some of the concepts from Program 21. After you answer the questions, use the chart on page 111 to help set your learning goals.

WORKPLACE LINK: Eduardo is watching a television program about the destruction of central Africa's rain forests. Eduardo gets bored and turns off the television. "Rain forests in Africa," he says. "What are rain forests to me?"

The Value of Rain Forests

Eduardo doesn't realize it, but what happens to a region half a world away can indeed affect his life. It is true that the rain forests are far away from Eduardo's home. In fact, most rain forests are located along the Equator, forming a ragged band around Earth's middle region. But the effects of the world's rain forests reach way beyond their locations.

For thousands of years, few people lived in the world's rain forests. Most of those who did were farmers. They cut and burned rain forest trees so they could more easily plant their crops. Because the soil layer of the rain forest is thin, after several harvests, the soil would lose nutrients. Then the farmers simply moved to another site. The rain forest at the first site quickly grew back while farmers cut and burned another part of the rain forests.

Today more and more people are trying to make their living from the rain forest. This spells danger for the region. With recent ranching, mining, and logging projects, millions of acres of rain forest are cleared every year.

Why should Eduardo care about the geography of the rain forests, so far from his home? Eduardo may not realize it, but every day he uses products from the rain forests. Rubber, wood, foods, dyes, and even the chicle that makes chewing gum all come from rain forest trees. Many medicines also have one or more ingredients from rain forest plants.

Eduardo should care about the rain forests because their geography affects him and all of us. The trees of the world's rain forests absorb carbon dioxide from the air we breathe, and they release oxygen into the air. The destruction of the rain forest could upset the balance of these gases in the atmosphere. Too much carbon dioxide or too little oxygen would make it very difficult for people and most other living things to survive on Earth.

Answer these questions based on the reading above.

1. Where are most rain forests located?

    (1)   in the United States
    (2)   at Earth's poles
    (3)   on the continent of Europe
    (4)   in the world's cold, northern regions
    (5)   along Earth's Equator

2. Who were the main inhabitants of the world's rain forests for thousands of years?

    (1) different types of animals but no people at all
    (2) farmers who practiced cut-and-burn agriculture
    (3) loggers who looked for the biggest trees to cut down
    (4) miners who were searching for gold
    (5) hunters who shot animals for sport

3. Expanding populations in rain forest regions has led to many problems in these regions. Which of the following is <u>not</u> one of the problems caused by expanding populations in the rain forests?

    (1) The nutrients in the rain forest soil do not get replenished, because farmers are clearing the land too quickly.
    (2) The soil is washing away rapidly after loggers cut down many trees.
    (3) Run-off from piles of mineral wastes is washing into the rivers of the rain forest, polluting them.
    (4) The climate in the rain forests is cooling off, because of increased carbon dioxide in the air.
    (5) Many species of rain forest plants and animals are being killed off when large areas are cleared for farming.

4. Which technological advance do you think has had the biggest effect on the movement of people into the rain forest in the past 50 years?

    (1) dams built to help bring electricity to rain forest residents
    (2) irrigation canals built so farmers can water their crops
    (3) hospitals built in the rain forest so people have access to health care
    (4) communications satellites launched to allow people in the rain forest to make long distance phone calls
    (5) roads and airports built so travel to remote regions is easier

Feedback

- If you got all of the answers right...   you have a firm understanding of the relationship between Earth's people and its geography.

- If you missed question 1...   you need to learn more about how people define regions to help them understand their world.

- If you missed question 2...   you need to learn more about how people interact with the geography of Earth.

- If you missed question 3...   you need to examine the impact humans have on their surroundings.

- If you missed question 4...   you need to find out how technology has helped overcome geographical barriers.

ANSWERS FOR SNEAK PREVIEW:
1. Choice (5)   2. Choice (2)   3. Choice (4)   4. Choice (5)

Vocabulary for *Geography*

adapt	to adjust
climate	a region's typical weather patterns
commute	to travel back and forth from home to a workplace regularly
delta	silt-built land at the mouth of a river
developing nation	a country that has not yet fully industrialized its economy
downsize	to decrease the number of employees for economic reasons
embargo	a ban, often enforced by a government, on trade with one or more nations
environment	the geography of our immediate surroundings
floodplain	the flat land located along the course of a stream or river that can flood easily
landform	a physical feature of Earth's surface
levee	artificial banks and walls built to control rivers
region	area of the Earth's surface defined by one or more physical or human characteristics
telecommuter	an employee who works at home using an electronic linkup with the office

---

➡ NOW WATCH PROGRAM 21:

You'll learn that Geography is a subject that encompasses a wide range of topics—from the physical look of the earth and satellite mapping to how cultures develop and a sense of place. Choose an aspect of geography that interests you for future study.

After you watch the program, work on:

- pages 113–128 in this workbook
- Internet activities at http://www.pbs.org/literacy

Geography

On the following pages, you will learn more about the ideas discussed in the video program and have an opportunity to develop and practice your GED social studies skills.

Key Points to Think About

In the video program, you explored:

- How places and regions help us define our world.
- How geographic factors help shape people's activities.
- How the surroundings influence social development.

On the GED Social Studies Test:

- You will be expected to recognize terms that are used to describe world geography.
- You will identify ways in which people change their surroundings.
- You should recognize the connection between geography and economics.

As you work through the lesson for Program 21:

- Identify ways in which your surroundings affect your daily life.
- Analyze ways in which the people who live in your region have changed the region's geography.
- Evaluate how the people of the world adapt to their surroundings.

Places and People

COMMUNITY LINK: Elise and her father run every morning along paths in a nearby woods. Elise's younger brothers play there. Now Elise hears that a land developer has bought the woodlands and plans to build a mall there. Elise worries about how this mall will change the quality of life in her neighborhood.

Each Place Is Unique

Like Elise's neighborhood, every place on Earth has physical characteristics that make it different from all other places. Physical characteristics include a place's **landforms,** or such natural features as mountains. Also included are a place's **climate,** or weather patterns, and its waterways. An area's plants, such as the trees in Elise's woods, are other physical characteristics that make one place different from other places.

Human characteristics also make a place special. People's languages, religions, and governments help form a unique place. A place's characteristics shape people's experiences. For example, in America's Midwest, the landforms and seasonal weather patterns sometimes encourage tornadoes. So in Columbus, Ohio, part of life is occasionally hearing sirens issuing tornado warnings. On the other hand, the climate of America's East Coast includes hurricanes. So part of life in Ocean City, Maryland, is seeing signs marking evacuation routes for hurricane emergencies.

The physical and cultural characteristics of a place influence many aspects of life, including what people eat, what they do for a living, and how they relax. People who live far from the ocean may eat less seafood than people living along the coast. People living in the coal-rich Appalachian region of West Virginia are more likely to make their living mining than those who live in a place with few mineral resources. Similarly, mountain climbing might be a more popular sport among those who live near Colorado's Rocky Mountains than among those who live on Kansas's flat plains.

All these factors cause places to be different from each other. It's important to read about places other than the place where you live, so that you can better understand the world's many people and their cultures.

SKILL PRACTICE

Check all of the statements that are true. There may be more than one true statement.

_____ 1. A place's climate, landforms, and waterways are part of its human characteristics.

_____ 2. People are influenced by a place's physical characteristics.

_____ 3. In the United States, all places are alike in terms of cultural characteristics.

_____ 4. A place's climate has a significant influence on what the place is like.

Answers and explanations start on page 260.

People Create the Concept of Regions

Physical and human characteristics help differentiate many places on Earth. To make sense of the great number and kinds of places, people classify areas into regions. A **region** defines an area of Earth's surface according to one or more physical or human characteristics. The concept of regions allows geographers to describe the world clearly. This concept helps us better understand our surroundings.

For example, many Americans live in cities. Whatever their origin, all the people living in the same city share a common culture. They all can watch the same local television shows and listen to the same local radio channels. They all can read the same local newspaper. They travel to work along the same main highways, and they shop at the same stores. This urban setting is one of the human characteristics that helps define the city as a cultural region.

The city also has a government, another human characteristic. This makes it a political region. Everyone in the city has the same mayor. Everyone chooses among the same set of candidates for city council. Each of the 50 states, as well as the United States, is a political region.

Economics, another human characteristic, also defines many regions. One economic region is the Cotton Belt, shown on the map. Most of the nation's cotton is raised in this part of the southern United States.

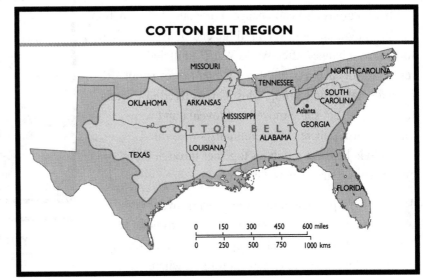

COTTON BELT REGION

PROGRAM 21: Geography

SKILL PRACTICE

Answer the questions based on the information above.

1. What are some human characteristics that help define cities as cultural regions?

    _____

2. List three regions in which an Atlanta resident lives.

    _____

3. What larger geographic region encompasses the Cotton Belt?

    _____

Answers and explanations start on page 261.

COMMUNITY LINK: Franjo spent the first ten years of his life in Yugoslavia. Then in 1991 the nation Franjo had always loved changed. The region in which Franjo lived became independent from Yugoslavia. It became the nation of Croatia.

Regions Change

Regions are changing all the time. Changes in resources, for example, can change a place's economy, population, and quality of life. The American West is proof of this. After its gold and silver mines were no longer profitable, mining towns changed into ghost towns. Changes in ways people use land and new technology also can change a region.

Political regions also can change. For example, the nation of Yugoslavia did not exist until the end of World War I. Its borders changed after World War II to include six republics. In each republic lived a majority of people from a single ethnic group. Most Croats lived in Croatia, for example, but some moved to Slovenia and were a minority group there. The communists who ruled Yugoslavia held the republics together through their government's strict, central control.

Then in 1990 pro-democracy movements swept the world, and communist governments began to fall. By 1991 Yugoslavia was breaking apart along some of its original ethnic lines. Five nations formed where once there was one. These nations were Yugoslavia (including Serbia, Montenegro, Volvodina, and Kosovo), Croatia (Franjo's new home), Slovenia, Bosnia and Herzegovina, and Macedonia. In many parts of the region, conflicts arose between a new nation's ethnic majority and its ethnic minority groups, creating more instability.

SKILL PRACTICE

Write *F* if the statement is a fact, *O* if it is an opinion.

_____ 1. Ghost towns are examples of how regions change over time.

_____ 2. Yugoslavia has changed too much in the last 15 years.

_____ 3. Former Yugoslavia's southernmost nation is Macedonia.

_____ 4. Franjo's loyalty today should be to Croatia, not Yugoslavia.

Answers and explanations start on page 261.

■ Apply What You Learn

Read the following article about the changing region of Rochester, New York. Then answer the questions that follow.

Change Comes to Rochester

More than a hundred years ago, George Eastman started what would later be called the Eastman Kodak Company in Rochester, New York. The company flourished, selling photographic film and cameras. Kodak became a major employer in the Rochester area and also donated large sums of money to support theater and performing arts in the region.

However, Kodak did not keep up with new technology in the camera film industry. Kodak lost sales to a rival film company, Fuji, in Japan. Kodak decided to cut costs by downsizing, or decreasing the number of its employees. Since 1981, it has cut its staff repeatedly, and the Rochester staff has been cut in half. Kodak also has cut its support of the city's arts.

With Kodak's tremendous downsizing, Rochester's economy has deteriorated. Average home prices in Rochester have not increased for a decade. People have moved from the region to find jobs elsewhere.

People are still working in Rochester, where unemployment is low. But that measure alone can be deceiving. It is estimated that today about one-third of the available jobs in Rochester are temporary. With these temporary jobs, workers generally receive no benefits. Their pay is lower than that of full-time employees who do the same work. Many work more than one job. The low unemployment rate also does not indicate how many workers have taken jobs for far less money than they used to make.

SKILL PRACTICE

Match the effect to its cause.

Cause	Effect
_____ 1. Kodak doesn't keep up with technological advances.	a. Half of Kodak's Rochester workers lose their jobs.
_____ 2. Kodak decides to downsize.	b. Fuji increases its film sales.
_____ 3. Kodak gives less money to the community.	c. Rochester's theaters cut the number of performances they give.

WRITING Connection

Landforms are the natural features that occur on the surface of Earth. Landforms can be mountains, hills, plateaus, or plains. River valleys, such as the Genesee River valley in Rochester, are also landforms.

Find a picture of a landform in an encyclopedia. Look closely at the characteristics of the landform. Then write a description of it in your own words.

Answers and explanations start on page 261.

Geography and Human Interaction

WORKPLACE LINK: Felina is happy today because the new highway extension close to her town just opened. The new extension will get Felina to work much faster than driving on roads full of stoplights.

Transportation and Communication Conquer Geography

Felina uses the nation's highway system to get to work. The highways allow her to get to work by **commuting,** or traveling back and forth from home to workplace regularly. In the days before cars, buses, and highways, the same trip would have taken many hours. Felina would have been forced to live nearer to her job.

Improvements in transportation also help goods move faster. In hours, airplanes travel distances that took weeks by ship, barge, or train. This makes it easier and cheaper to transport some goods all over the world. In addition, more efficient, faster shipping methods can bring other goods in by sea. Such improved movement opens up new markets, so people can buy and sell more and more goods.

Today the improved transportation system affects Felina's work life. Felina may find, however, that communication advances will soon have an even bigger impact on her work life. This is because computers, phones, and faxes have together made it possible for some people to work at home, at least part of the time. These workers are able to communicate electronically with their employers. They are called **telecommuters.** They save money on gas, parking fees, work clothes, and dry cleaning, for example. Their employers also save money, for they usually can rent smaller office space. The trend toward working at home has an impact on the surroundings, too, since fewer people commute to work. This means fewer cars and buses, which means less traffic and pollution.

SKILL PRACTICE

Write *F* if the statement is fact, *O* if is it an opinion.

_____ 1. The invention of the airplane was the greatest improvement in transportation the world has ever seen.

_____ 2. Telecommuting helps employers and employees save money.

_____ 3. Improvements in transportation have led to increased international trade.

_____ 4. Telecommuting is the best way people in the United States can help protect the environment.

_____ 5. Unfortunately, personal privacy is lost with some new communications technology.

Answers and explanations start on page 261.

SOCIAL STUDIES

Geography Influences the Economy

Improved transportation and communication systems link regions. They also link nations. They make it easier for one nation to get what it lacks from other nations. This is important, because no region or country has everything its people need.

For example, **developing nations**—those that have not yet fully industrialized their economy—often have raw materials that industrialized nations need. Many developing nations prepare raw materials and harvest food for export. For example, in Tonga, a nation in the South Pacific Ocean, 70 percent of the people farm. They take advantage of the rich soil their island offers to grow crops, such as vanilla beans, ginger, and black pepper. Industrialized countries want these food products, and so they trade their processed and manufactured goods. People in most developing nations also raise crops for their own use.

Recently, industrialized countries have been exporting more than just manufactured goods to developing nations. They are also exporting manufacturing jobs, because in developing nations, manufacturing costs are lower. For example, it costs an average of $17.20 an hour to employ someone in manufacturing in the United States. In Mexico, the cost drops to an average of $1.51 an hour. This savings has encouraged U.S. manufacturing companies to open factories in developing nations. And this has meant that more people in developing nations are taking industrial jobs.

This change from agriculture to industry has created another change as well. Most manufacturing jobs are in cities. This has made many people move from their rural homes to urban areas, causing massive population shifts in some nations. As a result of this shift, some developing nations have had to import food to their cities from elsewhere when food supplies have been unevenly distributed within their borders.

SKILL PRACTICE

Answer the questions based on the information above.

1. Why are many people in developing nations employed in agriculture? _____

    _____

2. Why are some industrialized nations sending manufacturing jobs to developing countries?

    _____

3. What has caused population shifts in some developing nations? _____

    _____

4. What do you think might happen if industrialized nations continue to send jobs to developing nations? _____

    _____

Answers and explanations start on page 261.

COMMUNITY LINK: Alex reads in the newspaper that the United States is taking Israel's side in a new Middle East conflict. Alex remembers that when this happened before, it led to an energy crisis in the United States. He wonders if another energy crisis will result.

The Problems of a Smaller World

The same economic links that encourage trade between regions also can lead to conflict. For example, by the 1970s, transportation improvements had encouraged the United States to rely more and more on petroleum, or oil, from the Middle East. Pipelines in the Middle East brought oil from the fields to ports, where tankers waited to bring the oil to the United States. The pipelines helped make imported Middle East oil cheaper than U.S. oil.

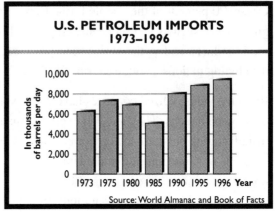

U.S. PETROLEUM IMPORTS 1973–1996

In thousands of barrels per day

Source: World Almanac and Book of Facts

Then in 1973 some Middle East countries went to war against Israel. The United States announced that it would supply Israel with weapons. In response, Saudi Arabia and other oil-producing nations in the region put an **embargo,** or stoppage, on their oil shipments to the United States. This plunged the United States into the energy crisis that Alex remembered. The energy crisis did not end until the Arab oil embargo ended in 1974. The graph shows how U.S. oil imports have changed since then.

Economic problems related to global trade, or the lack of global trade, are only one challenge of our increasingly linked world. Other problems relate to the ease of worldwide communications. For example, in 1998, the Environmental Protection Agency (EPA) considered posting on the World Wide Web details of what would happen if certain dangerous substances were released. Immediately, some groups, including some congressional representatives, the Federal Bureau of Investigation (FBI), and even the nation's firefighters, argued against releasing this information on the Internet. They argued that terrorists could use this information to increase terrorism against the United States.

SKILL PRACTICE

Check all the statements that are true. There may be more than one true statement.

_____ 1. In the early 1970s Middle East oil was cheaper than U.S. oil.

_____ 2. To protest a U.S. foreign policy decision, Saudi Arabia and other Middle East nations imposed an oil embargo on the United States in 1973.

_____ 3. According to the graph, the United States today is less dependent on imported petroleum than it was in 1973.

_____ 4. In 1998 the FBI was upset because the EPA was going to release information on how to stop chemical fires.

_____ 5. Increased worldwide communication could potentially pose increased risk of terrorist attacks.

Answers and explanations start on page 261.

■ Apply What You Learn

Read the following article about the technological world of the future. Then answer the questions that follow.

The World of the Future

In the future, experts predict that new technologies will break down many of the barriers geography presents to us today. For example, a new kind of airplane is being developed that will travel at three times the speed of sound. This plane will be able to fly for 10,000 miles, almost half way around the world, without refueling. In a decade, tests will start on a vehicle that will be part airplane and part spaceship. This vehicle will actually go into orbit and will deliver people from the United States to places as far away as Tokyo, Japan, and Sydney, Australia, in two hours.

Car travel also will change during this time. The first "intelligent highways" will be built. These highways will provide cruise control and help people navigate. Cars will be attached bumper to bumper to form trains. These car-trains will be guided electronically to their destination.

In the next century, tunnels and bridges will be used to connect continents. There are plans in the works to connect Europe and Africa at Gibraltar. A link also is proposed between Asia and North America across the Bering Strait.

SKILL PRACTICE

Match the effect to its cause.

Cause	Effect
_____ 1. Improvements in air transportation will allow people to travel around the world in hours.	a. Transcontinental trade will increase.
_____ 2. Tunnels will connect people across continents.	b. Road travel will be safer.
_____ 3. Cars will be linked and guided to their destination electronically.	c. People will be more likely to visit people in distant places and learn about other cultures.

SCIENCE Connection

Because geography is the study of Earth and its people, geographers also analyze population growth. Here are three ways in which experts think people will deal with the future's expanding world population:

1. Domed enclosures provide solar heat to new settlements in the Arctic.
2. Skyscrapers extend 200 stories into the air.
3. Permanent colonies will be built in space.

Think about what would be involved in building each of these structures. Then write down your prediction of the order in which you think the structures are most likely to be built. Finally, write an explanation why you think this order is most likely.

Answers and explanations start on page 261.

Environments and Social Development

FAMILY LINK: Julia is happily packing for her family's vacation. She folds up her shorts and T-shirts and thinks about the hot Miami sun waiting for her. She wishes she didn't have to wear her winter coat, because she knows she won't need it in Florida. But she'll need it on her way to the airport.

Geography Influences People

Julia has shown us one way in which people have **adapted,** or adjusted, to their environment. The **environment** is the geography of our immediate surroundings. It includes a place's soil, climate, natural features, and vegetation. Julia must adapt to her environment's climate. Her home is in a place where the winters are cold enough for people to adapt by wearing winter coats. She is going to vacation in Florida, where people adapt to the warm, sunny climate by wearing shorts and T-shirts. If Julia doesn't adapt to the environment in this way, she could be extremely uncomfortable.

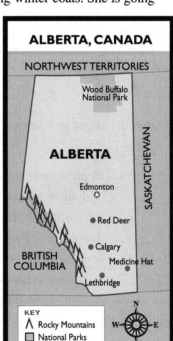

Just as people adapt their clothing to their environment, they also adapt their housing. Good examples of this can be seen in different Native American groups that were America's first people. The Algonquins of New England built dome-shaped shelters made of bark because trees were plentiful in their environment. In contrast, the Native Americans of the Great Plains lived in teepees made of buffalo skins because buffalo were plentiful there.

People's decisions on where to settle are also influenced by their environment. The map of Alberta, Canada, shows that the province's western border is quite mountainous. There are no cities in that area. Instead, much of this land has been set aside as National Parks.

SKILL PRACTICE

Answer the questions based on the information above.

1. What are two ways people adapt to the climate of the region where they live?

2. What did the Plains Indians use to build shelters, and why did they use these resources?

3. Why is Alberta's border with British Columbia sparsely settled? What interests might people have who visit the area?

Answers and explanations start on page 261.

Technology Conquers Geography

Using a variety of technologies, people have figured out ways to take advantage of all but Earth's harshest places. For example, in the 1940s, few people lived in Phoenix, Arizona. One reason for the sparse population was Phoenix's hot, dry climate. (High temperatures in summer often soar above 100° for weeks on end.) Then came a new technology—air conditioning. By the 1950s, air conditioning had widespread use. Phoenix began to attract manufacturing companies, especially companies that made computers and electronic equipment. Phoenix's population doubled, then doubled again. Today over a million people call Phoenix home. Because of technological advances such as air conditioning, the environment of Phoenix and many other hot places on Earth was tamed for human use.

Another example of technology overcoming geographical barriers is in Alaska. In 1968 one of the greatest oil discoveries of all time was made at Prudhoe Bay in northern Alaska, a frozen, forbidding region above the Arctic Circle. Now the problem was how to get the oil from Prudhoe Bay to a port where ships could take it to market. To solve this problem, seven oil companies banded together to build a pipeline from Prudhoe Bay to Valdez, the northernmost ice-free port in North America. The pipeline required special pipe that could withstand the harsh environment, and it would extend 800 miles from the Arctic Ocean in the north to southern Alaska and the Pacific Ocean. Just to get the 70,000 workers to the area to build the pipeline, the companies had to build hundreds of miles of roads. They even had to construct a 2,250-foot-long log-and-ice bridge across the Yukon River! After three years and at a cost of $8 billion, the Trans-Alaska Pipeline opened. It was the world's first Arctic pipeline, and it brings from Prudhoe Bay up to 20 percent of all the oil produced in the United States.

THE TRANS-ALASKA PIPELINE

SKILL PRACTICE

Match the effect to its cause.

Cause

_____ 1. A place's harsh climate presents challenges to people who live there.

_____ 2. Air conditioning becomes widely available.

_____ 3. Oil is found in northern Alaska.

_____ 4. The Arctic region where the Alaskan oil is located is extremely isolated.

Effect

a. Oil companies band together to plan the Trans-Alaska pipeline.

b. People develop methods and behaviors to adapt to their environment.

c. Oil companies built hundreds of miles of roads to transport workers and materials to the pipeline sites.

d. Manufacturers settle in Phoenix.

Answers and explanations start on page 261.

COMMUNITY LINK: The construction of a dam upstream from Carlos's town has brought new industry to the area. But it also has reduced the flow of water in the river. This has meant water shortages, with frequent bans on lawn watering and car washing, and rising water bills for Carlos and his neighbors.

The Impact of Humans on Their Environment

In almost every corner of the world, people have used technology to change the environment. But there are prices people must pay when they change geography. For example, in exchange for the dam that attracts new industry to town, the residents pay by having less available water.

Air conditioning and improved irrigation techniques have brought Americans to the dry Southwest, and the presence of people has increased the demand for water there. To meet their water needs, people build dams and canals, which bring the waters of the Colorado River to their cities and farms. The river water now flows to the houses, swimming pools, and lawns of 21 million people, and to 2 million acres of farmland. In fact, U.S. and Mexican residents take away so much water that, in most years, the river never reaches the sea anymore. It just disappears into the desert. This has turned the river's mouth, once rich with wildlife, into a mud-cracked flat.

Unlike the Colorado River, some of the waters of Egypt's Nile River still reach the sea. But damming has drastically altered the region fed by the Nile. For thousands of years, Egyptians have lived in the long strip of fertile land along the Nile created by the river's dependable floods. The floods brought both water and nutrients to the soil. However, they also limited the time crops could be grown to only four months of the year.

To allow for a longer growing season, Egyptians began damming the Nile. The Aswan High Dam, built in the 1960s, now controls the Nile's waters. Using damming and irrigation, the Nile provides water for more than 60 million people and more than 3 million acres of farmland. But the silt—fertile soil deposits—that used to travel with the floodwaters now stops behind the dam. This means farmers must use more fertilizer. It also means that the Nile's **delta**—silt-built land at the mouth of a river—is shrinking. Also, the silt that the delta receives often is polluted by the growing number of manufacturers upstream. Both these changes are affecting delta farming, which supplies much of Egypt's food.

SKILL PRACTICE

Write *F* if the statement is a fact, *O* if it is an opinion.

_____ 1. Because of damming on the Colorado River, the river's delta has become a dried-up mud flat.

_____ 2. The Nile's delta is shrinking because of the Aswan High Dam.

_____ 3. The Nile is a more important river than the Colorado.

_____ 4. The Aswan High Dam should never have been built.

_____ 5. It's okay to pollute if it doesn't affect our waterways.

Answers and explanations start on page 261.

■ Apply What You Learn

Read the following article about flooding along the Mississippi River. Then answer the questions that follow.

Flooding Continues; River Rages

Heavy rains started falling in the Midwest in the summer and fall of 1992. They fell on ground already soaked, in part, because a cool summer had not caused much water to evaporate. Then in April 1993, the rains started again and lasted for four months. The Mississippi River poured over its banks to flood 8 million acres in nine states. The land stayed flooded for two months. All in all, floodwaters overwhelmed 77 towns, destroyed 50,000 homes, and did up to $20 billion in damage.

Before the flood, the U.S. federal government had spent over a century building hundreds of **levees**—artificial banks and walls—to direct the Mississippi's waters. Assuming the levees would hold, many people built homes on the **floodplain,** the flat land along a stream or river that is apt to flood. More than 1,200 of the Mississippi's levees failed during the 1993 flood. That is why the damage from the flood was so great.

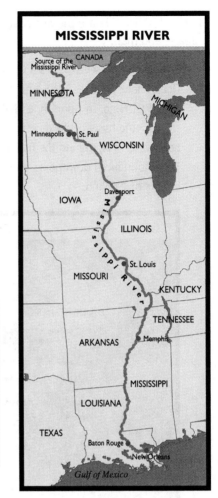

SKILL PRACTICE

Check all the statements that are true. There may be more than one true statement.

_____ 1. The purpose of a levee is to control the flow of river water.

_____ 2. The weather in 1992 was one cause of the 1993 flood.

_____ 3. The nine states most affected by the 1993 flood of the Mississippi River were Wisconsin, Iowa, Illinois, Indiana, Missouri, Kentucky, Tennessee, Arkansas, and Mississippi.

_____ 4. The federal government of the United States leaves flood control to state governments.

WRITING Connection

People in Wisconsin and Missouri learned from the 1993 flood. Cities there have moved houses and businesses from the floodplain to higher locations.

Imagine you live in a town on a floodplain. Write a letter to the mayor, explaining why the town must be moved to higher ground.

Answers and explanations start on page 261.

DIRECTIONS: Choose the <u>one best answer</u> to each question. <u>Questions 1 through 4</u> refer to the passage and map.

Every three to seven years a weather pattern occurs which involves the warming of the Pacific Ocean near the coast of South America. Peaking around Christmas time, the weather pattern is called El Niño. In Spanish, El Niño means "the child," a reference to the baby Jesus.

El Niño has worldwide effects. Along America's Pacific coast, warm water drives away the cold-water fish, ruining the fishing industry. In Chicago, daffodils bloom in mid-winter. In Peru, El Niño-induced downpours and once created a 2,300-square-mile lake. The map shows other effects of El Niño.

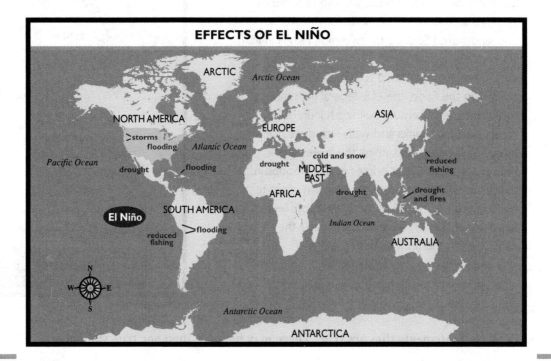

EFFECTS OF EL NIÑO

1. In which region of the world does El Niño warm the ocean waters?
   (1) the Arctic
   (2) the north Atlantic coast off Europe
   (3) the Pacific coast off South America
   (4) the Indian Ocean near India
   (5) the Antarctic

2. What does the occurrence of El Niño show?
   (1) People can have a huge effect on the environment of the entire planet.
   (2) Most people are at the mercy of the weather for their livelihood.
   (3) People have little control over some weather-related events.
   (4) People are more affected by changes in weather patterns than animals are.
   (5) The weather in one place does not affect the weather in other places.

3. Which statement <u>does</u> <u>not</u> apply to El Niño?
   (1) El Niño occurs every three to seven years.
   (2) El Niño affects the fish population of the Pacific Ocean.
   (3) El Niño usually occurs in the winter.
   (4) El Niño has caused flooding in every continent.
   (5) El Niño can bring snow to the Middle East.

4. What will improvement in the ability to forecast El Niño mean?
   (1) People will have time to prepare for its impact.
   (2) The United States can outlaw El Niño before it happens again.
   (3) People will move away from coastal regions.
   (4) People can change the weather patterns.
   (5) People will build more dams.

As the diagram shows, humans thrive because our atmosphere allows most sunlight to reach Earth, warming us. However, some scientists believe that human activity is contributing to a rising atmospheric temperature called global warming. Global warming occurs due to a buildup of certain gases in the air. These gases trap heat close to Earth. For example, over half of all electricity in the United States is generated from the burning of coal. However, burning coal releases carbon dioxide, one of the gases suspected of raising the atmosphere's temperature. Burning other fossil fuels, such as natural gas and oil, as sources of energy also releases extra carbon dioxide.

Some scientists predict that the temperature on Earth could increase by more than a degree in the next 25 years. That doesn't sound like a cause for concern, but thousands of years ago, ice covered most of North America. Why? Because Earth's temperature had dropped an average of nine degrees, creating the last Ice Age.

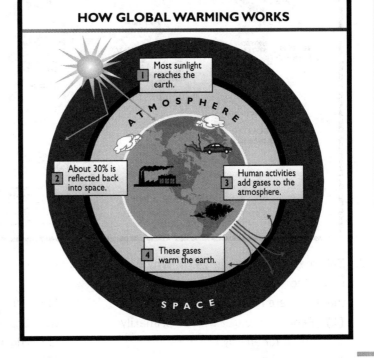

HOW GLOBAL WARMING WORKS

1 Most sunlight reaches the earth.

ATMOSPHERE

2 About 30% is reflected back into space.

3 Human activities add gases to the atmosphere.

4 These gases warm the earth.

SPACE

5. According to the diagram, about how much sunlight is reflected from Earth's atmosphere back into space?
   (1) none
   (2) about 20 percent
   (3) about 30 percent
   (4) about 40 percent
   (5) about 50 percent

6. Carbon dioxide released by human activity stays in the atmosphere for 500 years. What is one easy way to reduce the amount of carbon dioxide released?
   (1) stop using aerosol cans
   (2) increase electricity use
   (3) decrease electricity use
   (4) use more coal for heating
   (5) thicken the atmosphere with other gases

7. Which does not threaten Earth's atmosphere?
   (1) factories
   (2) cars
   (3) logging
   (4) fossil fuels
   (5) solar heating

8. Because experts record that Earth's temperature is increasing, what might we expect?
   (1) The world climate will become wetter, causing the deserts to bloom.
   (2) Record rain will fall, causing many rivers to flood.
   (3) Less sunlight will reach Earth.
   (4) The increase will be too small to have an effect.
   (5) Polar ice caps will shrink, causing flooding along sea coasts.

Questions 9 through 12 refer to the passage and map.

Resources are unevenly distributed across Earth. Rather than showing the nations of the world in their correct size, this map shows the size of nations in proportion to the oil resources they have.

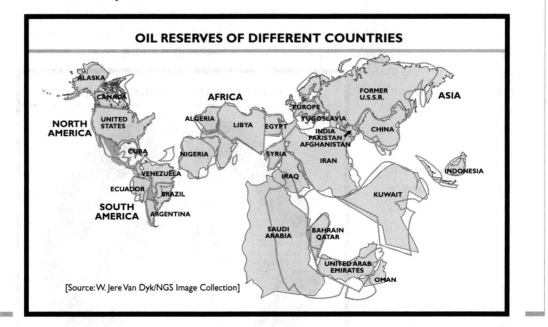

OIL RESERVES OF DIFFERENT COUNTRIES

[Source: W. Jere Van Dyk/NGS Image Collection]

9. This map was drawn in 1974. Why might the sizes of countries change if the map were redrawn today?
    (1) People no longer depend primarily on oil for energy.
    (2) Since 1974 nations have continued to use reserves and discover new ones.
    (3) The former Yugoslavia was split into five different countries.
    (4) The Trans-Alaska pipeline has closed down since 1974.
    (5) The energy crisis came to an end in 1974.

10. Why do you think Australia is not shown on this map?
    (1) Australia used up all its oil reserves before 1974.
    (2) Australia has no known oil reserves.
    (3) The map only covers the Northern Hemisphere.
    (4) The map only covers the Southern Hemisphere.
    (5) The map only covers the Western Hemisphere.

11. Which country holds South America's biggest oil reserves?
    (1) Venezuela
    (2) Ecuador
    (3) Nigeria
    (4) Brazil
    (5) Argentina

12. In 1990 Iraq invaded Kuwait, claiming that Kuwait was really part of Iraq. What might have been one reason for the invasion?
    (1) Kuwait wanted to be part of Iraq, because Iraq had more oil that could be used for home heating there.
    (2) Kuwait wanted to be part of Iraq to participate in Iraq's oil-rich economy.
    (3) Iraq wanted to take over the vast oil fields of Kuwait and gain power or income from selling the oil.
    (4) Iraq wanted to take over the vast oil fields of Kuwait to gain the oil for home heating in Iraq.
    (5) Since Iraq and Kuwait both have large oil reserves, the reason must have related to politics, not oil.

Answers and explanations start on page 261.

Social Studies Practice Test

DIRECTIONS: Choose the <u>one best answer</u> to each question.

<u>Questions 1 and 2</u> refer to the following passage.

In 1818 Frederick Douglass was born into slavery in Maryland. When he was 20, he escaped north and began speaking out against slavery. Douglass settled in Rochester, New York, a stop on the Underground Railroad. This was the secret system of about 3,000 households that helped African Americans journey from slavery in the South to freedom in the North or Canada.

The first runaway slave to give public speeches, Douglass was a great orator. He quickly became famous. With money he raised from public speaking, he and another abolitionist (person against slavery) started up a newspaper in 1847 to promote the anti-slavery cause. Douglass was also one of the persons who persuaded President Abraham Lincoln to go forward with the Emancipation Proclamation, which freed enslaved African Americans in the South during the Civil War.

1. Which statement does the passage <u>best</u> support?
   (1) Douglass worked against abolitionists.
   (2) Douglass thought that the North would win the Civil War.
   (3) Douglass worked toward helping women gain the right to vote.
   (4) Douglass thought the United States did enough to prevent racial discrimination.
   (5) Douglass worked toward ending slavery in the United States.

2. What conclusion can you draw from the passage?
   (1) Douglass's work was respected by abolitionists and other Americans.
   (2) Douglass was poor after the Civil War.
   (3) Douglass founded the Underground Railroad.
   (4) Douglass freed African Americans.
   (5) Douglass's newspaper was only for former slaves.

<u>Question 3</u> is based on the following passage.

When African-American soldiers returned home after World War II, they objected strongly to segregation. They had risked their lives for a country that, at home, kept their families separated from white Americans in places such as schools, restaurants, and buses. Then, in 1954 the U.S. Supreme Court ruled against segregation in public schools in *Brown* v. *Board of Education*. As a result, the civil rights movement grew during the 1950s.

Among the movement's leaders was Dr. Martin Luther King, Jr. A minister, King preached nonviolent ways of protesting segregation. He and other black leaders organized a march on Washington, D.C., in August 1963. More than 250,000 supporters heard King say: "In a sense we have come to our nation's capital to cash a check. When the architects of our republic wrote the magnificent words of the Constitution and the Declaration of Independence, they were signing a promissory note to which every American was to fall heir . . . America has given the Negro people a bad check; a check which has come back marked "insufficient funds." But we . . . refuse to believe that there are insufficient funds in the great vaults of opportunity of this nation."

3. Which statement best describes what King meant by "insufficient funds"?
   (1) The United States owed money to black Americans for its unjust treatment of them.
   (2) White business owners gave lower pay to black workers.
   (3) The United States had not provided blacks with the same rights as whites.
   (4) Schools in southern states treated African-American students unfairly.
   (5) African Americans in some states enjoyed better protection of their rights than those who lived in others.

Questions 4 through 7 are based on the following map.

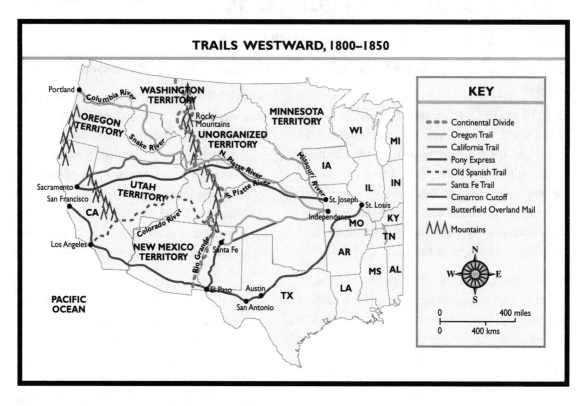

TRAILS WESTWARD, 1800–1850

KEY

- - - Continental Divide
— Oregon Trail
— California Trail
— Pony Express
- - - Old Spanish Trail
— Santa Fe Trail
— Cimarron Cutoff
— Butterfield Overland Mail
ΛΛΛ Mountains

4. What is the main purpose of this map?
   (1) to show when the eastern coast was settled
   (2) to show how the borders of the states were formed
   (3) to show how the United States claimed Mexico
   (4) to show how settlers and traders took a number of different routes west
   (5) to show the bodies of water and mountains the pioneers crossed

5. Which statement does the map support?
   (1) The Pony Express and the Santa Fe Trail both began at Independence, Missouri.
   (2) Some trails followed the Continental Divide.
   (3) The Cimarron Cutoff saved pioneers time.
   (4) The California Trail took pioneers to San Francisco.
   (5) All trails required crossing the Rocky Mountains.

6. Texas became a state in 1845. If the U.S. president wanted to get a message to the new governor in Austin, which trail would his messenger be most likely to use?
   (1) the Cimarron Cutoff
   (2) the Old Spanish Trail
   (3) the Pony Express route
   (4) the Butterfield Overland Mail route
   (5) the Santa Fe Trail

7. California became a state in 1850 while much of the Rocky Mountain region was called the Unorganized Territory. Based on this information, what can you infer about the settlement of the United States?
   (1) The North was settled before the South.
   (2) The South was settled before the North.
   (3) The Rocky Mountain region was settled before the East Coast.
   (4) The Rocky Mountain region was settled before the West Coast.
   (5) The West Coast was settled before the Rocky Mountain region.

Question 8 is based on the following passage and chart.

People originally called World War I the Great War, because they hoped that they would never see such terrible bloodshed again. The war began in 1914 when Archduke Francis Ferdinand of Austria-Hungary was assassinated. Because the killer had ties to Serbia, Austria-Hungary concluded that the Serbian government had encouraged the assassination. Austria-Hungary declared war on Serbia. Germany, Bulgaria, and the Ottoman Empire joined Austria-Hungary in the fight. They became known as the Central Powers. The Allies—Great Britain, France, Russia, and over a dozen other nations— were the nations that sided with Serbia.

Both sides thought the war would not last long. They were wrong. World War I dragged on for four years. It did not end until the United States, angered at the German sinking of unarmed ships, including American boats, added its strength to the Allies in 1917. A year later, the Central Powers admitted defeat.

MILITARY CASUALTIES IN WORLD WAR I (1914–1918)*

THE ALLIES	Dead	Wounded
Belgium	14,000	44,700
British Empire	908,400	2,090,200
France	1,385,000	4,266,000
Greece	5,000	21,000
Italy	650,000	947,000
Portugal	7,200	13,800
Romania	335,700	120,000
Russia	1,700,000	4,950,000
Serbia and Montenegro	48,000	143,000
United States	116,516	204,002
THE CENTRAL POWERS		
Austria-Hungary	1,200,000	3,620,000
Bulgaria	87,500	152,400
Germany	1,773,700	4,216,100
Ottoman Empire	325,000	400,000

*Except for the United States, all figures are approximate.

8. What is the most likely explanation for the relatively low number of casualties experienced by the United States?
   (1) The United States did not send soldiers to fight in World War I.
   (2) The United States did not enter the war at its start.
   (3) Italy, France, and Romania all have bigger populations than the United States.
   (4) The United States sided with Germany.
   (5) Most U.S. casualties were civilians, not soldiers.

Question 9 is based on the following passage and table.

Germany used to be a divided nation. The nations that World War II in 1945 divided Germany so it could not create conflict again. Occupied after the war by the United States, Great Britain, and France, West Germany eventually became a democracy. The Soviet Union placed East Germany under communist control. The capital, Berlin, deep in East German territory, also was split into West (democratic) and East (communist). The Soviets built the Berlin Wall to prevent people from East Germany from escaping to the West.

FACTS ABOUT THE BERLIN WALL

total length	96 miles
total length through Berlin	27 miles
total miles of concrete wall (12'–15' high)	67 miles
total miles of wire mesh fencing	42 miles
total miles of watch towers	302
number of persons successful in crossing the Wall	~5000
number of persons killed in border area	>150
date construction began	8/13/1961
date destruction began	11/9/1989

9. Which fact provides evidence that East Germany was not a democracy?
   (1) The Berlin Wall was 96 miles long.
   (2) The Soviets built a concrete wall.
   (3) The Berlin Wall no longer stands.
   (4) People trying to escape were killed.
   (5) Germany was a divided nation.

Questions 10 and 11 are based on the following map.

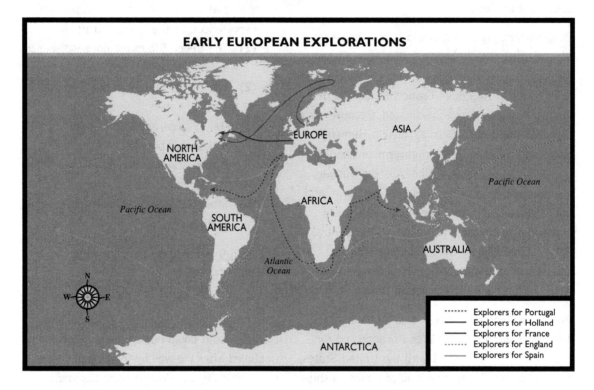

EARLY EUROPEAN EXPLORATIONS

10. What is the main purpose of this map?
    (1) to show which explorers landed in the Americas
    (2) to show that no European explorers went to China
    (3) to show how large Antarctica is
    (4) to show when world exploration was ending
    (5) to show the places to which European explorers traveled

11. Which conclusion is <u>not</u> supported by the map?
    (1) Explorers from Holland traveled the farthest north.
    (2) Some Spanish explorers went all the way around the world.
    (3) Portuguese explorers got the closest to what is now Alaska.
    (4) France sponsored fewer explorers than Spain.
    (5) The English and the French both sent explorers to North America.

Question 12 is based on the following quote.

"Slowly . . . the remains of the passage debris that encumbered [blocked] the lower part of the doorway were removed, until at last we had the whole door clear before us. The decisive moment had arrived. With trembling hands I made a tiny breach in the upper left-hand corner. . . . Widening the hole a little, I inserted the candle and peered in . . . At first I could see nothing . . . but presently, as my eyes grew accustomed to the light, details of the room within emerged slowly from the mist, strange animals, statues, and gold."

12. Archaeologist Howard Carter describes the opening of the tomb of Egyptian king Tutankhamen, often called King Tut. Which statement would Carter probably support?
    (1) Archaeologists should not be trusted with treasures.
    (2) Tutankhamen was a very rich king.
    (3) Archaeologists are afraid to explore tombs.
    (4) Egypt doesn't have any valuable archeological sites.
    (5) King Tut was a strange king.

Questions 13 and 14 are based on the following passage.

The freedoms enjoyed by U.S. citizens include many economic freedoms. For example, everyone in this nation is free to buy and sell; free to earn a living (legally); and free to make, save, and spend money. These freedoms have helped make the United States one of the richest nations on Earth.

One reason for this economic success is that the U.S. economy follows what is called the law of supply and demand. This is a general economic rule that says the price of an item is determined at any particular time by how many of the items are for sale (supply) and how many people want to buy them (demand). So, when a shortage of peanuts causes a shortage of peanut butter, the price of peanut butter can go up, because demand will stay pretty much the same for the item. Similarly, if a manufacturer makes more radios than there are customers to buy radios, the price of the radios may go down.

13. A new computer game has just come on the market. Many people want to buy the few copies available. What generalization can you make about the price of the computer game?
    (1) The price will go up in six months.
    (2) The price will be the same in six months.
    (3) The price will be higher than the price of more commonly available computer games.
    (4) The price will be higher if the manufacturer makes more copies of it.
    (5) The price is set by the highest bidder.

14. The price of lettuce drops, then drops again. What is most likely the cause of these price drops?
    (1) The supply is greater than the demand.
    (2) Growers are going out of business.
    (3) Growers are trying to reduce lettuce sales.
    (4) The demand is greater than the supply.
    (5) The supply and demand remain equal.

Question 15 is based on the following cartoon featuring Uncle Sam, a symbol of the U.S. government.

BIG CITIES AND UNCLE SAM

'A Couple Hundred Billion Would Help'

[Source: Don Hesse, *St. Louis Globe-Democrat*]

15. What does this cartoon imply?
    (1) Cities get most of their money from state governments.
    (2) People who live in big cities pay higher taxes.
    (3) The United States refuses to give money to the nation's cities.
    (4) The federal government has fewer problems than the big cities.
    (5) Cities need financial help from the federal government.

Questions 16 and 17 are based on the following form.

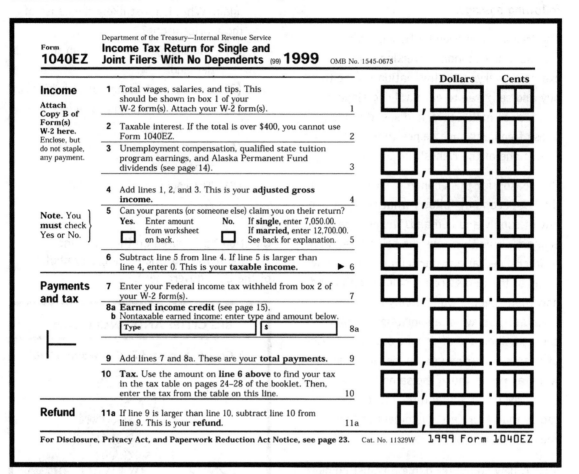

16. Which conclusion does the form support?

(1) Single people should not use this form.

(2) Adjusted gross income includes unemployment compensation.

(3) If you've made over $100 in taxable interest, you cannot use this form.

(4) No one gets money refunded from the government.

(5) This form is for use by people under the age of 30.

17. If the amount of taxes you paid is more than the taxes you are supposed to pay, then what can you expect?

(1) to owe the government money

(2) to have more federal income taxes withheld

(3) to get a refund

(4) to need additional tax forms

(5) to owe no taxes next year

Question 18 is based on the following quote by President Franklin D. Roosevelt in 1932.

"Taxes are paid in the sweat of every man who labors. If those taxes are excessive, they are reflected in idle factories, in tax-sold farms, and in hordes of hungry people tramping the streets and seeking jobs in vain. Our workers may never see a tax bill, but they pay. They pay in deductions from wages, in increased cost of what they buy, or in unemployment throughout the land."

18. What did President Roosevelt mean by those words?

(1) There are serious consequences to imposing high taxes.

(2) If you don't see a tax bill, you don't have to pay taxes.

(3) Income tax is the most important source of tax money for the government.

(4) Workers pay few taxes.

(5) People who pay taxes perspire.

SOCIAL STUDIES

Questions 19 through 21 are based on the following passage.

The word *democracy* means "government by the people." Sometimes this means that people vote directly for the laws that will govern them. This was true in the ancient city-state of Athens. Because every citizen participated in the government, it was a *direct* democracy. Today, however, most democracies are *representative* democracies. In these nations, people vote for those who will represent them in government.

19. Based on the information in the passage, which statement explains the most likely reason that most present-day democracies are representative democracies?
    (1) Populations are too large for everyone to vote on every issue.
    (2) People today get too bored to participate in government.
    (3) The bureaucracies now do most of the government's work.
    (4) Direct democracies worked well only in ancient times.
    (5) More and more countries want to be like the United States.

20. Which is an example of a direct democracy?
    (1) All the people of Ohio elect two senators.
    (2) A monarch rules the nation.
    (3) All the people of the town meet to vote on two proposed laws.
    (4) A ruling council makes the government decisions.
    (5) One person uses force to gain control of the village government.

21. The king has died. As has been true for generations, the king's oldest son will now be crowned king and will become the sole ruler of the land. What type of government does this situation illustrate?
    (1) the kind of government found in the United States
    (2) a monarchy
    (3) a republic
    (4) a direct democracy
    (5) a representative democracy

Questions 22 and 23 are based on the following bar graph.

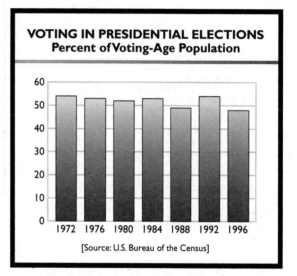

22. According to the graph, in which two years was voter turnout the highest?
    (1) 1976 and 1984
    (2) 1922 and 1992
    (3) 1972 and 1992
    (4) 1972 and 1976
    (5) 1988 and 1996

23. Which general conclusion does the graph support?
    (1) Most Americans vote.
    (2) Many Americans don't take advantage of their right to vote.
    (3) Most Americans are not represented on this graph because they are not of voting age.
    (4) American participation in the election process is gradually increasing.
    (5) In 1992, Americans didn't care who became president.

Questions 24 and 25 are based on the following document.

Voter Registration Application

Check one:
☐ New Registration ☐ Address Change ☐ Name Change

Last Name	First Name	Middle Initial	Jr. Sr. II III

Street Address Where You Live			Apt. #

City or Town	County	Zip Code

Address Where You Get Your Mail (if different from above)

Date of Birth - Month, Day, Year	Telephone Number (optional)

Name and Address Of Your Last Voter Registration

	County

Declaration - I swear or affirm that:	For Office Use Only

Declaration - I swear or affirm that:
- I am a U.S. citizen
- I live at the above address
- I will be at least 18 years old on or before the next election
- I am not on parole, probation or serving sentence due to a conviction for an indictable offense under any federal or state laws.
- I understand that any false or fraudulent registration may subject me to a fine up to $1000, Imprisonment up to 5 years or both pursuant to R.S. 19:34-1

Signature or Mark	Date

24. Which of the following is part of the declaration that people must make when completing this voter registration form?
(1) I have traveled extensively.
(2) I will make informed voting decisions.
(3) I have lived at my current address for 18 years.
(4) I know I can be punished for giving false information.
(5) I will vote in all elections.

25. What is the most likely explanation for listing the name and address of your last voter registration?
(1) to make sure the voter doesn't vote in two places
(2) to make sure the voter has actually lived at the current address for at least 30 days
(3) to determine if the voter is disabled
(4) to see where the voter gets mail
(5) to give the voter the old registration number

26. Built in the early 1900s by the United States, the 51-mile long Panama Canal enables ships to travel from the Atlantic Ocean to the Pacific Ocean without going all the way around South America.

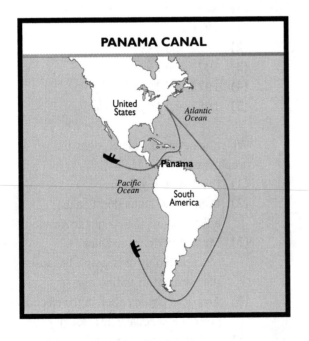

PANAMA CANAL

The building of the canal took years of draining and clearing disease-infested swamps and digging through hillsides. What is the most likely reason engineers chose Panama as the site of an ocean-to-ocean canal?
(1) Panama was the only country that could afford the canal.
(3) Panama was a relatively disease free country.
(3) The United States owned Panama.
(4) Panama's swamps would take less time to drain.
(5) Panama had a very narrow strip of land separating the two oceans.

SOCIAL STUDIES

Questions 27 through 29 are based on the following map. The number for each shaded state gives the percentage of population increase for that state between 1990 and 1997.

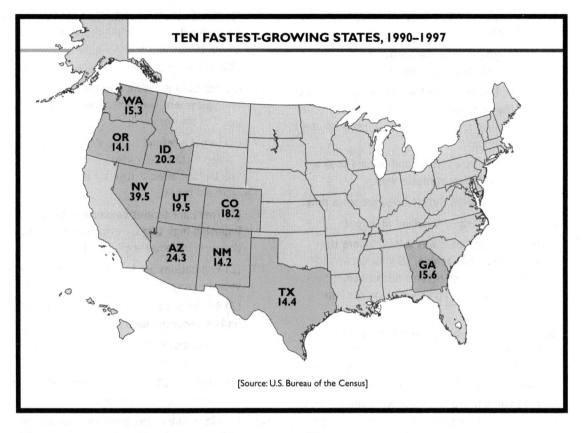

TEN FASTEST-GROWING STATES, 1990–1997

WA 15.3

OR 14.1

ID 20.2

NV 39.5

UT 19.5

CO 18.2

AZ 24.3

NM 14.2

TX 14.4

GA 15.6

[Source: U.S. Bureau of the Census]

27. Which is the only state in the Southeast to make the top ten list in population increases?
    (1) South Carolina
    (2) Idaho
    (3) Nevada
    (4) Georgia
    (5) Texas

28. Over the eight-year period represented on the map, which state's population averaged growth of about 5 percent annually?
    (1) Georgia
    (2) Texas
    (3) New Mexico
    (4) Arizona
    (5) Nevada

29. Which generalization about U.S. population growth does the map support?
    (1) Few Americans moved between 1990 and 1997.
    (2) Many Americans are moving to the West.
    (3) The Northeast is experiencing a growth in population.
    (4) Hawaii has the nation's highest standard of living.
    (5) Immigration accounts for the nation's population growth in the West.

Answers and explanations start on page 138.

Social Studies Practice Test Answers and Explanations

1. **(5) Douglass worked toward ending slavery in the United States.**

2. **(1) Douglass's work was respected by abolitionists and other Americans.**

3. **(3) The United States had not provided blacks with the same rights as whites.** Choices 1 and 2 discuss money, which King only mentions as a symbol of rights.

4. **(4) to show how settlers and traders took a number of different routes west**

5. **(3) The Cimarron Cutoff saved pioneers time.**

6. **(4) the Butterfield Overland Mail route**

7. **(5) The West Coast was settled before the Rocky Mountain region.** California, which is on the West Coast, became a state before the Rocky Mountain region was organized into territories.

8. **(2) The United States did not enter the war at its start.** According to the text, by the time the United States entered the war, the other Allies had been experiencing casualties for years.

9. **(4) People trying to escape were killed.** In a democracy, people can leave without having to escape. None of the other facts in the table addressed specific government policies.

10. **(5) to show the places to which European explorers traveled**

11. **(3) Portuguese explorers got the closest to what is now Alaska.** English explorers got the closest, not Portuguese.

12. **(2) Tutankhamen was a very rich king.**

13. **(3) The price will be higher than the price of more commonly available computer games.** If demand is high while supply is low, the price will be relatively high. Other similar products that are readily available would cost less.

14. **(1) The supply is greater than demand.** When supply exceeds demand, prices tend to drop.

15. **(5) Cities need financial help from the federal government.** The "cities" figure is poor and is asking Uncle Sam for "A couple hundred billion" dollars.

16. **(2) Adjusted gross income includes unemployment compensation.** Refer to line 4 of the document.

17. **(3) to get a refund** According to point 11a, "If line 9 (total payments) is larger than line 10 (tax owed)," then the person will receive a refund.

18. **(1) There are serious consequences to imposing high taxes.** President Roosevelt describes the adverse effects of high taxes.

19. **(1) Populations are too large for everyone to vote on every issue.**

20. **(3) All the people of the town meet to vote on two proposed laws.**

21. **(2) a monarchy** Monarchy is the term used for a government ruled by a hereditary king.

22. **(3) 1972 and 1992** In 1972 and 1992, about 55% of voting-age population voted.

23. **(2) Many Americans don't take advantage of their right to vote.** The graph shows that between 44% and 51% of Americans of voting age do not vote in presidential elections.

24. **(4) I know I can be punished for giving false information.**

25. **(1) To make sure the voter doesn't vote in two places.** The form shows the old address so it can be checked against voting records.

26. **(5) Panama had a very narrow strip of land separating the two oceans.** The shortest distance the canal needed to span would be best.

27. **(4) Georgia**

28. **(5) Nevada** According to the map, Nevada experienced a 39.5 percent population change.

29. **(2) Many Americans are moving to the West.**

Circle the question numbers that you got incorrect. Use this information to determine the skills and content areas in which you need more work.

	Comprehension	Application	Analysis	Evaluation
U.S. History	4, 7	6	2, 3	1, 5
World History	10	12	8, 9	11
Economics	15, 18	14	17	13, 16
Civics and Government	22, 24	20, 21	19, 25	23
Geography	27		26, 28	29

Science Pretest

DIRECTIONS: Choose the <u>one best answer</u> to each question.

<u>Question 1</u> refers to the following diagram.

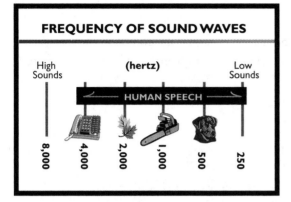

1. The higher the frequency of a sound wave, the higher its pitch. As people age, they lose the ability to hear higher-frequency sounds. To improve an older person's ability to understand speech, what sounds should a hearing aid be designed to amplify?
   (1) all sounds
   (2) sounds between 250 and 500 hertz
   (3) sounds between 500 and 1,000 hertz
   (4) sounds between 1,000 and 6,000 hertz
   (5) sounds over 6,000 hertz

2. Some skin infections are caused by fungi. The most common fungi cause ringworm, athlete's foot, jock itch, and vaginal yeast infections. They are transmitted by contact. These conditions are all similar, but they were given different names because they occur in different parts of the body. For example, athlete's foot is a fungal infection on the foot. What is the best way to avoid getting athlete's foot?
   (1) Avoid exercising in gyms and health clubs.
   (2) Wash your hands frequently.
   (3) Avoid going barefoot in places where many people walk.
   (4) Wear a different pair of shoes on alternate days.
   (5) Stay away from people who have ringworm.

<u>Question 3</u> refers to the following table.

Meteor Shower	Can Be Seen
Quadrantids	January 1–6
Perseids	August 9–13
Geminids	December 11–16

3. When a comet revolves around the sun, it leaves a trail of dust and debris that remains for many years. As Earth moves through these trails, the dust and debris burn in the atmosphere, and a meteor shower occurs. Which of the following is the best explanation of why each meteor shower can be seen at the same time each year?
   (1) Comets take one year to revolve around the sun, and Earth is stationary.
   (2) Earth takes one year to revolve around the sun, and the comets take many years.
   (3) Earth takes one year to revolve around the sun, and the comet trails stay in the same area.
   (4) The dust and debris burn in Earth's atmosphere, making it visible.
   (5) The dust and debris reflect the sun's light, making it visible.

4. Many turkeys are sold with pop-up thermometers that indicate when the bird is cooked to the proper temperature. These thermometers have a tightly coiled spring anchored by a solid metal alloy. When the meat reaches a certain temperature, the alloy melts and the spring is released, pushing the indicator up. For which of the following properties is the metal alloy used in a pop-up thermometer chosen?
   (1) its ability to reflect heat
   (2) its elasticity
   (3) its melting point
   (4) its expansion when heated
   (5) its ability to conduct electricity

In the 1980s, doctors began offering advanced breast cancer patients a treatment that had been used successfully on leukemia patients, even though there was no evidence that it would work on breast cancer. The treatment consists of high-dose chemotherapy followed by a bone marrow transplant.

In five studies done during the 1990s, advanced breast cancer patients who had regular chemotherapy and patients who had high-dose chemotherapy with transplants were compared. Here are the results.

Study	Number of Patients	Results
Eastern Cooperative Oncology Group (U.S.)	553	No difference in survival; 30 to 40 percent survival in both groups.
Cancer and Leukemia Group B (U.S.)	874	No difference in survival after 3 years, but study is continuing.
The Scandinavian Breast Cancer Study Group	525	No difference in survival.
University of Witwatersrand Medical School (South Africa)	154	Longer survival, fewer relapses in transplant patients. It was later found that these results may have been falsified.
PEGASE Group (France)	61	No difference in survival. Transplant recipients took longer to relapse.

5. Which of the following is a reason doctors might offer advanced breast cancer patients the new treatment?
   (1) Regular chemotherapy is not used on advanced breast cancer.
   (2) Patients are wary of the latest advances in treatment.
   (3) The treatment is successful with other types of cancer.
   (4) The patients are likely to die if they do not receive the new treatment.
   (5) The new treatment is much more effective than conventional chemotherapy.

6. When the Witwatersrand results were first published, many scientists doubted their accuracy. Why did doubts arise about the accuracy of these results?
   (1) The study consisted of 154 patients.
   (2) The study took place over years.
   (3) The study was conducted by a university.
   (4) Breast cancer patients usually survive.
   (5) No other study had similar results.

7. How long did these studies take to complete?
   (1) hours
   (2) days
   (3) weeks
   (4) months
   (5) years

8. Which of the following conclusions do the results of these studies support about treatment for advanced breast cancer?
   (1) The new treatment is more effective than regular chemotherapy.
   (2) High-dose chemotherapy is more effective without bone marrow transplant.
   (3) There is no clear benefit from high-dose chemotherapy with bone marrow transplant.
   (4) Neither treatment is effective, so patients should not choose them.
   (5) Most advanced breast cancer patients survive as a result of treatment.

9. Symbiosis is an arrangement in which two or more organisms of different species help one another. Which of the following is an example of symbiosis?

    (1) An ant removes eggs that are harmful to an aphid, and the aphid provides honeydew to the ant.
    (2) Some ants protect the nest, and others hunt for food outside the nest.
    (3) Fungus grows on termite dung in a termite nest, and the termites eat the fungus.
    (4) Gypsy moth larvae eat the leaves of oak trees, and the trees sometimes die.
    (5) A treehopper insect looks like a thorn on a stem, and the plant provides it with sap.

Question 10 refers to the following graph.

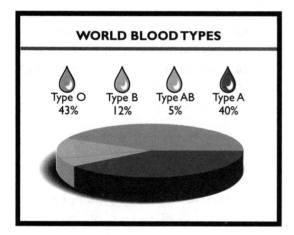

10. People who have type O blood can safely donate their blood to anyone. People with types A, B, or AB can safely donate blood to people with the same blood type. Anyone can donate blood to a person with type AB blood.

    What percentage of people worldwide can donate blood to anyone?

    (1) 5 percent
    (2) 12 percent
    (3) 40 percent
    (4) 43 percent
    (5) 100 percent

Question 11 refers to the following table.

Metropolitan Area	Days Did Not Meet Air Quality Standards	
	1990	**1996**
Atlanta, GA	17	6
New York, NY	18	4
St. Louis, MO	8	4
Denver, CO	9	1
Los Angeles, CA	180	88

11. Which of the following statements is supported by the information in the table?

    (1) In terms of air quality, the most polluted city is Denver.
    (2) The air quality in St. Louis declined from 1990 to 1996.
    (3) Between 1990 and 1996, air quality improved in all the cities.
    (4) Most of the air pollution in Los Angeles comes from vehicle exhausts.
    (5) Los Angeles did not meet air quality standards on 180 days in 1996.

12. In 1992, astronomers found two or three planets circling a type of star called a pulsar. In 1995, a single planet was found orbiting a normal, shining star. In 1999, astronomers found three large planets orbiting a star similar to the sun. This last discovery was the most promising, because by studying this planetary system, scientists may discover more about the origin and development of

    (1) the universe.
    (2) the galactic cluster.
    (3) the Milky Way galaxy.
    (4) the solar system.
    (5) Earth.

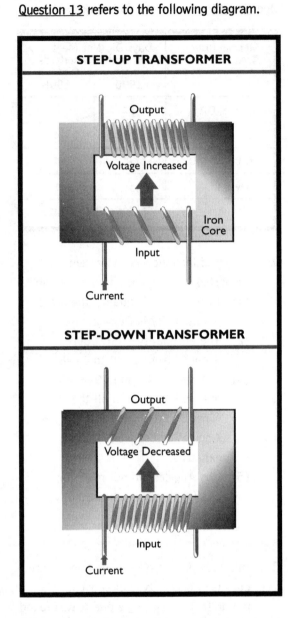

STEP-UP TRANSFORMER

Output

Voltage Increased

Iron Core

Input

Current

STEP-DOWN TRANSFORMER

Output

Voltage Decreased

Input

Current

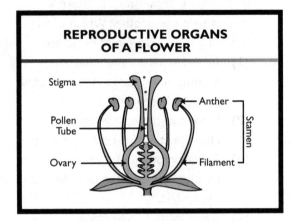

REPRODUCTIVE ORGANS OF A FLOWER

Stigma

Anther

Pollen Tube

Ovary

Filament

Stamen

14. When pollen is transferred from the male stamens into the female stigma of a flower, pollination occurs. This process is most similar to the
    (1) reproduction of bacteria by cell division.
    (2) fertilization of a human egg by sperm.
    (3) replication of viruses by taking over the DNA of cells.
    (4) growth of the embryo in the uterus.
    (5) differentiation of cells during development.

15. Plate tectonics is a theory that explains the movement of continents over millions of years. According to the theory, Earth's crust is made of several giant plates of rock that "float" on the mantle below. New crust is formed at the boundaries of plates, where molten material comes up from the mantle. Which of the following is evidence supporting the theory of plate tectonics?
    (1) Sedimentary rocks form from particles of rock.
    (2) The mantle is the layer of Earth below the crust.
    (3) Volcanoes are usually located along the edges of plates.
    (4) Earth's crust is weathered by wind, water, and ice.
    (5) More than two-thirds of Earth's crust is covered by water.

13. A transformer changes an electrical signal from one voltage to another. The voltage can be increased or decreased. To increase the voltage, the transformer must have
    (1) only a current input.
    (2) only a current output.
    (3) more turns of the output coil.
    (4) more turns of the input coil.
    (5) a battery providing electricity.

16. Commercial fishing boats use weighted nets and dredges to catch cod, haddock, shrimp, flounder, and other bottom-feeding fish. This gear scoops up everything in its path as it plows the ocean floor. Which of the following is an unintended result of this fishing technology?

(1) The price of fish has fallen as the supply decreases.

(2) In many areas, the number of fish has dropped dramatically.

(3) Commercial fishing boats travel from one place to another to fish.

(4) A single fishing trip yields a large catch.

(5) Commercial fishing boats process the fish on board.

17. Robert Boyle is considered one of the first modern scientists. In the 17th century, he used scientific methods to analyze phenomena. For example, he was the first to conclude that materials must absorb something during oxidation, or rusting.

Which of the following methods would yield evidence that metal absorbs something during oxidation?

(1) looking at the metal before and after oxidation

(2) scraping the metal before and after oxidation

(3) measuring the temperature of the metal before and after oxidation

(4) measuring the weight of the metal before and after oxidation

(5) measuring the time it takes the metal to oxidize

Question 18 refers to the following diagram.

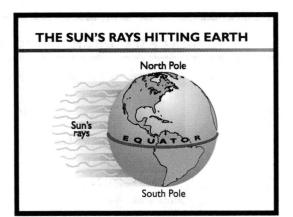

THE SUN'S RAYS HITTING EARTH

18. Areas near the equator, where the sun shines directly overhead, have hotter climates than areas near the poles. Why do areas near the poles have colder climates?

(1) The sun's rays come in at a low angle so they are not so direct and intense.

(2) The sun's rays do not reach the poles.

(3) The ozone layer is thinner at the poles than it is at the equator.

(4) The days are shorter at the poles than at the equator.

(5) The land masses at the poles are smaller than those at the equator.

19. Natural selection is the process by which organisms that are poorly adapted to their environments are eliminated from a population, leaving those with features best adapted to survival to breed and continue the species. Which of the following is an example of natural selection?

(1) Wolves have been reintroduced to Yellowstone National Park.

(2) Bears have been trained to do tricks in the circus.

(3) A frog has tried eating a monarch butterfly but spits it out because it is bitter.

(4) A couple who had trouble getting pregnant adopted a child.

(5) Head lice have developed resistance to the active ingredient in delousing products.

Questions 20 and 21 refer to the following graph.

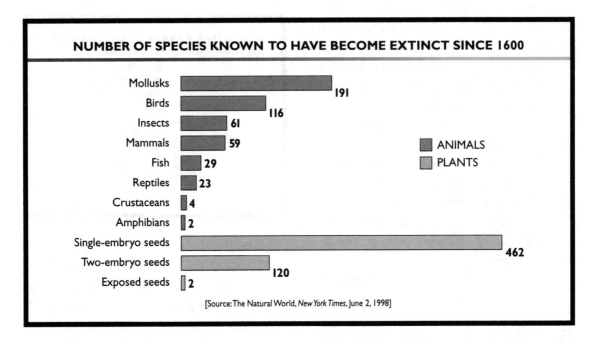

NUMBER OF SPECIES KNOWN TO HAVE BECOME EXTINCT SINCE 1600

- Mollusks 191
- Birds 116
- Insects 61
- Mammals 59
- Fish 29
- Reptiles 23
- Crustaceans 4
- Amphibians 2
- Single-embryo seeds 462
- Two-embryo seeds 120
- Exposed seeds 2

ANIMALS
PLANTS

[Source: The Natural World, *New York Times*, June 2, 1998]

SCIENCE

20. How many known species of plants have become extinct since 1600?

   (1) 2
   (2) 23
   (3) 120
   (4) 462
   (5) 584

21. Which of the following is the most likely reason that no microscopic forms of life, such as bacteria and protozoa, are known to have become extinct since 1600?

   (1) Microscopic forms of life never become extinct, as do larger organisms.
   (2) The microscope was invented in the 1600s, so only then were such life forms discovered.
   (3) Microscopic forms of life are so small that extinctions are difficult to verify.
   (4) Humans do not hunt microscopic forms of life and deplete their populations.
   (5) Microscopic forms of life reproduce more rapidly than larger organisms.

Question 22 refers to the following diagram.

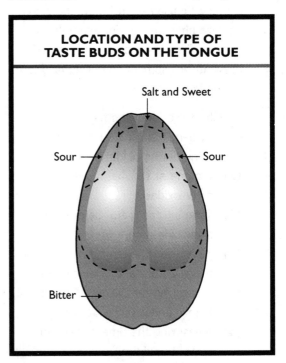

LOCATION AND TYPE OF TASTE BUDS ON THE TONGUE

Salt and Sweet

Sour — Sour

Bitter

22. If you wanted to avoid tasting a pill before you swallow it, where on your tongue should you place it?

   (1) the tip
   (2) the back
   (3) the center
   (4) the left side
   (5) the right side

Questions 23 and 24 refer to the following passage and diagram.

Rainwater soaks into layers of permeable rock and flows downward. If the permeable rock layer is sandwiched between rock layers that do not let the water through, the water collects in the permeable layer. In this type of formation, water is under pressure from the water above. Thus when a well is drilled, pressure forces water to the surface. This kind of well is called an artesian well.

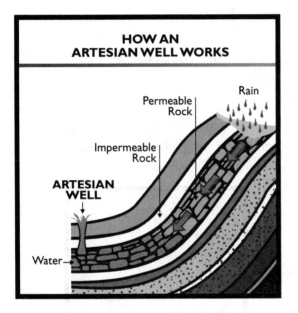

HOW AN ARTESIAN WELL WORKS

23. If the layer of rock above the water were also permeable, which of the following would result?
    (1) Rainwater would not soak into the ground except during periods of heavy rainfall.
    (2) Water would not flow downward through the rock to lower elevations.
    (3) Water would rise into the permeable layer during periods of heavy rainfall.
    (4) Water would flow farther downward toward the center of Earth.
    (5) Rainwater would collect in lakes and ponds on Earth's surface.

24. A farming region with little rainfall has been drawing irrigation water from artesian wells faster than it can be replaced. As a result, the water pressure is now too low to force water to the surface. Which of the following is a short-term solution that would not jeopardize the crops?
    (1) Ration water for irrigation.
    (2) Pump water to the surface.
    (3) Build an aqueduct to bring water from another region.
    (4) Build a dam to collect water.
    (5) Rely on rainfall to water crops.

25. In physics, work is done when an object on which a force is acting moves in the direction of that force. Which of the following is <u>not</u> an example of work?
    (1) rolling a car down a hill
    (2) lifting a bag of groceries
    (3) pushing a tack into a corkboard
    (4) pulling a child on a sled
    (5) holding a board in a vice grip

26. The Gulf Stream is a warm ocean current that flows from the Caribbean and Gulf of Mexico, up the coast of North America, and across the Atlantic Ocean to northern Europe. Like other ocean currents, the Gulf Stream influences climate. Which of the following statements is supported by this information about ocean currents?
    (1) The coast of northern Europe is warmer than inland places as far north.
    (2) Most ocean currents flow south to north.
    (3) Water in the south Atlantic is colder than water in the north Atlantic.
    (4) The Gulf Stream brings cold weather to the north Atlantic.
    (5) Most ocean currents carry warm water from one part of the ocean to another.

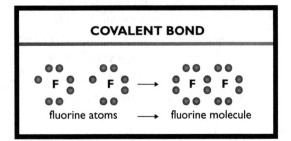

COVALENT BOND

fluorine atoms ⟶ fluorine molecule

27. In a covalent bond, two or more atoms share the electrons (shown by dots) in their outermost electron shells. Two or more atoms joined by covalent bonds form molecules. In a fluorine molecule, how many electrons are there in each atom's outermost electron shell?
    (1) one
    (2) two
    (3) four
    (4) seven
    (5) eight

Question 28 refers to the following diagram.

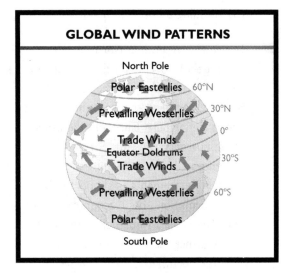

GLOBAL WIND PATTERNS

North Pole
Polar Easterlies 60°N
Prevailing Westerlies 30°N
Trade Winds 0°
Equator Doldrums
Trade Winds 30°S
Prevailing Westerlies 60°S
Polar Easterlies
South Pole

28. Global wind patterns are influenced by the rotation and uneven heating of Earth. Which of the following shipping routes takes advantage of one of these wind patterns?
    (1) west to east along the equator
    (2) east to west along the equator
    (3) west to east near 40 degrees north
    (4) east to west near 40 degrees south
    (5) north to south near 60 degrees south

29. Sedimentary rocks are formed from particles of other rocks or hard animal and plant remains. The particles are usually deposited in the ocean by water, wind, or ice, and eventually they harden into rock as more layers are piled on top.

    Which of the following is necessary for the formation of sedimentary rock?
    (1) chemical change
    (2) heat
    (3) pressure
    (4) friction
    (5) wind

Question 30 refers to the following information.

Experts have ranked problem substances from most to least addictive. The more addictive a substance is, the harder it is to quit using it.

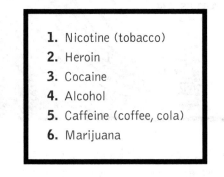

1. Nicotine (tobacco)
2. Heroin
3. Cocaine
4. Alcohol
5. Caffeine (coffee, cola)
6. Marijuana

30. Which of the following conclusions is supported by the information given?
    (1) It is easier to stop smoking tobacco cigarettes than to stop smoking marijuana.
    (2) Trying nicotine is more likely to lead to addiction than trying alcoholic beverages.
    (3) Cocaine is the most addictive problem substance included in the rankings.
    (4) It is easier to give up alcohol than to give up caffeine.
    (5) Marijuana is the most addictive problem substance included in the rankings.

Answers and explanations start on page 147.

Science Pretest Answers and Explanations

1. **(4) sounds between 1,000 and 6,000 hertz** This frequency range includes the higher-pitched speech sounds that older people have difficulty hearing.

2. **(3) Avoid going barefoot in places where many people walk.** Since these fungal skin infections are transmitted by contact, not walking where other people walk and may have deposited fungi is the best way to prevent athlete's foot.

3. **(3) Earth takes one year to revolve around the sun, and the comet trails stay in the same area.** Because the dust and debris in the comet trails remain behind, Earth encounters each trail once a year as it orbits the sun.

4. **(3) its melting point** The melting of the alloy triggers the pop-up indicator, so the alloy needs to melt at the temperature at which the turkey is fully cooked.

5. **(3) The treatment is successful with other types of cancer.** Since the new treatment has been used successfully on leukemia patients, doctors may feel the treatment would potentially work on breast cancer patients.

6. **(5) No other study had similar results.** Four other major studies showed no indication that the high-dose chemotherapy and bone marrow transplant improved survival rates among advanced breast cancer patients. Therefore, the Witwatersrand results were inconsistent with the other results.

7. **(5) years** Survival after treatment must be measured in years; thus the studies took place over several years.

8. **(3) There is no clear benefit from high-dose chemotherapy with bone marrow transplant.** According to the table, most of the studies reported no difference in survival rates.

9. **(1) An ant removes eggs that are harmful to an aphid, and the aphid provides honeydew to the ant.** The ant helps the aphid by removing its enemies, and the aphid helps the ant by providing it with food. Since both species benefit, this is an example of symbiosis.

10. **(4) 43 percent** According to the pie chart, 43 percent of people worldwide have Type O blood and thus can donate blood to anyone.

11. **(3) Between 1990 and 1996, air quality improved in all the cities.** According to the table, the number of days each city did not meet air quality standards dropped from 1990 to 1996. Thus the air quality improved in each city during this period.

12. **(4) the solar system.** The planetary system discovered in 1999 is most similar to the solar system, and by studying it, the astronomers may learn more about our solar system.

13. **(3) more turns of the output coil.** According to the diagram, to increase voltage there must be more turns of the output coil than turns of the input coil.

14. **(2) fertilization of a human egg by sperm.** Pollination is the seed plant's version of fertilization, when the male sex cell penetrates the female sex cell.

15. **(3) Volcanoes are usually located along the edges of plates.** Volcanic activity consists of molten material coming up from the mantle, which is characteristic of the edges of plates.

16. **(2) In many areas, the number of fish has dropped dramatically.** Commercial fishing gear disturbs the bottom of the ocean and collects so many fish that not enough are left to reproduce and maintain the population. Option 4 is incorrect because it is an intended result.

17. **(4) measuring the weight of the metal before and after oxidation** If metal absorbs a substance during oxidation, it will weigh more after oxidation than before. Thus, weighing the metal before and after oxidation would provide objective evidence.

18. **(1) The sun's rays come in at a low angle so they are not so direct and intense.** At the poles, the sun is low in the sky. Its rays come in at a low angle, covering more area but providing less heat to the poles.

19. **(5) Head lice have developed resistance to the active ingredient in delousing products.** Lice that have developed the ability to survive the delousing products survive and reproduce, passing this characteristic down to their offspring. The lice that are poisoned by the delousing products die and do not reproduce. None of the other examples relate to a species' ability to survive in habitat and reproduce.

20. **(5) 584** According to the graph, 462 single-embryo seed plants, 120 two-embryo seed plants, and 2 exposed seed plants have become extinct since 1600, for a total of 584.

21. **(3) Microscopic forms of life are so small that extinctions are difficult to verify.** Given the total number of species, it is likely that some microscopic life forms have become extinct since 1600. But since these organisms cannot be seen with the naked eye, their extinctions are difficult to verify.

22. **(3) the center** According to the diagram, the center of the tongue has few taste buds, so placing the pill on the center will prevent you from tasting it.

23. **(3) Water would rise into the permeable layer during periods of heavy rainfall.** Permeable rock would absorb any excess water caused by heavy rainfall.

24. **(2) Pump water to the surface.** This solution is short term because it does not increase the total supply of water. Rationing water or relying on rainfall is a long-term solution that would require a change in crops; in the short term, these solutions would jeopardize the crops.

25. **(5) holding a board in a vice grip** Of all the choices, this is the only one in which movement is not occurring. Since movement is necessary for work to be done in physics, this is the correct answer.

26. **(1) The coast of northern Europe is warmer than inland places as far north.** The warm water of the Gulf Stream warms the climate of northern Europe, making it warmer than comparable inland regions as far north.

27. **(5) eight** Because the two atoms share electrons when they bond, each has eight.

28. **(3) west to east near 40 degrees north** The prevailing wind pattern at 40 degrees north is from west to east (the westerlies). Ships traveling from west to east take advantage of that wind.

29. **(3) pressure** The weight of the layers on top eventually hardens the lower layers into sedimentary rock.

30. **(2) Trying nicotine is more likely to lead to addiction than trying alcoholic beverages.** Nicotine is listed as the most addictive of these six substances.

Circle the question numbers that you got incorrect. Use this information to determine the skills and content areas in which you need more work.

	Comprehension	Application	Analysis	Evaluation
Life Science	7, 10, 20, 22	2, 9, 14, 19	5, 16, 21	6, 8, 30
Earth and Space	28, 29	12	3, 18, 23, 24	11, 15
Chemistry	27		4	17
Physics		25	1, 13	26

This program helps you get ready to watch the other four science programs by introducing you to science and the scientific method. You'll also learn what's expected of you on the GED Science Test, and you can try some sample test questions.

Passing the GED Science Test

OBJECTIVES

1. Introduce the types of passages and graphics on the test.

2. Determine the number of items and how long you will have to take the test.

3. Investigate the types of questions on the test.

4. Explore the general science concepts on the test.

You should become familiar with the scientific method on page 274 of the Reference Handbook.

We eat genetically engineered tomatoes, get vaccinated against polio, and go to the beach when the forecaster predicts hot, sunny weather. We get X-rayed when we break a bone. At work, we use computers and other technology to improve productivity. So science and technology play important roles in our daily lives.

The purpose of the GED Science Test is to assess your ability to apply what you know about science, to analyze scientific information you see or read, and to evaluate the scientific information that comes your way.

This lesson and the four that follow will help you prepare for the GED Science Test. You can also prepare on your own. Pay attention when science stories appear on TV or in the newspaper. Observe the world around you and analyze causes and effects in nature and with technology. If you do these things, you will soon become familiar with many of the topics that are on the GED Science Test.

For additional practice, visit *LiteracyLink* **online at http://www.pbs.org/literacy.**

GED Science Test Overview

The GED Science Test assesses your ability to understand, analyze, and apply science information. It does <u>not</u> require that you memorize science facts. However, familiarity with key science concepts will help you pass the test.

You will have 80 minutes to answer 50 multiple-choice questions. Each question has five possible answers, and you must select the best answer. The questions will test your understanding of reading passages, tables and charts, bar graphs, line graphs, circle graphs, and diagrams. This workbook will give you plenty of practice with these types of materials.

The questions on the GED Science Test come from four main content areas. These correspond to the videos you will see and the next four workbook lessons.

- **Life Science (45%)**—including cells, genetics, evolution, organisms, and ecosystems.
- **Earth and Space Science (20%)**—including the universe, the solar system, Earth itself, and interactions between people and the environment.
- **Physical Science (35%)**
  - **Chemistry**—including the structure and states of matter, chemical bonds and reactions, and specific types of substances such as solutions and hydrocarbons.
  - **Physics**—including the laws of motion, work, and heat; waves; nuclear physics; and electricity and magnetism.

Many of the questions on the GED Science Test cover core concepts in the content areas above. The other questions on the GED Science Test fall into major themes in science. The video you are about to see and this lesson will explain these themes further. The themes include:

- **Science as Inquiry**
- **Science and Technology**
- **Science in Personal and Social Perspectives**
- **History and Nature of Science**
- **Unifying Concepts and Processes**

Finally, GED Science Test items assess your ability to use thinking skills to answer questions about science reading passages and graphics. These skills, covered in depth in Lesson 16: Passing the GED Social Studies Test, are:

- **Comprehension**—requires an understanding of the meaning or intent of science material.
- **Application**—requires the use of information in a concrete situation.
- **Analysis**—requires an exploration of the relationship between ideas, such as a cause-and-effect relationship.
- **Evaluation**—requires a judgment about the soundness or accuracy of scientific information or methods.

→ **NOW WATCH PROGRAM 22:**

Pay particular attention to the host's explanations of why answer choices are correct or incorrect. You'll pick up some tips to use as you practice additional questions in the workbook and online.

PBS LiteracyLink®

After you watch the program, work on:
- pages 151 – 160 in this workbook
- Internet activities at http://www.pbs.org/literacy

22

Key Science Concepts and Skills

The video program presented an overview of the GED Science Test. The rest of this workbook lesson will give you the opportunity to learn some of the basic skills and concepts you will need to pass the GED Science Test.

KEY SKILLS

The GED Science Test will assess your knowledge and understanding of science topics through the following types of skill questions:

- Comprehension
- Application
- Analysis
- Evaluation

You can review these skills on pages 13-19 of this book.

Science as Inquiry

Science is not simply a group of facts. Science is actually a process of asking and answering questions. Scientists use inquiry to build on accepted concepts and to test new ideas. They collect data and analyze evidence. Then they try to explain the evidence. Slowly, a body of scientific knowledge grows.

On the GED Science Test, you will be expected to evaluate scientific data, studies, explanations, and conclusions. You will need to use logic and common sense. Try it on the following passage.

> Dr. James S. Reilly and his colleagues reviewed 5,588 cases in which children were admitted to the hospital for choking. Of these cases, 78 percent involved children under four. Researchers reported that the foods most likely to choke children were nuts (544), chunks of meat (125), chicken parts (121), seeds (116), carrots (83), hotdogs and sausages (70), fish bones (52), apples (47), and hard candy (34). Dr. Reilly said that most young children don't have all their teeth and thus have trouble with certain foods.

GED PRACTICE

This question requires you to identify an implication of the study.

Based on the results of the study, what advice would you give caregivers of young children?
(1) Never leave a young child alone.
(2) Supervise young children when they eat.
(3) Cut food into small pieces for young children.
(4) Do not give young children meat.
(5) Feed pureed baby food to children under five.

Science and Technology

Understanding the relationship between science and technology is important. The knowledge gained through scientific inquiry is often put to use by technology. For example, physicists' research in magnetism (science) led to the development of the television (technology). However, technology also influences science. A dramatic example is the invention of the microscope (technology). By allowing us to see tiny organisms, the microscope opened up new fields of study (science).

On the GED Science Test, many passages involve technology. Here is an example.

One source of geothermal energy is underground hot water. Cold groundwater seeps downward until it reaches hot rocks. The water heats up and some of it turns to steam and expands. The pressure of the steam forces the rest out in a jet of boiling water, called a geyser. When a geyser is capped, the steam can be forced through a turbine to generate electricity.

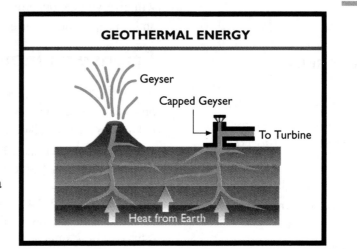

GEOTHERMAL ENERGY

Geyser

Capped Geyser

To Turbine

Heat from Earth

Most electrical power plants produce steam by burning coal or oil or using nuclear reactions. In a geothermal power plant, steam is produced by

   a. the natural heat of the underground rocks.

   b. cold groundwater seeping downward.

In a geothermal plant, steam is produced by **a. the natural heat of the underground rocks.** This is stated in the passage and shown in the diagram.

GED PRACTICE

This question requires you to identify a summary of an important scientific principle.

When rocket fuel burns, a jet of gas is propelled out the back of the rocket, causing the rocket to move forward. Which of the following scientific principles describes how a rocket works?

   (1) For every action there is an equal and opposite reaction.

   (2) An object moving in a straight line continues to do so unless acted upon by a force.

   (3) Gravity is a force that pulls objects toward one another.

   (4) Gaseous elements combine in proportions by volume, expressed as simple whole numbers.

   (5) The pressure of a gas stays the same if the temperature and the volume both double.

Answers and explanations start on page 263.

SCIENCE

Science in Personal and Social Perspectives

Science and technology affect individuals, nations, and the whole human race. In turn, social and political forces influence the directions science and technology take. For example, unless nations agreed to cooperate, the International Space Station would probably not have been started even though the technology to build it exists. Science, people, and societies interact in areas of personal health and nutrition, population growth, the use of natural resources, environmental quality, and natural and man-made disasters. Many passages on the GED Science Test address these issues. Here is an example.

There are more elderly Americans today than ever before, and in general they are healthier. The number of people over 65 with high blood pressure, arthritis, and emphysema has declined. The death rates from stroke and heart disease have also declined. One reason that older people are healthier today is that they are better educated, and educated people tend to make changes in diet and life style to improve their health. They also tend to seek medical treatment when needed. In addition, the elderly of today have benefited from 20th-century improvements in public health, nutrition, and medical care.

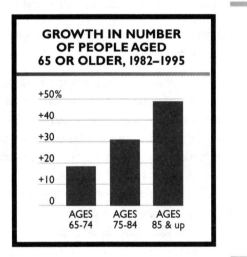

GROWTH IN NUMBER OF PEOPLE AGED 65 OR OLDER, 1982–1995

What are two reasons that older Americans are healthier today than in the past?

_____

_____

To find the answer, review the paragraph. Reasons for improved health are listed from the fourth sentence to the end. The reasons are **(1) more education, which leads people to improve their diet and life style and to seek medical treatment;** and **(2) improved public health, nutrition, and medical care.**

GED PRACTICE

This question requires you to draw a conclusion about the aging process.

The elderly of today are the parents of the baby boom generation born after World War II. Given the large size of the baby boom generation and continued progress in nutrition and health, over the next 50 years the number of elderly in the United States will probably

    (1)   decrease.
    (2)   remain about the same.
    (3)   continue to increase.
    (4)   decrease, then increase.
    (5)   increase, then decrease.

Answers and explanations start on page 263.

History and Nature of Science

Science is a human enterprise. It may involve individuals working alone, like Charles Darwin making observations and formulating the theory of evolution. Or, it may involve hundreds of people, like NASA planning and carrying out a planetary mission.

As we have seen, scientific knowledge changes and grows through the process of observation and experimentation. Over the years, scientists have contributed discoveries, observations, and theories that have advanced our understanding of the world and the universe. While doing so, they have confronted ethical, social, and political issues that influenced their work.

Some questions on the GED Science Test involve the history and nature of science. Here is an example.

> In 1975, Polly Murray, a woman in the tiny wooded town of Lyme, Connecticut, became concerned about the number of children with symptoms of rheumatoid arthritis—swollen, stiff joints. She was put in touch with Dr. Allen C. Speere, a specialist in rheumatology.
>
> Speere took Murray's list of thirty-nine children and tried to discover what they had in common. Some residents blamed a nearby nuclear power plant; some blamed the drinking water; others thought the disease was communicable. But Speere observed that the children's symptoms began in the summer or fall. He hypothesized that the children had an insect-related disease.
>
> Two years later, Speere found the insect by chance. An ecologist brought him a tick that had bitten him. This tick, carried on the backs of deer and mice, was new to the area. When they compared the map showing the areas infested by this tick with the map showing where victims of the disease lived, they found a match. The cause of Lyme disease had been identified.

Why did Speere think that the children's disease was insect-related?

_____

The answer to this question is in the second paragraph. Because symptoms started in the summer or fall, when children played outdoors, Speere thought the cause might be an insect.

GED PRACTICE

This question asks about how a scientist used data to solve a problem.

What was the primary means of data collection that led to the identification of the tick that carries Lyme disease?

- **(1)** measurement
- **(2)** reading
- **(3)** experimentation
- **(4)** modeling
- **(5)** observation

Answers and explanations start on page 263.

Unifying Concepts and Processes

Scientific facts are very specific. For example, it is a fact that Earth is the third planet from the sun. Yet this specific fact can be thought of in a more general context: that of the solar system. Science has many systems that function in an orderly way, from the solar system to the digestive system.

Besides the concept of orderly systems, there are other unifying concepts in science. Unifying concepts are general ideas that cross science content areas. For example, the objective nature of scientific evidence, constancy and change, and evolution and equilibrium are some general scientific concepts that can be used to understand particular facts. On the GED Science Test, you will often be asked specific questions that involve these general ideas.

The following passage and diagram involve the unifying concept of systems.

All living things contain the element carbon. Through the carbon cycle, carbon is transferred between the atmosphere and Earth's surface. Plants take carbon dioxide from the air during photosynthesis. They return some carbon dioxide to the air through respiration. Animals eat the plants. During respiration, they return carbon dioxide to the air. Both plants and animals eventually die. Decomposers, including fungi and bacteria, feed on plant and animal remains. In the process, they absorb the carbon and give out carbon dioxide.

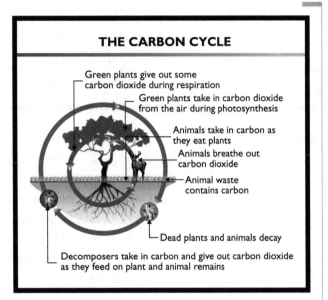

THE CARBON CYCLE

Green plants give out some carbon dioxide during respiration

Green plants take in carbon dioxide from the air during photosynthesis

Animals take in carbon as they eat plants

Animals breathe out carbon dioxide

Animal waste contains carbon

Dead plants and animals decay

Decomposers take in carbon and give out carbon dioxide as they feed on plant and animal remains

What is the role of decomposers in the carbon cycle? _____

To find the answer to this question, read the last sentence of the passage or look at the label about decomposers in the diagram. **Decomposers absorb carbon from decaying plants and animals and give off carbon dioxide.**

GED PRACTICE

This question requires an application of a scientific principle to the problem of global warming.

Carbon dioxide is one of the "greenhouse gases" that contributes to the warming of Earth's atmosphere. The more carbon dioxide in the atmosphere, the more heat is trapped, causing global warming. Based on the information above, which of the following would be a practical way to help decrease the amount of carbon dioxide in the atmosphere?

- **(1)** increase the number of green plants
- **(2)** decrease the number of green plants
- **(3)** increase the number of animals
- **(4)** increase the number of decomposers
- **(5)** eliminate the decomposers

Answers and explanations start on page 263.

Reading Charts and Tables

Scientists often need to present data, or information. When the information is related to one topic—for example, the characteristics of the moons of Jupiter—it can be shown in a chart or table. Let us say that a chemist wants to present information about common esters. Esters are organic chemicals that have a sweet smell and are used in foods and scented products. The chemist summarizes the basic information in a table such as this.

COMMON ESTERS		
Name	**Chemical Formula**	**Characteristic Odor**
Ethyl butyrate	$C_3H_7COOC_2H_5$	Pineapple
Amyl acetate	$CH_3COOC_5H_{11}$	Banana, pear
Methyl salicylate	$C_6H_4(OH)COOCH_3$	Wintergreen
Amyl valerate	$C_4H_9COOC_5H_{11}$	Apple
Methyl anthranilate	$C_3H_4(NH_2)COOCH_3$	Grape

When you read a chart or table, look for these parts.

- **Title.** The title tells you the topic—what the information is about. The topic of this table is common esters.
- **Columns.** Each vertical section of a table is a column. The column head tells what information is found in that column. For example, the third column tells what odor each ester has.
- **Rows.** Each horizontal section of a table is a row. The first item in a row indicates what the information in that row is about. For example, the last row of this table has information about methyl anthranilate.

To find information in a table, you must use the column heads and the first column as guideposts. For example, to find the characteristic odor of amyl valerate, look for the column head "Characteristic Odor." Then go down that column until you get to the row for amyl valerate. The characteristic odor of amyl valerate is apple.

Using the table, find the answer to this question: What is the name of the ester whose chemical formula is $CH_3COOC_5H_{11}$? _____

First locate this chemical formula in the table. It is the second formula listed. Now, look at the name of the chemical in that row. It is **amyl acetate.**

GED PRACTICE

This question requires drawing a conclusion from the chart.

Which of the following esters would a chemist formulating a new purple chewing gum be most likely to use?

(1) ethyl butyrate   (4) amyl acetate
(2) methyl salicylate   (5) methyl anthranilate
(3) amyl valerate

Answers and explanations start on page 263.

Reading Bar Graphs

Scientists often use graphs to present numerical data. Graphs make numerical data easier to understand because they present information visually. For example, suppose you wanted to compare how much energy several nations produced and consumed. You could show this information using a bar graph. **Bar graphs** are used to compare quantities.

When you read a bar graph, you should note the following items.

- **Graph Title.** The title tells you the topic. The topic of this graph is energy production and consumption in several nations.
- **Axis Titles.** Each axis, or side, of a bar graph has a title. These titles tell what is shown on that axis. For example, the vertical axis shows the amount of energy in quadrillion Btus, a measure of energy.
- **Legend.** The legend explains any symbols or colors used: Purple bars show energy production, and red bars show energy consumption.
- **Bars.** The bars show numerical data. For example, Russia's purple bar shows that Russia produced 40 quadrillion Btus of energy in 1996.

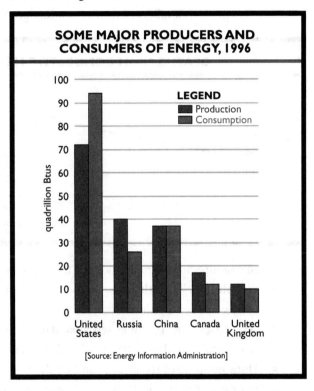

Note that this graph is a double bar graph. It compares two amounts—production and consumption—for each nation. Double bar graphs are used to compare and contrast data.

Now, look at the bar graph. Which nation consumes more energy than it produces? _____

If you answered the **United States,** you are correct. Of the nations shown, only the United States has a "taller" bar for consumption than production.

GED PRACTICE

This question asks for an evaluation of each statement to see if it is supported by the data on the graph.

Which of the following statements is supported by the graph?

(1) Russia consumes about 10 quadrillion Btus more energy than China.

(2) Most of Canada's energy is produced in the form of natural gas.

(3) Canada and China produce about the same amount of energy.

(4) The United States produces more energy than any other nation shown.

(5) The United Kingdom consumed about 20 quadrillion Btus in 1996.

Reading Line Graphs

As you've seen, a bar graph is useful for comparing quantities. Another type of graph, a line graph, shows how quantities change. Line graphs are useful for showing trends.

For example, a scientist who studies a particular disease may want to show the number of people who die from that disease over a period of time. She could make a chart listing each year and the number of deaths. The data would be there but it would be hard to see a trend. In contrast, if she plotted the years and numbers of deaths in a line graph, the trend would be visible right away.

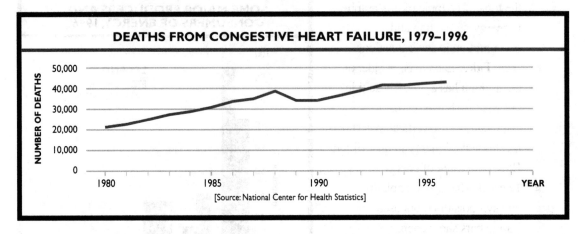

DEATHS FROM CONGESTIVE HEART FAILURE, 1979–1996

[Source: National Center for Health Statistics]

When you examine a line graph, look for the following items.

- **Graph title.** The title tells you the topic. The topic of this graph is deaths from congestive heart failure from 1979 to 1996.
- **Axis titles.** The axis titles tell what data is shown on that axis. For example, the horizontal axis shows the years, and the vertical axis shows the number of deaths.
- **Data points and trends.** A point on the line gives a single value; for example, the numbers of deaths in 1988. The line itself indicates the trend—rising, falling, or remaining the same.

Now, answer this question: In what year did about 20,000 people die of congestive heart failure?

_____

To find this answer, you must first locate 20,000 on the vertical axis, then draw an imaginary or real horizontal line from that point on the axis to the trend line. Once you have a point on the trend line, draw a real or imaginary line down to the horizontal axis to locate the year: **1980.**

GED PRACTICE

This question requires an analysis of the data on the graph.

During which of the periods below did the number of deaths from congestive heart failure decrease?

- **(1)** 1979 to 1988
- **(2)** 1988 to 1989
- **(3)** 1989 to 1992
- **(4)** 1992 to 1993
- **(5)** 1993 to 1996

Answers and explanations start on page 263.

Reading Circle Graphs

A circle graph is a good way to show the parts of a whole. The whole is the circle, and the parts are the wedges.

For example, suppose a chemist wanted to show the most common elements in Earth's crust. He could draw a circle graph that looks like this.

When you read a circle graph, look for these items:

- **Title.** The title of the graph tells you the topic. In this case, the topic is the most common elements in Earth's crust.
- **Labels.** The labels identify each wedge, or part, of the whole and tell the amount. In this case, you can see that oxygen is the most common element, accounting for almost half of the crust by mass.

**MOST COMMON ELEMENTS
IN EARTH'S CRUST, BY MASS**

Aluminum **7%**
Iron **4%**
Calcium **3%**
Silicon **26%**
Others **11%**
Oxygen **49%**

Look at the circle graph. Which element makes up about one quarter of Earth's crust?

_____

To answer this question, you can look for the wedge that is about one-quarter of the circle. Or, you can read the labels for each element and look for a label close to 25%. The answer is **silicon.**

GED PRACTICE

This question requires comparing the parts of the circle to draw a conclusion.

Most of the nutrients in this cookie are in the form of

- **(1)** saturated fat.
- **(2)** monounsaturated fat.
- **(3)** carbohydrates.
- **(4)** sugar.
- **(5)** protein.

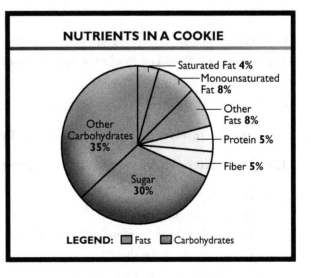

NUTRIENTS IN A COOKIE

Saturated Fat **4%**
Monounsaturated Fat **8%**
Other Fats **8%**
Protein **5%**
Fiber **5%**
Other Carbohydrates **35%**
Sugar **30%**

LEGEND: ▨ Fats ▨ Carbohydrates

Answers and explanations start on page 263.

Interpreting Science Diagrams

In science, diagrams usually show the parts of something, like an electric circuit, or the steps in a process, like the life cycle of a frog. In addition to providing the "big picture," diagrams provide many details as well. This diagram shows how muscles work in pairs to move the forearm.

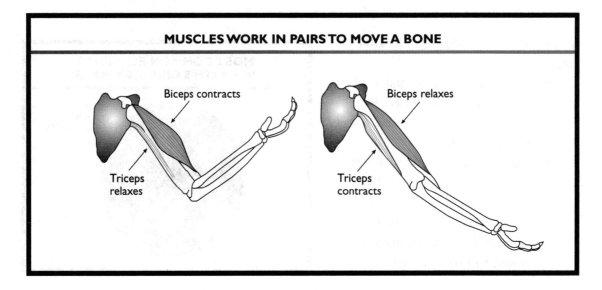

MUSCLES WORK IN PAIRS TO MOVE A BONE

Biceps contracts

Triceps relaxes

Biceps relaxes

Triceps contracts

When you read a science diagram, look at these parts first to get an idea of what is being shown. Then study the details.

- **Title or caption.** Most GED science diagrams have a title that tells the topic and possibly the main idea; a few have captions. The main idea of this diagram is that muscles work in pairs to move a bone.
- **Labels.** Labels are words that describe a part of the diagram. They point to the part being described. In this diagram, the labels point to the two upper arm muscles and explain what they do.

Now, study the diagram and answer this question: Which muscle contracts to bend the arm at the elbow? _____

First look at the part of the diagram that shows the arm bent. Then read the label to find which muscle is contracting. The label says that the **biceps** is contracting.

GED PRACTICE

This question involves an analysis of a cause/effect relationship.

The muscles work in pairs to bend the arm because as the biceps contracts, the

    (1)   triceps contracts.
    (2)   triceps relax.
    (3)   shortened biceps alone pulls the forearm.
    (4)   triceps pulls the shoulder.
    (5)   triceps pulls the forearm.

Answers and explanations start on page 263.

This program is packed with information relating to the diverse and fascinating subject of living things. At locations ranging from a farm that preserves traditional breeds of animals to an aquarium featuring a man-made coral reef, scientists will explain key concepts in life science, including cell structure, photosynthesis, and ecosystems.

Life Science

OBJECTIVES

1. Realize that all living things are made of cells, and describe cell characteristics and processes.
2. Understand the processes that contribute to diversity in nature.
3. Explore how organisms interact with each other and with their environments.

DNA, the genetic material of living things, was first described by life scientists only fifty years ago. Yet today, DNA has many scientific uses. It is used to identify crime suspects, establish paternity, create genetically altered foods, and pinpoint genes that carry diseases. All these are uses for a molecule smaller than a cell—one of the most important molecules in life science.

Life science is an important part of the GED Science Test. Almost half of the test items cover life science. Many test items will require you to apply life science concepts to everyday concerns, including health and nutrition. Learning the concepts of life science will help you on the GED Test as well as help you make decisions affecting the well-being of yourself and your family.

On the following pages, you will find a brief exercise called *Sneak Preview*. It is designed to introduce you to the topics that will be featured in the video program and the corresponding lesson. After you complete the exercise and check your answers, turn to the vocabulary page. There you will find terms that will help you better understand the video and the lessons that follow. After reviewing page 164, you will be ready to watch Program 23.

For additional practice, visit *LiteracyLink* online at http://www.pbs.org/literacy.

Sneak Preview

This exercise previews some of the concepts from Program 23. After you answer the questions, use the chart on page 163 to help set your learning goals.

WORKPLACE LINK: Steve Cooley, a Wyoming game warden, once relied solely on tire and shoe prints, witnesses, fingerprints, and ballistics tests to identify people suspected of wildlife crimes. Now he has another tool to use against wildlife crime.

DNA Fingerprinting

The use of DNA samples to identify suspects has become well known through sensational murder trials. Each individual's DNA is unique. So a match between a suspect's DNA and DNA taken from a crime scene can provide evidence in a trial. Now officials can use DNA "fingerprinting," as it is called, to identify and prosecute poachers. But in these cases, it's not the poacher whose DNA is being examined. It's the DNA of the animal that has been killed illegally.

In one Wyoming case, six headless antelope were found rotting near a city dump. After asking around, the game warden, Steve Cooley, came up with Kenneth Nelson as a possible suspect. Cooley tracked down one of the antelope heads waiting to be mounted in a taxidermist's shop. The antelope head had been brought in by Kenneth Nelson. Its DNA matched that of one of the headless antelope near the dump. This was the only physical evidence connecting Nelson with the crime. He was convicted of six charges of wanton destruction for illegally killing the antelope.

DNA testing in wildlife crimes is not limited to cases involving the illegal killing of animals. Officials also use it to identify species in crimes involving illegally obtained animal substances. For example, it is against the law to trade in elephant and rhinoceros horns and tusks. When these materials are found in products like jewelry, DNA testing can identify the materials' species source. Traders of these products can be prosecuted.

Answer these questions based on the reading above.

1. What is the main idea of the article?

   (1) One of a game warden's jobs is to track down poachers.
   (2) It is illegal to kill some animals, whether for sport or commercial use.
   (3) DNA evidence is used in sensational murder trials.
   (4) DNA fingerprinting is now being used in wildlife crimes.
   (5) Each individual's DNA is as unique as his or her fingerprint.

2. What evidence caused Kenneth Nelson to be convicted of wanton destruction?

   (1) Six headless antelope were found near a Wyoming city dump.
   (2) Steve Cooley, the game warden, suspected Kenneth Nelson.
   (3) Kenneth Nelson's DNA was found at the scene of the crime.
   (4) The DNA of Nelson's antelope head matched the DNA of an illegally killed antelope.
   (5) The antelope head was found in a taxidermist's shop frequented by Kenneth Nelson.

3. A game warden finds a patch of bloody fur, some cigarette butts, and a half-full soda can on private property where hunting is prohibited. She later finds elk meat belonging to a hunter in the freezer of a hunting lodge. To prove that the elk was illegally killed on private property, which of the following should she have DNA fingerprinted?

   (1) the bloody fur and the frozen elk meat
   (2) the bloody fur and the hunter
   (3) the cigarette butts and the frozen elk meat
   (4) the cigarette butts and the hunter
   (5) the soda and the hunter

4. Which of the following is supported by information in the article?

   (1) DNA fingerprinting has replaced more traditional evidence in trials.
   (2) Game wardens are trained to do DNA fingerprinting.
   (3) DNA fingerprinting is used to identify individuals and species.
   (4) As a result of DNA fingerprinting, wildlife crimes are decreasing.
   (5) DNA fingerprinting can only be used on animals and people.

Feedback

- If you got all of the answers right...

  you're doing great! Concentrate on adding to your knowledge of science.

- If you missed question 1...

  you need to improve your ability to understand the main point of an article.

- If you missed question 2...

  you need to learn to analyze the relationships among ideas.

- If you missed question 3...

  you need to learn to take general concepts and apply them in specific situations.

- If you missed question 4...

  you need to learn to evaluate whether specific information supports a conclusion.

Vocabulary for *Life Science*

cell	the basic living unit of all organisms
cell membrane	the structure surrounding a cell that allows substances to pass in and out
cell wall	a cellulose structure surrounding the cell membrane in a plant cell
cellular respiration	the process by which cells use oxygen to release energy from glucose
chloroplasts	in plant cells, the green structures that absorb the sun's energy, enabling the plant to produce sugar
classification	the identification, naming, and grouping of organisms into a formal system
DNA	deoxyribonucleic acid; the molecule that carries genetic instructions
ecosystem	a community of plants, animals, and other organisms along with the nonliving things in the environment
evolution	the process by which the genetic makeup of a population changes over a period of time
food web	a feeding pattern that shows the energy transfer throughout an ecosystem
gene	a unit of DNA by which traits are passed from parent to offspring
genetics	the scientific study of how traits are inherited
genome	the entire genetic code of an individual or species
habitat	the place in an ecosystem where a species lives
immune system	the body system that attacks disease-causing agents
mitosis	the process by which most cells reproduce; cell division
nucleus	in a cell, the structure that contains genetic material and controls the cell's activities
photosynthesis	the process by which green plants use carbon dioxide, water, and energy from sunlight to make their own food
species	a group of organisms that resemble one another and that produce fertile offspring when they interbreed

---

➡ NOW WATCH PROGRAM 23:

Don't worry about trying to remember every fact or definition mentioned in the program. As you watch the various segments, think about what living things have in common and how they affect each other. You can review specific information about topics such as cells, genetics, photosynthesis, and food webs in the workbook and online.

PBS
LiteracyLink®

After you watch the program, work on:

- pages 165–180 in this workbook
- Internet activities at http://www.pbs.org/literacy

23

Life Science

On the following pages, you will learn more about the ideas discussed in the video program and have an opportunity to develop and practice your GED science skills.

GED TIPS

When taking the GED Test, you should:

- Give yourself extra time to get to the test site.
- Bring a watch with you so you can pace yourself.
- Avoid spending too much time on any one question. If a question is giving you trouble, skip it, but be sure to come back to it at the end.

Key Points to Think About

In the video program, you explored:

- Cells, the basic living units of all organisms.
- Some of the processes that contribute to diversity in nature.
- How organisms interact with one another and their environments.

On the GED Science Test:

- You will be expected to know some basic facts about cells, organisms, and ecosystems.
- You should know how to apply general concepts to specific, real world situations.
- You will be given passages to read and diagrams, charts, and graphs to interpret.

As you work through the lesson for Program 23:

- Concentrate on understanding the relationships among the different areas of life science.
- Remember that life science covers everything from the tiniest forms of life to the largest ecosystems.
- Relate what you are learning to your own life and environment, not just to the GED Science Test.

Similarities in Living Things

The Cell

A cell is the basic living unit of all organisms. Cells perform the following life processes: growing, using energy to perform various functions, and reproducing. All living organisms are made of cells. Some, like bacteria, are made of a single cell. Others, like animals and flowering plants, are made of millions of cells. In multicelled organisms, cells are specialized and perform different functions. For example, human nerve cells, bone cells, and muscle cells all look different and have different jobs.

A typical cell consists of cytoplasm, a watery material. The cytoplasm is surrounded by a **cell membrane,** which allows nutrients and oxygen to enter the cell and wastes to pass out. In a plant cell, the cell membrane is surrounded by a cell wall made of cellulose. The cell wall helps give a plant its shape.

In the cytoplasm are a number of structures. The **nucleus** controls the way the cell functions and reproduces. The endoplasmic reticulum is a network that transports substances and makes proteins. Vacuoles are sacs that hold food, water, or wastes. In the mitochondria, the sugar glucose is broken down to release energy.

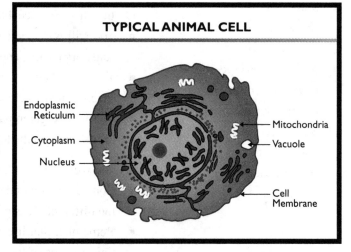

TYPICAL ANIMAL CELL

Endoplasmic Reticulum

Cytoplasm

Nucleus

Mitochondria

Vacuole

Cell Membrane

SKILL PRACTICE

Match each part of a cell with its function.

Cell Part	Function
_____ 1. nucleus	**a.** a barrier that allows some substances to pass
_____ 2. mitochondria	**b.** the control center of a cell
_____ 3. cytoplasm	**c.** structure that produces energy from glucose
_____ 4. cell membrane	**d.** structure that produces proteins
_____ 5. cell wall	**e.** the watery material a cell is made of
_____ 6. endoplasmic reticulum	**f.** stiff structure that gives plants their shape

Answers and explanations start on page 263.

SCIENCE

Photosynthesis and Respiration

Photosynthesis is a complex process by which green plants, algae, and some bacteria make their own food using the energy from sunlight. Photosynthesis is the ultimate source of food for life on Earth, because all animals eat plants or eat animals that eat plants.

During photosynthesis, plants use light energy, water, and carbon dioxide to produce both the sugar glucose and oxygen. Sunlight is absorbed by **chloroplasts,** cell structures containing the green pigment chlorophyll. Water enters from the soil and travels up through the roots and stems to the leaves, where most photosynthesis takes place. Carbon dioxide enters the leaves through openings called stomata.

Photosynthesis takes place in two stages, called the light reactions and the dark reactions. In the light reactions, the energy from sunlight is used to split water into hydrogen and oxygen. The oxygen is released into the air.

The second set of reactions is called the dark reactions, because light is not necessary for them to take place. In the dark reactions, the hydrogen produced during the light reactions is combined with carbon dioxide from the air to produce glucose and water.

The glucose produced during photosynthesis contains the energy that once was in the form of light. Now this energy is in chemical form, and it can be used by the plant for its own cell growth, reproduction, and other functions. When animals eat the glucose in plants, it can be used as a source of energy for the animals' cell growth, reproduction, and other functions. The process by which energy is released from glucose in the cells is called **cellular respiration.** In cellular respiration, oxygen from the air reacts with the glucose to produce energy, carbon dioxide, and water.

SKILL PRACTICE

Fill in each blank in the sentences below with the best term.

photosynthesis   cellular respiration   dark reactions   light reactions   chloroplasts

1. During _____, green plants use the light energy from the sun to produce their own food.

2. Plant cells contain _____, the structures that absorb light energy from the sun.

3. During the _____, the light energy from the sun is used to split water into hydrogen and oxygen.

4. During the _____, hydrogen and carbon dioxide combine to form glucose and water.

5. The process by which oxygen reacts with glucose in the cells, producing energy, carbon dioxide, and water is called _____.

Answers and explanations start on page 263.

WORKPLACE LINK: Tyrell works in a lab, helping to screen tissue samples. He is looking for cancer—cells that grow and divide abnormally. Tyrell's job requires patience, care, and a sharp eye. People's lives depend on his accuracy.

Cell Division

Almost all cells reproduce by simple cell division, a process called **mitosis.** In this process, the cell's chromosomes, which contain the genetic material called **DNA,** duplicate themselves. The duplicate sets of chromosomes line up along the equator of the cell. During division, the chromosomes separate, each set moving to opposite sides of the cell. The cell membrane begins to pinch in, and two new "daughter" cells are formed. Each daughter cell has a complete set of genetic material identical to that of the "mother" cell.

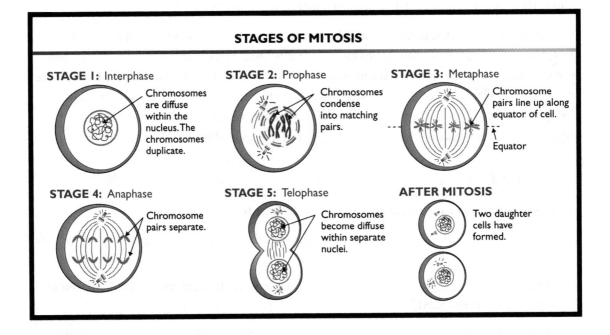

STAGES OF MITOSIS

STAGE 1: Interphase
Chromosomes are diffuse within the nucleus. The chromosomes duplicate.

STAGE 2: Prophase
Chromosomes condense into matching pairs.

STAGE 3: Metaphase
Chromosome pairs line up along equator of cell.
Equator

STAGE 4: Anaphase
Chromosome pairs separate.

STAGE 5: Telophase
Chromosomes become diffuse within separate nuclei.

AFTER MITOSIS
Two daughter cells have formed.

SKILL PRACTICE

Answer the questions based on the above information and diagrams.

1. What happens to the DNA of a cell during mitosis?_____

2. During which stage of mitosis does the cell membrane pinch in and two nuclei form?
   (1) metaphase   **(2)** anaphase   **(3)** telophase

3. Why is a daughter cell identical to its mother cell after mitosis?_____

Answers and explanations start on page 263.

SCIENCE

■ Apply What You Learn

Read the following article about the life span of cells. Then answer the questions that follow.

Immortality for Cells

In multicelled organisms, cell division cannot go on forever. Most human cells, for example, can divide about fifty times. After that, the cells do not reproduce properly, the body begins to break down, and the person dies. The upper limit on our life span—thought to be about 120 years—is the result of the limit on cell division.

However, one type of human cell that *can* divide indefinitely is the embryonic stem cell. In the early embryo, there is a cluster of about twenty of these cells, which eventually give rise to all the varied types of cells in the body. Once these cells specialize—that is, develop into skin or muscle or bone—the upper limit on cell division kicks in. But before they specialize, these cells can divide indefinitely, as long as they remain embryonic.

Biologists tried for years to isolate and grow embryonic stem cells in the laboratory. They hoped to use such cells to create tissues of different types. These healthy tissues could then be injected into a person whose tissues were diseased. In 1998, scientists finally succeeded in growing embryonic stem cells from embryos left over from a fertility clinic and from an aborted fetus.

This research has caused a legal and ethical debate. There is a ban on using federal funds for fetal research, so the question has arisen as to whether the ban applies to embryonic stem cells. The much larger question is ethical. Is it morally right to experiment with an entity that might have the potential to grow into a human being? This question is not likely to be resolved soon.

SKILL PRACTICE

1. Why do multicelled organisms eventually die of "old age"?

   _____

   _____

2. Do you think that research on human embryonic stem cells is ethical? Explain your thinking.

   _____

   _____

Connection

History and Nature of Science

In 1920, the average U.S. life expectancy was about 54 years. Today, that figure is about 76 years. On your own or with a partner, consider reasons why U.S life expectancy has lengthened so dramatically. List three possible reasons.

Answers and explanations start on page 263.

Diversity in Nature

FAMILY LINK: Janna and Marc and their daughter Katie all have dark brown hair and eyes. But their son Will has blond hair and blue eyes. Will feels like the odd person out in this family. Janna and Marc want to explain to Will how he can be blond and blue-eyed and still be their child.

Genetics

When you inherit a trait, you get it from your parents. Many features, including eye color and blood type, arise because the fertilized egg from which a person develops contains two sets of instructions, one from each parent. These instructions are called genes, and they are made of DNA. The scientific study of heredity is called **genetics.** Modern genetics began with Gregor Mendel, an Austrian monk and amateur botanist who published a paper on inheritance patterns in 1866.

Mendel studied heredity by using pea plants. By cross-breeding plants with different characteristics and keeping careful records through the generations, Mendel noticed some patterns. For example, when he crossed a tall pea plant with a short pea plant, all the offspring were tall. But when he crossed two of these offspring, in the next generation about one in four plants was short. Shortness had been hidden for one generation, but clearly it was still there.

To explain this, Mendel proposed that each offspring inherited two factors relating to height—one from each parent. (We now call these factors genes.) In pea plants, the tall factor was dominant over the short factor, which was recessive. This meant that when a plant got a tall gene from one parent and a short gene from the other, the plant grew tall. It also grew tall when it got a tall gene from each parent. The only time a plant grew short was when it inherited the short gene from both parents.

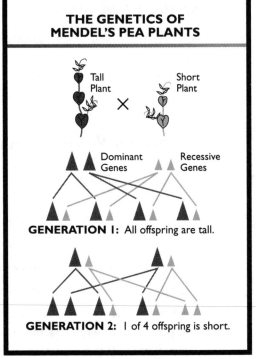

THE GENETICS OF MENDEL'S PEA PLANTS

Tall Plant × Short Plant

Dominant Genes   Recessive Genes

GENERATION 1: All offspring are tall.

GENERATION 2: 1 of 4 offspring is short.

SKILL PRACTICE

Answer the questions based on the above information.

1. What is genetics?

    a. the scientific study of how traits are inherited
    b. the study of plants and their offspring

2. Brown eyes are dominant over blue eyes.
    Explain how brown-eyed Janna and Marc can have a blue-eyed child like Will.

Evolution

Mendel's work helped explain why parents and their offspring are both alike and different. But it did not explain why one **species** is different from another and how these differences arose. Charles Darwin, a British naturalist, tried to explain how species change over time in his 1859 book, *Origin of Species*.

Evolution is the process by which the genetic makeup of a population changes over a period of time. As a result of evolution, distinctive characteristics of a population develop and new species emerge. Some important ideas in Darwin's theory of evolution include:

- *Variation.* Not all members of a species are exactly alike. For example, some may run faster; others may have better camouflage.
- *Competition.* Because resources like food are scarce, individuals have to compete for them. Some obtain resources, others don't.
- *Natural selection.* The individuals with variations best adapted to their environments are mostly likely to compete successfully, survive, and reproduce. They then pass these characteristics to their offspring.
- *Different environments.* Since environments differ, a variation that is an advantage in one place may not be an advantage in another. So members of a species in different environments develop differently. In time, the populations become so different that they are different species.

Advocates of the theory of evolution cite two types of evidence to support the theory. First, there are several series of fossils from rocks of different ages that show how species may have developed and changed. For example, there is a series of fossils that show how elephants may have descended from pig-sized animals. Second, there are structural similarities between species. For example, a whale's flipper, bat's wing, and human arm have similar bones even though their functions are different. This structural similarity may be evidence of evolution from a common ancestor.

SKILL PRACTICE

Answer the questions based on the information above.

1. An individual who succeeds in competing for scarce resources is likely to survive and

    (1) become a different species.
    (2) have offspring with his or her characteristics.
    (3) move to a different environment.

2. Why do populations in different environments develop differently?

    _____

3. What two types of evidence can support the theory of evolution?

    _____

Answers and explanations start on page 264.

Classifying Living Things

Individual organisms belong to species, the only category that actually exists in nature. A species is a group of organisms that resemble one another and that can interbreed and produce fertile offspring. However, biologists have a system that they use to further group organisms. **Classification** is the identification, naming, and grouping of organisms into a formal system. Groups of organisms have shared traits that make them like one another and unlike organisms in other groups. Modern classifications also try to place groups into categories that reflect evolutionary relationships.

In the present classification system, species that are closely related are grouped into a genus. Genera with similar characteristics are grouped into families. Families are grouped into orders, orders into classes, and classes into phyla. Groups of related phyla are placed into kingdoms, the largest categories of living things.

The five kingdoms generally recognized today are Animalia, Plantae, Fungi, Protista, and Monera. Organisms in each kingdom are characterized by similarities in their cells and their source of nutrition.

Nutrition	Multicellular			Unicellular	
	PLANTAE	**FUNGI**	**ANIMALIA**	**PROTISTA**	**MONERA**
Photosynthesis	Plants (rose)			Algae	
Absorption (take in through cells)		Fungi (mushroom)			Prokaryotes (bacteria)
Ingestion (take in by mouth)			Animals (lion)	Protozoa	

SKILL PRACTICE

Write *True* if the statement is true, *False* if it is false.

_____ 1. Human beings belong to the kingdom Animalia.

_____ 2. Organisms in the kingdom Fungi are made of a single cell.

_____ 3. A species is a group of organisms that belong to the kingdom Monera.

_____ 4. Both animals and protozoa get their nutrition by ingestion.

_____ 5. Unicellular organisms belong either to the kingdom Protista or the kingdom Monera.

Answers and explanations start on page 264.

SCIENCE

172

■ Apply What You Learn

Read the following article about bacteria and antibiotics. Then answer the questions that follow.

Bacteria That Antibiotics Can't Kill

In 1928, antibiotics were discovered by accident when Alexander Fleming noticed that a spot of green mold killed some bacteria he was growing in his lab. From this mold later came penicillin, the first antibiotic to kill disease-causing bacteria. Today we have many antibiotics that target different bacteria.

When a new antibiotic is developed, it is usually very effective for many years. Gradually, however, the bacteria it targets evolve. They develop resistance to the antibiotic, and eventually the drug is no longer effective for use against the bacteria. So far, new antibiotics have been developed faster than bacteria can evolve. But now it seems that the bacteria are catching up. Soon the evolution of new types of bacteria may outpace the development of new drugs. If that happens, doctors will be powerless to treat infections that were once routine.

This has already happened in the case of one family of bacteria, the enterococci. Enterococci are among the leading causes of blood infections in hospitalized patients. The bacteria tend to attack only the sickest people, and the infection can be deadly. Only one antibiotic, vancomycin, still works against enterococci. However, recent data have shown a sharp increase in the number of enterococci that are resistant to vancomycin. What this means is that of the 19,000 cases of infection with these bacteria each year, many are untreatable.

And drug resistance is not limited to the enterococci. Drug resistance is evolving among the bacteria that cause tuberculosis, pneumonia, and meningitis. Drug companies are reviving their research into antibiotics to head off possible medical crises.

SKILL PRACTICE

Answer the questions based on the above information.

1. What are antibiotics? _____

2. Some bacteria adapt to antibiotics and develop resistance to them. What is this an example of?

   (1) cell division   **(2)** evolution   **(3)** photosynthesis

Connection

Science as Inquiry

Different antibiotics destroy different types of bacteria. Suppose you were a researcher for a pharmaceutical company. How might you test whether a new antibiotic you have developed is effective against bacteria that cause ear infections?

▶▶ **For information about the scientific method, see page 274.**

For information about the scientific method, see page 274.

Answers and explanations start on page 264.

Organisms and Their Environments

FAMILY LINK: Keisha's children wanted goldfish as pets. So a month ago they bought a tank, gravel, plants, charcoal filter, and six fish. But the tank isn't doing well. Three fish have died. The pet store owner tells Keisha she's probably upsetting the balance in the tank by cleaning it too often.

Ecosystems

If you have ever had a fish tank, you know it is not so easy to keep fish and plants healthy. A fish tank is a small **ecosystem**—a community of plants, animals, and other organisms along with the nonliving things in the environment. Ecosystems can be small, like a fish tank or a tree, or big, like an ocean or forest. In a healthy ecosystem, all the elements are balanced. The plants provide all the food and oxygen needed by the animals, and all the wastes are recycled as nutrients to help produce new plants.

One way to think about what goes on in an ecosystem is to analyze its food web. A **food web** is a feeding pattern that shows how energy is transferred throughout the ecosystem. The first energy level of any food web is occupied by green plants, called producers. Through photosynthesis, they use the light energy of the sun to produce food. The second energy level is occupied by primary consumers, animals that eat plants. The third energy level consists of the secondary consumers, animals that eat other animals. Finally, the decomposers recycle dead animal and plant matter to provide nutrients for plants.

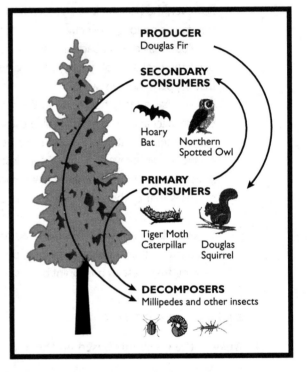

PRODUCER
Douglas Fir

SECONDARY CONSUMERS
Hoary Bat   Northern Spotted Owl

PRIMARY CONSUMERS
Tiger Moth Caterpillar   Douglas Squirrel

DECOMPOSERS
Millipedes and other insects

SKILL PRACTICE

Answer the questions based on the above information.

1. What is an ecosystem? _____

2. In the Douglas fir food web, which organism is ultimately the source of all food?

   (1) the Douglas fir   **(2)** the Douglas squirrel   **(3)** millipedes

3. What is the role of the decomposers in a food web? _____

Answers and explanations start on page 264.

The Human Body and Disease

Your body is the **habitat**—the home—of many living organisms. Many of these organisms do you no harm and even help body processes. For example, the bacteria in your intestines aid the digestion process. However, some organisms do cause trouble. Tapeworms, for example, disrupt digestion. Plasmodia are parasites that lodge in the liver and blood of a person with malaria, a potentially deadly disease spread by mosquito bites. Other bacteria cause illness by releasing poisons or by doing other damage.

When the body is invaded by a disease-causing agent, called an antigen, the **immune system** reacts to restore our health. White blood cells produce antibodies, substances that destroy the antigens. The first time we have a particular disease, it takes a while for the antibodies to be produced. During this period we feel sick. However, once our bodies have learned to make a particular antibody in reaction to a specific antigen, the next time we are exposed to the antigen, the antibody can be made quickly. We have become immune to that disease because the immune system can respond quickly enough to prevent the disease from taking hold.

Vaccinations work by using the body's ability to make antibodies. A vaccine contains altered or dead antigens for a particular disease such as tetanus or polio. These treated antigens do not cause the disease—except in very rare cases—but they do trigger the immune system to create antibodies. If the person later comes in contact with the antigen that causes the disease, the immune system can respond immediately.

Widespread vaccination has dramatically cut the incidence of several deadly diseases. A vaccination program against smallpox has rid the world of this disease. In many developed nations, vaccinations have almost eliminated diphtheria and polio. In the United States, almost all children are vaccinated against these diseases by the time they enter school. One of the goals of the World Health Organization is the vaccination of all children everywhere.

SKILL PRACTICE

Write *True* if the statement is true, *False* if it is false.

_____ 1. A habitat is the place where a particular organism lives.

_____ 2. The human body provides a habitat for many organisms, including disease causing bacteria.

_____ 3. When a person is exposed to an antibody, his or her white blood cells produce antigens to fight off the disease.

_____ 4. Vaccinations work by providing a drug to cure the symptoms of a particular disease.

_____ 5. Smallpox was completely eradicated by a worldwide vaccination program.

Human Activity and Ecosystems

People have moved into, or used resources from, ecosystems all over the world. One important result of increasing human activity is the destruction of habitats. As people settle an area, they push out plant and animal species. Many of these species become extinct. Others hang on in reduced numbers in smaller areas. Still others learn to adapt to humans.

KEY

■ Estimated current range of cougar

One story of decline and recovery is that of the cougar, or mountain lion. When Europeans first settled in the Western Hemisphere, the range of the cougar extended from Canada to the southern tip of South America. Because it posed a risk to human life and livestock, the cougar was hunted nearly to extinction in North America by the mid 1900s.

Restrictions on cougar hunting were imposed in all the western states. In addition, limits were set on hunting deer and elk, the main prey of cougars. These laws, coupled with mild winters, caused a population explosion among the deer and elk. As a result, the cougar population increased as well. Today cougars are again common in much of the West.

Unfortunately, much of the cougar's present habitat is also occupied by humans. There were 43 known cougar attacks on humans in the United States between 1970 and 1998, 11 of them fatal. Although these numbers are much smaller than the number of deaths caused by cars hitting deer, for example, the attacks are dramatic and make the news. Pressure is building to repeal the laws prohibiting cougar hunting.

SKILL PRACTICE

Answer the questions based on the above information.

1. What effect does human activity have on the plants and animals of an ecosystem?

    _____

2. Why was the cougar hunted nearly to extinction in North America?

    _____

3. What caused the number of cougars to increase in recent years?

    _____

■ Apply What You Learn

Read the following article about a new way to mop up oil spills. Then answer the questions that follow.

Oily Hair

When the *Exxon Valdez* spilled oil in Prince William Sound in 1989, the oil destroyed fish, birds, and other animals that depend on the ocean. A TV news clip of an otter soaked in oil from the spill gave Phillip McCrory an idea.

McCrory, a hairdresser from Huntsville, Alabama, wondered: If an otter's fur soaks up oil, would human hair do the same thing? McCrory decided to experiment. He collected four pounds of hair from the floor of his salon and stuffed it into a pair of tights. Then he filled his son's wading pool with water, added a gallon of used motor oil, and dumped in the hair. In two minutes, the hair had soaked up the oil and the water was clear.

McCrory's customers from the Marshall Space Flight Center in Huntsville referred him to Maurice Hale, a NASA technology transfer expert. Hale gave McCrory an opportunity to try his idea on a slightly larger scale. When some diesel oil spilled in a ditch at the center, McCrory made a filter—16 pounds of hair in a barrel. The oily water was pumped through the barrel and came out clean enough to dump in a sewer. Hale estimated that 1.4 million pounds of hair in mesh containers would have been able to soak up the *Exxon Valdez* oil in about a week. Perhaps someday McCrory's idea will be put to use in another oil spill.

SKILL PRACTICE

1. McCrory got his idea that hair might soak up oil by seeing the similarity between human hair and _____ .

2. Describe how McCrory first tested his idea. _____

   _____

3. What problem might arise if it was decided to use hair to mop up a large oil spill?

   _____

   _____

Connection

Science in Personal & Social Perspectives

Human activity can create pollution that damages ecosystems. For example, the *Exxon Valdez* spill disrupted wildlife in the area for several years. Farming, dumping toxic waste, and suburban development are other activities that often damage ecosystems.

Think about the area where you live. What human activity damages wildlife where you live?

DIRECTIONS: Read the passage. Then answer the questions that follow.

The custom of sending flowers to people in the hospital may have arisen in the late 18th century. At that time it was found that plants produce oxygen from carbon dioxide during photosynthesis. Soon after, a new trend arose: people started putting flowers in sickrooms to "purify" the air. A Dutch botanist, Jan Ingenhousz, was skeptical about the benefits. His experiments showed that only the green parts of the plants added oxygen, and only in strong light. The flowers, nongreen parts, and even green parts left in the dark all used up oxygen in the process of respiration, just as animals do. And the amounts of gases produced by just a few plants, day and night, were too small to make a difference in a sickroom. Ingenhousz concluded that a few plants in the sickroom did not "purify" the air. Still, the custom of sending flowers has persisted, although some people today remove the flowers from their rooms at night.

1. Before concluding that plants did not add oxygen to the air at night, Ingenhousz would have had to
   (1) measure the oxygen given off during the day and during the night.
   (2) measure the oxygen given off by the green parts and other parts.
   (3) measure the carbon dioxide given off during the day and during the night.
   (4) measure the carbon dioxide given off by the green parts and other parts.
   (5) observe whether people had difficulty breathing near the plants.

2. In Jason's hospital room are three plants sent by well-wishers. Jason's wife Alinda wants to remove them at night. Jason wants them to stay. Who is right?
   (1) Alinda, because the plants compete with Jason for carbon dioxide at night
   (2) Alinda, because the plants compete with Jason for oxygen at night
   (3) Jason, because the plants add oxygen to the air at night
   (4) Jason, because the plants add carbon dioxide to the air at night
   (5) Jason, because there are too few plants to make any difference

3. Based on the article, which is the best reason to send flowers to sick people?
   (1) to add carbon dioxide to the air at all times
   (2) to add carbon dioxide to the air at night
   (3) to add oxygen to the air at all times
   (4) to add oxygen to the air at night
   (5) to cheer them up

Study the graph. Then answer the question that follows.

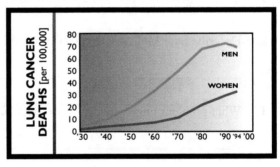

4. If the trends shown were to continue, lung cancer deaths would likely
   (1) decrease for both women and men.
   (2) increase for both women and men.
   (3) level off for both men and women.
   (4) decrease for men; increase for women.
   (5) stabilize at 30 deaths per 100,000.

SCIENCE

Read the passage and study the diagram. Then answer the questions that follow.

Genetic information is stored in the nucleus of the cell in a coded sequence recorded in the structure of DNA. The genetic code of DNA is carried outside the nucleus to the protein-producing areas of the cell by a single-stranded messenger, called mRNA, or the "sense" strand. There, depending on its code sequence, the sense strand binds the building blocks of proteins in a particular order to produce a protein. Most diseases occur when bacteria, viruses, or defective genes cause a cell to make abnormal proteins.

Scientists theorized that a disease-causing sense strand could be deactivated by binding an "antisense" drug to it before it can start making defective proteins. The first antisense drug, called fomivirsen, was approved by the Food and Drug Administration in 1998. It treats CMV retinitis, a viral infection that often causes blindness in AIDS patients.

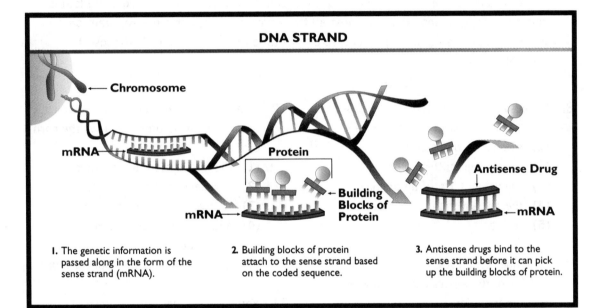

DNA STRAND

Chromosome

mRNA

Protein

mRNA

Building Blocks of Protein

Antisense Drug

mRNA

I. The genetic information is passed along in the form of the sense strand (mRNA).

2. Building blocks of protein attach to the sense strand based on the coded sequence.

3. Antisense drugs bind to the sense strand before it can pick up the building blocks of protein.

5. Which part of a cell leaves the nucleus to direct the production of proteins?
   (1) DNA
   (2) mRNA
   (3) CMV retinitis
   (4) formivirsen
   (5) FDA

6. The structure of a protein, produced by a particular sense strand, is determined by
   (1) the nucleus of the cell.
   (2) the sense strand's coded sequence.
   (3) the antisense drug.
   (4) formivirsen.
   (5) the cell's protein-producing areas.

7. Which of the following conclusions is supported by the information in the passage and diagram?
   (1) To work, an antisense drug must target a particular sequence of mRNA.
   (2) Antisense drugs are useful only to treat viral diseases.
   (3) Antisense drugs are useful only to treat AIDS-related diseases.
   (4) Development of antisense drugs has been slow because of their side effects.
   (5) Food and Drug Administration approval of formivirsen was based on animal and human data.

Read the passage. Then answer the questions that follow.

The larvae of the western corn rootworm beetle eat away at corn roots, causing the plants to fall over in a high wind. For years, Midwestern farmers controlled the beetle by crop rotation. The adult beetles, which eat corn silk and pollen, would lay their eggs in cornfields during the summer. Their larvae, the rootworms, would emerge late the next spring. But farmers would have planted soybeans instead of corn in those fields, and the rootworms would starve to death. By the following spring planting time, the field would be free of rootworms, and farmers would again plant corn.

But in a surprise development, some adult beetles have acquired a taste for soybeans. Now these beetles also lay their eggs in soybean fields. When corn is rotated onto these fields the next spring, the rootworms are there, ready to eat.

According to one scientist, planting a soybean field where rootworm eggs are laid is similar to applying insecticide. Almost all the insects will die, but a few resistant ones will survive. These insects reproduce, so crop rotation no longer controls the insect population.

8. Based on the information in the passage, which phrase best describes larvae?
   (1) single-celled organisms
   (2) always agricultural pests
   (3) the young form of an animal
   (4) the sexually mature form of an animal
   (5) beetles

9. Why does crop rotation no longer work to control the western corn rootworm beetle population?
   (1) There are too many of the beetles now.
   (2) More beetles have migrated from other areas.
   (3) The beetles have evolved to eat soybeans as well as corn.
   (4) Crop rotation reduces nutrients in the soil.
   (5) Farmers have been using pesticides against the beetles.

10. In a field with western corn rootworm beetles, what actually destroys the corn crop?
    (1) the application of insecticides
    (2) soybeans rotating with corn
    (3) rootworms eating the corn roots
    (4) adult beetles eating corn silk and pollen
    (5) farmers plowing the rootworm under

11. You are a farmer with a soybean crop planted. Which of the following would work to save next year's corn crop?
    (1) apply pesticides to the soybean and corn fields
    (2) rotate soybeans with corn
    (3) rotate a third crop in after the corn
    (4) apply pesticides to the corn crop to attack the adult beetle
    (5) hire people to pick off the larvae from the corn roots next year

Answers and explanations start on page 264.

From earthquakes to everyday weather, our earth is constantly changing. In this program you'll visit an earthquake center, a lake ecosystem, and a renewable energy research center to learn how natural events and cycles, as well as human activities, affect our planet and its resources.

Earth and Space Science

OBJECTIVES

1. Learn about our planet and its place in the solar system and universe.

2. Understand how Earth changes and how the atmosphere and oceans interact.

3. Explore how people affect the environment by polluting it and by using Earth's resources.

Chances are that you'll hear a story on the news today that relates to earth and space science. The story might be about the latest discovery of the Hubble space telescope or a space probe exploration on Mars. Perhaps the news will be about an earthquake in Italy or a flood in Bangladesh. Or it might be about the cleanup of a toxic waste dump.

Earth and space science is an important part of the GED Science Test. Some test items will require you to analyze familiar matters that you may never have thought much about—the weather, for example. Learning the concepts of earth and space science will help you on the GED test as well as enrich your understanding of everyday life.

On the following pages, you will find a brief exercise called *Sneak Preview.* It is designed to introduce you to the topics that will be featured in the video program and the corresponding lesson. After you complete the exercise and check your answers, turn to the vocabulary page. There you will find definitions of terms that will help you better understand the video and the lessons that follow. After reviewing page 184, you will be ready to watch Program 24.

For additional practice, visit *LiteracyLink* online at http://www.pbs.org/literacy.

Sneak Preview

This exercise previews some of the concepts from Program 24. After you answer the questions, use the chart on page 183 to help set your learning goals.

WORKPLACE LINK: Rosa works for the Department of Public Works in a large city. One of the department's jobs is snow removal. People in her office are discussing the weather. The forecast is for a 30 percent chance of snow tomorrow. Should they be getting the snow plows and crews ready?

Years ago, people looked outside for clues about the weather. A ring around the moon, for example, meant that snow or rain was probably coming. Today, forecasters use a global network of weather information sources to predict the weather.

Weather satellites transmit data about all parts of the world. Weather planes and balloons are sent up daily to gather information on conditions in the **atmosphere.** About 10,000 weather stations throughout the world report on local weather every three hours. All this information is processed by computers that provide forecast models.

Meteorologists interpret the models and data. They must consider the local conditions as well as the larger patterns forecast by the models. One forecasting method is to classify weather patterns into types and assign the present conditions to one of these types. Forecasters make predictions by referring to what has happened in the past. For example, if a cold front is expected in late January in mid-morning, and it has snowed 3 times out of 10 in such a situation in the past, the forecast is for a 30 percent chance of snow.

How accurate are weather forecasts? According to Sam Perugini, a meteorologist at Pennsylvania State University, "We can be pretty accurate up to about three days or so, in my opinion." After that, only general trends can be forecast.

Answer these questions based on the reading above.

1. What is the main idea of the article?

   (1) People used to look for clues in nature to forecast the weather.
   (2) A global network of sources provides accurate data about weather conditions.
   (3) Weather forecasting is usually accurate up to three days out.
   (4) Weather forecasting is based on information, computer models, and human interpretation.
   (5) Snow often accompanies the passing of a cold front during the month of January.

2. Which of the following statements expresses an opinion stated in the article rather than a fact?

   (1) People look for clues outside to forecast the weather.
   (2) Approximately 10,000 weather stations report local conditions.
   (3) Weather forecasting is accurate up to three days out.
   (4) Computer models are the basis for making local forecasts.
   (5) Present forecasts are based on similar situations in the past.

3. It is July, and a cold front is expected tomorrow afternoon. In the past, it has rained 7 out of 10 times during late afternoon or evening in such a situation. Which of the following is the best forecast for tomorrow?

   (1) 30 percent chance of rain in the late afternoon
   (2) 30 percent chance of rain in the late afternoon or evening
   (3) 70 percent chance of rain in the late afternoon
   (4) 70 percent chance of rain in the late afternoon or evening
   (5) rain in the late afternoon or evening

4. Why would it be unwise for meteorologists to rely entirely on computer models to forecast the weather?

   (1) Computer systems may go down at any time.
   (2) The models are too specific to use in everyday situations.
   (3) Global data is not included in the computer models.
   (4) Weather satellites report conditions in large areas of the world.
   (5) Specific local conditions are not included in the computer models.

Feedback

- If you got all of the answers right...   you're doing great! Concentrate on adding to your knowledge of science.

- If you missed question 1...   you need to improve your ability to understand the main point of an article.

- If you missed question 2...   you need to learn the difference between a fact and an opinion.

- If you missed question 3...   you need to learn to take information from one source and use it in another situation.

- If you missed question 4...   you need to learn to evaluate whether specific information supports a conclusion.

ANSWERS FOR SNEAK PREVIEW:
1. Choice (4)   2. Choice (3)   3. Choice (4)   4. Choice (5)

Vocabulary for *Earth and Space Science*

atmosphere	the layer of gases around Earth
climate	average weather conditions over a long period of time
crust	the top, rocky layer of Earth
earthquake	movement of Earth's crust caused by shifting plates
fault	crack in Earth's crust
fossil fuel	coal, oil, and natural gas; so-called because they form from ancient plant and animal remains
galaxy	a huge group of stars, dust, and gas held together by gravity
greenhouse effect	the atmosphere's role in heating Earth by trapping the sun's energy
light year	the distance light travels in one year (5,880,000,000,000 miles); used to measure huge distances in space
magma	molten rock below Earth's surface
mantle	the layer of Earth below the crust
nonrenewable resource	a resource, such as oil and minerals, that is limited in supply and cannot be replaced once it is used up
renewable resource	a resource, such as solar energy, whose supply is limitless
plate	large selection of Earth's crust that moves
plate tectonics	a theory explaining how Earth's crust changes over time
rock cycle	the processes that change one type of rock to another
solar system	the sun and the objects that revolve around it: planets, their satellites, asteroids, comets, and meteoroids
subduction	the sliding of one plate under another when they collide
water cycle	the processes by which water moves between the atmosphere, land, and oceans

---

→ NOW WATCH PROGRAM 24:

Use the "Thinking Connection" segments as an opportunity to reflect on and analyze what you hear from the scientists. Also think about the main idea in each segment of the program. Then look for more information on these concepts in the workbook lesson and online.

After you watch the program, work on:

- pages 185–200 in this workbook
- Internet activities at http://www.pbs.org/literacy

SCIENCE

24

Earth and Space Science

On the following pages, you will learn more about the ideas discussed in the video program and have an opportunity to develop and practice your GED science skills.

GED TIPS

When taking the GED Test, you should:

- Read each passage carefully and study the charts, diagrams, and graphs before you answer the questions.
- Be sure the answer you mark on the answer sheet matches the number of your answer choice.
- Answer every question, even if you have to guess.

Key Points to Think About

In the video program, you explored:

- The nature of the planet Earth and its place in the universe.
- How Earth changes and how the atmosphere and oceans interact.
- How people affect the environment by using resources and by polluting it.

On the GED Science Test:

- You will be expected to know some basic facts about Earth, our solar system, and the universe.
- You should know how to read a passage to get the main point as well as to analyze the logical relationships among ideas and facts.
- You will be given passages to read and diagrams, charts, and maps to interpret.

As you work through the lesson for Program 24:

- Concentrate on mastering basic concepts, not memorizing details.
- Remember that in science, there has to be measurable evidence to support theories.
- Relate what you are learning to your own life, not just to the GED Science Test.

Earth's Place in the Universe

FAMILY LINK: It's a clear, moonless summer night, and your family is relaxing after a barbecue. Someone points out the Milky Way, but no one really knows exactly what it is. You decide to find out more.

The Milky Way Galaxy

Galaxies are huge collections of stars, dust, and gas held together by gravity. Although astronomers estimate that there are about 50 billion galaxies, the only one we can see without a telescope is our own galaxy, the Milky Way. It looks like a luminous band of faint light stretching across the night sky. Its hazy appearance is due to the combined light of stars so far away that we cannot distinguish them with the naked eye.

The Milky Way is a large spiral galaxy with a central bulge where stars are close together. The central bulge is the band of light we see in the night sky. Spiraling outward from the center are arms where stars are further apart, and clouds of dust and gas are found. Our sun is a star in one of the spiral arms. The bulge and spiral arms form a disk shape. This disk is surrounded by a large cloud of hydrogen gas and clusters of stars above and below. Spiral galaxies contain many newly formed stars as well as old stars. Everything in the galaxy rotates around the center.

The Milky Way galaxy is huge. It is so large that scientists use **light years** instead of miles to measure it. A light year is the distance light travels in one year—about 9,461,000,000,000 km (5,880,000,000,000 mi). The distance across the Milky Way is about 100,000 light years.

Galaxies have other forms besides the spiral. Elliptical galaxies have an overall round shape with a bright center. They consist primarily of old stars and little gas or dust. There are few newly formed stars in elliptical galaxies. Galaxies with no particular shape are called irregular galaxies. Like spiral galaxies, they have large amounts of gas, dust, and young stars. A galaxy is usually not alone in space. Instead, galaxies occur in groups, which in turn form large clusters of galaxies. The Milky Way is a member of a group of about twenty galaxies called the Local Group.

SKILL PRACTICE

The photographs show three types of galaxies. Write the label *spiral, elliptical,* or *irregular* to identify each type of galaxy.

1. _____
2. _____
3. _____

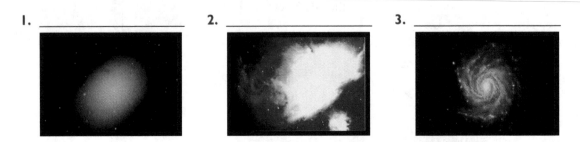

Answers and explanations start on page 265.

The Solar System

In one of the spiral arms of the Milky Way, the sun was born about 4.6 billion years ago. Revolving around the sun was a disk of material that formed the other bodies of our solar system: the planets, their satellites, asteroids, comets, and meteoroids. Together with the sun, these objects form our **solar system.**

There are nine major planets, usually divided into two groups. The inner planets are those closest to the sun. They are Mercury, Venus, Earth, and Mars. The inner planets are relatively small and rocky. The outer planets (with the exception of Pluto) are much larger and are made of gas and ice. The outer planets include Jupiter, Saturn, Uranus, Neptune, and Pluto.

Between the inner and outer planets is a band of asteroids, or tiny planets. Some asteroids are as tiny as a small house; others, such as Ceres, are as many as 620 miles across. Comets are small chunks of rock particles and ice. They have long, narrow orbits, or paths, around the sun. When comets come close to the sun, the ice turns to vapor and trails behind in a visible tail.

MAJOR PLANETS OF THE SOLAR SYSTEM

Planet	Distance from Sun (million miles)	Diameter (miles)	Year Length (1 revolution around the sun)	Day Length (1 complete rotation)	Number of Known Satellites
Mercury	36	3,030	88 days	59 days	0
Venus	67	7,545	225 days	117 days	0
Earth	93	7,927	365 days	23 hr 56 min	1
Mars	142	4,220	687 days	24 hr 37 min	2
Jupiter	483	88,700	11.9 years	9 hr 50 min	16
Saturn	887	75,000	29.5 years	10 hr 14 min	18
Uranus	1,783	32,300	84 years	17 hr 18 min	17
Neptune	2,794	30,800	164.8 years	16 hr	2
Pluto	3,660	1,800	248 years	6 days 9 hr	1

SKILL PRACTICE

Write *True* if the statement is true, *False* if it is false.

_____ 1. The solar system consists of the sun and all the objects that revolve around it.

_____ 2. All the outer planets are extremely large, except Pluto.

_____ 3. Uranus has 15 known satellites.

_____ 4. The farther from the sun a planet is, the shorter its day.

_____ 5. The farther from the sun a planet is, the longer it takes to revolve once around the sun.

Answers and explanations start on page 265.

COMMUNITY LINK: You've been watching news images of the planet Earth taken from the space shuttle. These images are in sharp contrast to the wars and crimes you see on the nightly news. They show that Earth looks calm and peaceful, a single community.

The Planet Earth

Photos of the planet Earth taken from space show a beautiful blue ball with patches and swirls of white clouds. Imagine slicing that ball in half to see a cross section of the planet. The cross section shows that Earth is made of layers of different materials.

The outermost layer of the planet is the **atmosphere,** the air that surrounds us. The atmosphere extends several hundred miles above the surface of Earth.

On Earth's surface is the hydrosphere. The hydrosphere consists of the oceans and other surface water. Water covers about 71 percent of the planet, which is why Earth looks so blue from space.

The solid planet itself is the geosphere, which also has layers. The top layer is the **crust,** which is made of a wide variety of rock types. Below the crust is the **mantle,** in which material rises and falls as a result of heating and cooling. Next is the liquid outer core, composed mainly of iron and nickel. The innermost layer is the inner core, made of solid iron and nickel.

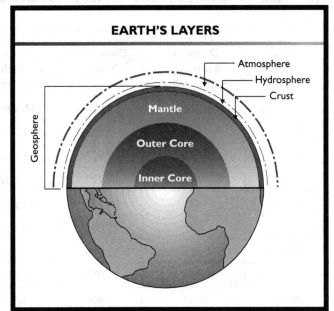

EARTH'S LAYERS

SKILL PRACTICE

Match the layer of Earth with its description.

	Earth's Layer	Description
_____	1. geosphere	a. consists of liquid iron and nickel
_____	2. inner core	b. the layer of water on the surface
_____	3. outer core	c. the solid planet itself
_____	4. atmosphere	d. top rocky layer
_____	5. mantle	e. consists of solid iron and nickel
_____	6. crust	f. layer in which materials rise and fall
_____	7. hydrosphere	g. layer of air

Answers and explanations start on page 265.

SCIENCE

■ Apply What You Learn

Read the following article about the Earth and its close neighbors in the solar system. Then answer the questions that follow.

Earth-Crossers

In the movies, actors like Bruce Willis save us from disasters ranging from tornadoes and volcanoes to asteroid and comet collisions. Natural disasters such as tornadoes do occur, but can we really believe that Earth might be hit by an asteroid or comet, causing widespread destruction and death?

Actually, yes. According to scientists, among the many thousands of asteroids and comets in the solar system, at least 1,700 are large enough to cause global damage if they hit us. Large asteroids and comets can cause so much damage because of their speed. On impact, they would explode with the force of millions of nuclear weapons. However, the odds of a major collision are small: about once every 300,000 years or so. Near misses occur frequently, however. In 1989, for example, a 1,000-foot asteroid passed relatively close to Earth, within 400,000 miles.

The U.S. government takes the threat of collision seriously. Scientists use an Air Force telescope in Hawaii and NASA cameras to take a census of the asteroids and comets whose orbits intersect with Earth's orbit. These asteroids and comets are called Earth-crossers because their orbits cross Earth's orbit. Within a few months of starting, census takers found four new Earth-crossers, one of them 1.8 miles across. The high rate of discovery suggests that there are many unknown Earth-crossers in the solar system.

SKILL PRACTICE

Answer the questions based on the above information.

1. According to scientists, about how often does a large comet or asteroid hit the Earth?

   _____

2. What is the purpose of the project that tracks asteroids and comets?

   _____

Connection

Science in Personal and Social Perspectives

Although the possibility of an asteroid striking Earth is relatively small, our society seems fascinated with this type of "doomsday" scenario. For instance, people flock to movies such as *Armageddon* and *Deep Impact* that tell of a heavenly body on a collision course with Earth. Moreover, science fiction stories about alien invasions remain wildly popular.

Why are people in our society so curious about "doomsday" events such as these? Write a paragraph expressing your opinion. Be sure to include a topic sentence summing up your main point.

Answers and explanations start on page 265.

The Changing Earth

COMMUNITY LINK: A news article tells of the discovery of a new fault line near your town. You decide to find out more about the causes of earthquakes so that you can talk with your neighbors about working together to protect lives and property.

The Movement of Earth's Plates

We live on Earth's crust, the 5- to 25-mile uppermost layer of Earth. The crust is not one unbroken piece. Instead, it is actually a patchwork of broad plates that fit together much like a roughly made jigsaw puzzle. The plates float on Earth's mantle, a hotter and more fluid layer of rock. The shifting of these plates often causes **earthquakes.** As dwellers on a moving surface, we should prepare for earthquakes, especially if we live near the boundary of two plates.

Three types of zones can be found along these plate boundaries. A certain type of movement characterizes each type of zone. Each type of movement can create **faults,** or cracks within Earth's crust. All the movements can cause earthquakes and volcanic activity.

- In a spreading zone, two plates move apart, forming cracks in Earth's crust. **Magma,** or melted rock, rises up to form ridges, mountain ranges, and volcanoes.

- Plates in a subduction zone collide. When two plates are forced into the same space, one plate may be subducted, or forced to slide under the other. It then melts into Earth's mantle. Sometimes, two plates collide and neither subducts. Then the plates push against each other, forming mountain chains. The world's most destructive earthquakes and volcanoes occur along subduction zones.

- In a transform zone, plates try to slide past each other. Since the edges of plates are not smooth, they often snag on each other. When enough pressure builds, the plates move past each other. With each slip and slide, earthquake tremors rock the landscape.

SKILL PRACTICE

The drawings show movement conditions along plate boundaries. Write the label *Spreading,* *Subduction,* **or** *Transform* **to identify each type of zone.**

1. _____   2. _____   3. _____

Answers and explanations start on page 265.

The Rock Cycle

Geologists learn about Earth by examining rocks. Rocks can be classified into three groups according to the way they were formed.

Igneous rocks are formed from molten rock, or magma. As magma nears Earth's surface, it cools and crystallizes to form rocks. Sedimentary rocks are formed when particles called sediment are compressed by the weight of layers of Earth or are cemented together. Metamorphic rocks are formed when great heat or pressure changes igneous, sedimentary, or older metamorphic rocks.

Rocks are transformed into new ones in a process known as the **rock cycle.** Once any rock reaches Earth's surface, it is slowly eroded and broken down into sediment. The sediment is carried by glaciers, rivers, and wind and deposited in layers where it forms sedimentary rock.

If the new sedimentary rock is forced deeper into the Earth by the movement of Earth's plates, heat and pressure will transform it into metamorphic rock. Then it may be pushed to the surface to erode once again, or it may go deeper into the Earth where it will melt, form magma, and cool to form igneous rock. This has been a continuous cycle since the formation of the Earth's crust.

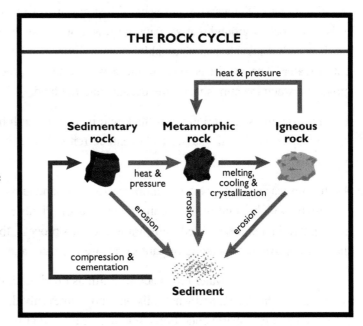

THE ROCK CYCLE

SKILL PRACTICE

Answer the questions based on the above information.

1. Metamorphic rocks have been exposed to which of the following?

    (1) erosion
    (2) heat and pressure
    (3) cementation

2. What kind of rock would you expect to find

    a. in a riverbed? _____
    b. near an active volcano? _____

3. What kind of rock do you think is most common? Why?

Answers and explanations start on page 265.

The Water Cycle

Water is vital to all life on Earth. About 71 percent of the Earth's surface is covered with water, but 97 percent of the water is salt water. Most of our fresh water is frozen in glaciers or polar ice or is so far below ground that we cannot draw it out. Less than $\frac{1}{2}$ of 1 percent of the water on the Earth is both drinkable and obtainable. With so little fresh water available, why haven't we run out of water? The answer is found in the **water cycle,** the process by which water constantly moves between the atmosphere, the oceans, and the land.

The atmosphere is about 350 miles thick and is held to Earth by gravity. Changing conditions in the atmosphere affect air masses and ocean currents. These, in turn, influence Earth's weather and **climate.**

As the sun warms Earth, water evaporates from the land and bodies of water. Evaporation is the process by which liquid water becomes water vapor. Plants also release water into the atmosphere in a process called transpiration. In this process, they lose moisture through pores in their leaves. Animals perspire or pant to release moisture and cool their bodies.

From the atmosphere, water falls back to Earth as precipitation. Much of the world's rain and snow falls in the ocean, and what falls on land is unevenly distributed. But by observing seasonal patterns and atmospheric conditions, scientists can predict floods and droughts and help us to manage our water resources.

SKILL PRACTICE

Write *True* if the statement is true, *False* if it is false.

_____ 1. In the summer, Maggie will lose less water to evaporation if she waters her lawn in the cool evening instead of the hot afternoon.

_____ 2. Most of Earth's water is drinkable.

_____ 3. Earth's water supply is affected by changes in the atmosphere.

_____ 4. Through the water cycle, salt water from the ocean becomes drinkable.

5. Using the information in the passage, draw a simple diagram of the water cycle.

Answers and explanations start on page 265.

SCIENCE

■ Apply What You Learn

Read the following article about the changing Earth. Then answer the questions that follow.

Robot Explorers

Mount Erebus in Antarctica may hold the secret to understanding the long-term effects of pollutants on Earth's environment. This active volcano continues to expel debris, steam, and gases once or twice per day. For twenty years, scientists had been looking for a safe way to explore the dangerous volcano and gather important data. None existed until recently.

In 1992, researchers at Carnegie Mellon University in Pittsburgh built an 8-legged, 990-pound robot that could descend safely into the heart of a volcano. Named Dante, the nearly 10-foot-long robotic spider was programmed to climb down a 325-foot cable to the floor of the crater. There, Dante would use a laser range-finder to avoid molten lava pools and volcanic cracks. After gathering samples of gas and dust, Dante was programmed to return to the cable and climb out. The robot was equipped with cameras to allow researchers to follow its progress.

Unfortunately Dante's mission was not a complete success. The cable snapped, and Dante fell deep within the crater, never to be recovered. Still, the mission proved to be valuable. Dante had led researchers to develop new laser technology. They learned more about how to program a robot to perform routine tasks in dangerous conditions. Scientists hope that future robots will help them learn more about volcanic rocks and processes.

SKILL PRACTICE

Answer the questions based on the above information.

1. What scientific problem brought about the need for Dante?

    _____

2. From building Dante, scientists learned and developed new technology. Name two things that they learned.

    a. _____

    b. _____

Connection

Science as Inquiry

In 1994, Dante II successfully collected data from inside Mount Erebus. In 1997, the robotic vehicle Sojourner explored the landscape of Mars and sent back pictures and data.

If you were a scientist studying plate boundaries on the ocean floor, for which step(s) of the scientific method could you use a robotic explorer? Explain.

▶▶ **For more information about the scientific method, see page 274.**

Answers and explanations start on page 266.

People and the Environment

The Greenhouse Effect

One function of the atmosphere is to warm Earth. The sun's rays are absorbed by Earth's surface and then radiated outward. Atmospheric gases such as carbon dioxide, methane, and ozone reflect the radiation back down toward Earth. The reflected radiation keeps Earth at temperatures that are suitable for life. This role of the atmosphere is called the **greenhouse effect,** and the gases that reflect the radiation are called greenhouse gases.

In recent years, the amount of greenhouse gases in the atmosphere has risen. The most important of these gases, carbon dioxide, has been on the rise because it is a byproduct of burning fossil fuels like oil, gas, and coal. The slash-and-burn clearing of forests also contributes to the carbon dioxide in the atmosphere. Although there are international agreements to hold steady or reduce the emission of greenhouse gases such as carbon dioxide, these emissions are still increasing.

CARBON EMISSIONS IN SELECTED COUNTRIES, in millions of metric tons					
Year	United States	Former USSR	Germany	Japan	China
1990 (actual)	1,338	1,014	265	310	649
2000 (projected)	1,483	868	292	395	907
2010 (projected)	1,632	1,037	325	443	1,170

Some scientists predict that the amount of carbon dioxide in the atmosphere will double by the year 2100. If this happens, they expect that average global temperatures will rise by 3° to 8° F. Other scientists argue that the present global warming is the result of natural climate cycles, not industrial pollution, and thus may not be so severe.

SKILL PRACTICE

Answer the questions based on the above information. Use a separate sheet of paper.

1. What is the greenhouse effect?
2. Why has the amount of carbon dioxide in the atmosphere been increasing?
3. List the nations in order of their 1990 carbon emissions, with the largest emission first.

Answers and explanations start on page 266.

SCIENCE

Nonrenewable Resources

For most of history, wood was the main source of energy for heating and cooking. After the industrial revolution, more concentrated sources of energy were needed, and people began to use coal, oil, and natural gas for heating, cooking, making electricity, transportation, and manufacturing. Today these fossil fuels are still our major sources of energy.

Coal, oil, and gas are called **fossil fuels** because they are made from animal and plant remains that have formed fossils. Coal formed 350 to 250 million years ago from the rotting plants of tropical forests. Buried under layers of rock that exert great pressure, the plant remains gradually turned into coal.

Natural gas and oil form from both animal and plant remains. They are often found together in porous rock, with the gas above the oil because gas is lighter. The oil and gas seep upward until they reach a barrier of impermeable rock through which they cannot pass.

Although coal, oil, and gas are excellent sources of energy, their use poses problems. First, burning fossil fuels releases carbon and other pollutants into the atmosphere. In addition to causing local air pollution, these emissions increase the level of greenhouse gases, contributing to global warming. Second, these fuels are **nonrenewable resources.** Once they are used up, they cannot be replaced. Eventually, people will need to find alternative sources of energy to replace fossil fuels.

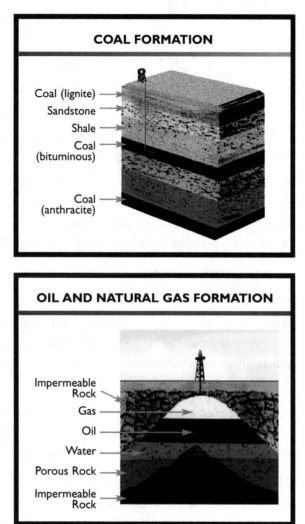

COAL FORMATION

Coal (lignite)
Sandstone
Shale
Coal (bituminous)
Coal (anthracite)

OIL AND NATURAL GAS FORMATION

Impermeable Rock
Gas
Oil
Water
Porous Rock
Impermeable Rock

SKILL PRACTICE

Write *True* if the statement is true, *False* if it is false.

_____ 1. Fossil fuels form from the remains of plant and animal life.

_____ 2. Wood is a more concentrated form of energy than coal, oil, and natural gas.

_____ 3. The use of fossil fuels contributes to global warming.

_____ 4. A nonrenewable resource is one that cannot be replaced once it is used.

_____ 5. If we run out of fossil fuels, we can use electricity for our energy needs.

Answers and explanations start on page 266.

Alternative Sources of Energy

During the 1970s, the world experienced its first shortage of oil and natural gas. The energy crisis sparked interest in alternative sources of energy such as solar energy, wind power, water power, and geothermal energy to lessen our dependence on oil and gas. These forms of energy are **renewable resources** because their supply is limitless.

Solar energy comes directly from the sun's rays and can be used to provide heat and hot water. Buildings designed to capture winter sun and keep out summer sun require less fossil fuel for heating and air conditioning. In most solar-powered buildings, water heats up as it flows through a solar panel on the roof. This water flows through pipes throughout the building, providing hot water as well as heat.

Wind power uses the energy of moving air. In areas with strong steady winds, windmill "farms" drive generators that produce electricity.

Water power uses the energy of falling water to produce electricity. Generally, a dam is built across a river and a large lake builds up behind it. Some water is allowed to pass through the dam, driving generators that produce electricity. At present, about 20 percent of the world's electricity is produced by water power.

Geothermal energy uses the heat energy stored deep in Earth. When the heat is brought up to the surface, it drives a turbine that generates electricity. Geothermal energy is practical only in areas where the heat sources are fairly close to the surface, as in earthquake zones.

All these energy sources are renewable and quite clean compared to fossil fuels, but they are far more expensive. For example, to generate one kilowatt hour of electricity using natural gas costs about 3 cents. In contrast, the same amount of electricity generated by wind or geothermal energy is about 5 cents, and by solar energy, about 14 cents. The high cost of alternative energy sources has limited their use.

SKILL PRACTICE

Match the type of energy with its source.

	Type of Energy	Source
_____	1. geothermal energy	a. sun's rays
_____	2. water power	b. falling water
_____	3. wind power	c. underground heat
_____	4. solar energy	d. moving air

Answers and explanations start on page 266.

SCIENCE

■ Apply What You Learn

Read the following article about global warming and its possible effects. Then answer the questions that follow.

Polar Ice Meltdown?

According to current predictions of global warming, melting glaciers and polar ice may cause the sea level to rise about 1.5 feet by the year 2100. If that happens, many low-lying coastal areas will be under water. However, some scientists are now predicting that the West Antarctic Ice Sheet could collapse in a few hundred years, sending enough water into the oceans to raise the sea level by 13 to 20 feet. Such a rise in sea level would be a catastrophe. A large portion of the Eastern Seaboard of the United States, for example, would be under water. So would many of the island nations of the Pacific, Caribbean, and Indian Ocean.

On what is this prediction based? In sediments taken from the land below the West Antarctic Ice Sheet, scientists have found evidence that marine life existed there within the last two million years. This evidence suggests that the ice sheet collapsed at least partially sometime during this period, allowing ocean life to exist there. If this happened once, they reason, it might happen again.

SKILL PRACTICE

Answer the questions based on the above information.

1. By how much would the sea level rise if the West Antarctic Ice Sheet collapsed?

   _____

2. Why would the collapse of the West Antarctic Ice Sheet be catastrophic?

   _____

3. On what evidence is the prediction of a West Antarctic Ice Sheet collapse based?

   _____

   _____

Connection

Science in Personal and Social Perspectives

A rise in sea level is a global problem that may affect millions of people who live in low-lying coastal areas. Although the rise discussed in this article may not happen for hundreds of years, if at all, even a small rise may affect many communities.

Think about the effects that rising sea levels may have on coastal communities. Then brainstorm ideas to help coastal communities combat the effects of rising sea levels. List three ideas.

Answers and explanations start on page 266.

DIRECTIONS: Read the passage and study the diagram. Then answer the questions that follow.

Earthquakes produce seismic waves that can travel long distances and cause great damage. Scientists measure seismic waves using a seismograph. This machine measures the amplitude, or size of the waves, in millimeters. To use the data, scientists must calculate the distance of the seismograph from the epicenter, or point of origin, of the quake.

The Richter Scale estimates the magnitude, or force, of an earthquake based on the relationship between the distance from the epicenter and the amplitude. The diagram shows that an earthquake at a distance of 100 kilometers with an amplitude of 1 millimeter is rated at magnitude 3.0 on the Richter Scale. Note that an earthquake of magnitude 4.0 at the same distance would produce 10 millimeters of amplitude. The change of one unit in magnitude produces an earthquake ten times more powerful!

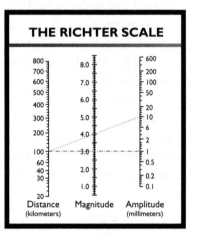

Someday, scientists hope to use seismographs and other instruments to predict earthquakes. Until then, cities are reinforcing existing buildings and designing new ones to withstand strong quakes without collapsing. However, most cities would suffer major damage if hit by a strong quake.

1. What does a seismograph measure?
   (1) the amount of destruction caused by the earthquake
   (2) the amplitude of seismic waves
   (3) the magnitude of the quake on the Richter Scale
   (4) the epicenter of the quake
   (5) the depth of the quake

2. In 1906, an estimated 8.2-magnitude earthquake destroyed much of San Francisco. In comparison, if the same earthquake were to strike San Francisco today, the loss of life and property damage would probably be
   (1) greater because San Francisco has increased in population and size.
   (2) greater because of the new location of the fault.
   (3) much less because people know how to stay safe during earthquakes.
   (4) much less because San Francisco is no longer in a fault zone.
   (5) much less because of our ability to predict earthquakes.

3. According to the diagram, what would be the amplitude of a 5.0 magnitude quake at a distance of 100 kilometers?
   (1) 20 millimeters
   (2) 50 millimeters
   (3) 100 millimeters
   (4) 200 millimeters
   (5) The amplitude is impossible to calculate.

4. Knowing the Richter Scale ratings for two earthquakes can help you compare
   (1) the amounts of energy they released.
   (2) the lengths of time they lasted.
   (3) the costs in loss of life and property.
   (4) the distances of the epicenters from major cities.
   (5) the effects of both earthquakes on Earth's surface.

Read the passage and study the diagram. Then answer the questions that follow.

Stars are born, shine for billions of years, and then run out of fuel. Stars form from clouds of gas and dust, which come together because of gravity. Some of them grow into blue giants, which eventually explode into supernovas and may become black holes or neutron stars. Other young stars grow to medium size. Toward the end of their life cycle, they expand and become red giants. Then they shrink into dim white dwarfs.

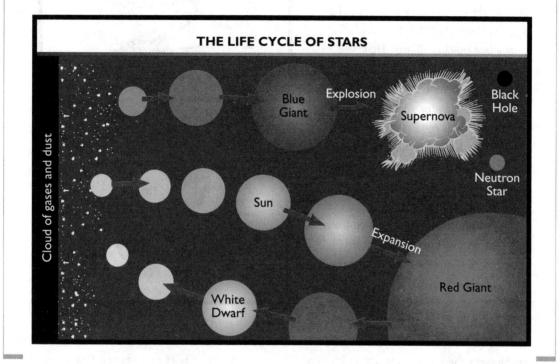

THE LIFE CYCLE OF STARS

5. A white dwarf star develops from
   (1) a shrinking red giant.
   (2) a shrinking blue giant.
   (3) an expanding neutron star.
   (4) an expanding black hole.
   (5) a supernova.

6. Which of the following conclusions is supported by the information in the passage and diagram?
   (1) All stars are at the same stage of their life cycle at any given time.
   (2) Only neutron stars eventually become supernovas.
   (3) Increased star size is associated with higher temperatures.
   (4) The life cycle of the solar system is tied to that of our star, the sun.
   (5) Distant stars appear dimmer than stars nearby.

7. Why do clouds of gases and dust eventually become stars?
   (1) Their energy disappears into space.
   (2) Gravity causes the particles to come together.
   (3) Nuclear reactions produce heat and light.
   (4) Black holes and supernovas disintegrate.
   (5) Blue giants explode into supernovas.

8. Our sun is a medium-sized star about 4.6 billion years old. Eventually, the sun will become a
   (1) supernova.
   (2) neutron star.
   (3) black hole.
   (4) blue giant.
   (5) red giant.

Read the passage and study the diagram. Then answer the questions that follow.

Communications satellites, which beam phone calls, beeper messages, TV programs, and computer data around the world, work best in geosynchronous orbit above the equator. That means they circle Earth at the same speed as Earth rotates, appearing to stay still above one point on Earth. However, satellites launched from north and south of the equator wind up in orbits at an angle to the equator. Moving them into the proper orbit requires course corrections and more fuel. Boeing and companies from other countries have joined to build a mobile launching platform to be used in the Pacific Ocean at the equator. Rockets launched from the platform will get a boost from Earth's rotation. They will also travel a relatively short distance to release satellites into orbit above the equator.

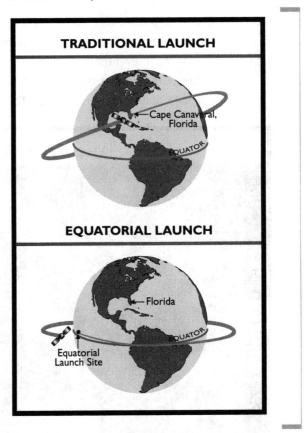

9. What was the most important reason for developing the equatorial ocean launch platform?
   (1) to improve communications satellites
   (2) to increase international cooperation
   (3) to cut the cost of satellite launches
   (4) to launch scientific experiments
   (5) to improve rocket technology

10. From the information and diagram, you can infer that one reason Cape Canaveral, Florida, is the site of U.S. launches is that Cape Canaveral
    (1) is relatively close to the equator.
    (2) is relatively far from the equator.
    (3) is near aerospace manufacturers.
    (4) has many communications satellites.
    (5) is on a major hurricane path.

Read the passage. Then answer the question that follows.

Since the first Earth Day in 1970, environmental regulations have succeeded in reducing the emission of air pollutants in 41 states. Still, according to the Environmental Protection Agency, two out of every five Americans live in areas where the air is unhealthful.

11. Since 1970, the emission of hazardous air pollutants has
    (1) decreased in most states.
    (2) increased in most states.
    (3) reduced the need for environmental regulations.
    (4) ceased to be a problem.
    (5) increased every year.

Answers and explanations start on page 266.

Think that chemistry happens only in laboratories? Think again. In this program you'll see fascinating chemical changes occur in a glassblower's studio, even in the kitchen! Then you'll hear about the world of atoms behind those reactions, and why chemistry is an important part of life and industry.

Chemistry

OBJECTIVES

1. Learn about the structure and states of matter.

2. Understand how elements behave when combined.

3. Explore the characteristics of different types of chemicals.

When you scramble an egg or try to get rid of the rust spots on your car, you are using the principles of chemistry. Chemistry is the study of the composition and properties of matter. Since matter is all around us, we use the principles of chemistry all the time, even though we may not be aware of them.

Chemistry is an important part of the GED Science Test. Many test items cover chemistry. Learning the concepts of chemistry will help you on the GED Test as well as enrich your understanding of everyday life.

On the following pages, you will find a brief exercise called *Sneak Preview*. It is designed to introduce you to the topics that will be featured in the video program and the corresponding lesson. After you complete the exercise and check your answers, turn to the vocabulary page. There you will find definitions of terms that will help you better understand the video and the lessons that follow. After reviewing page 204, you will be ready to watch Program 25.

For additional practice, visit *LiteracyLink* online at http://www.pbs.org/literacy.

Sneak Preview

This exercise previews some of the concepts from Program 25. After you answer the questions, use the chart on page 203 to help set your learning goals.

FAMILY LINK: Sam is preparing breakfast for his children. He sets out melamine plates and cups. He flips pancakes with a nylon spatula. The children pour syrup from a plastic bottle. After breakfast, they cover the leftovers with plastic wrap.

It's hard to imagine life without plastics. Bags, bottles, toys, computer and TV cases, helmets, electrical insulation, floor coverings, synthetic fibers—the list of plastic items is almost endless. Yet, plastics did not exist 150 years ago. Before 1860, natural materials like ivory and amber were used where plastic is used today. As these materials became scarcer, the need for a substitute grew.

The first plastic was made by Alexander Parkes from cotton fibers. These fibers contain cellulose, a long molecule called a **polymer.** Parkes dissolved cellulose in nitric acid and added camphor. Then he evaporated the solvent. The result was a substance that could be molded into various shapes.

The first synthetic plastic was Bakelite, invented by Leo Baekeland in 1907. Baekeland developed a synthetic polymer from phenol and formaldehyde. Bakelite was hard, heat-resistant, and a good insulator. It was used for many things like radio and clock cases. Bakelite was a dark color. By the 1920s, multicolored plastics were developed. Today there are hundreds of plastics and synthetic fibers like nylon, most of them made from petroleum.

All plastics are categorized into one of two main groups depending on how they act when heated. Thermoplastic materials like polyvinyl chloride (PVC) soften when they are heated. This is because heat breaks the links between the polymers, so the molecules can slide past one another. In contrast, thermosetting plastics like epoxy resins do not soften when heated. Their polymers are cross-linked in a network that gives them a permanent rigid structure.

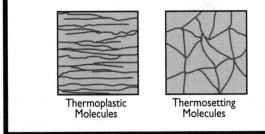

MOLECULAR STRUCTURES OF THERMOPLASTIC AND THERMOSETTING

Thermoplastic Molecules

Thermosetting Molecules

Answer these questions based on the reading above.

1. What is the main idea of the last paragraph?

    (1) Most modern plastics are synthesized from petroleum.
    (2) Bakelite's color was one of its main drawbacks.
    (3) Polymers are long chain molecules.
    (4) When plastics are heated, they soften.
    (5) There are two main types of plastics.

SCIENCE

2. Care instructions for a synthetic fleece pullover made from recycled plastic indicate it should be washed in cold water and briefly tumble dried on a low setting. It should not be ironed. What is the reason for these instructions?

   (1) Heat will damage the molecular structure of the fabric.
   (2) Washing is better than dry cleaning for cleaning this fabric.
   (3) The fabric is manufactured from thermosetting plastic.
   (4) The fabric is made from cotton cellulose polymers.
   (5) The polymers are cross-linked in a strong, rigid network.

3. The main difference between the molecular structures of thermosetting plastics and thermoplastic materials is that in thermosetting plastics the polymers are

   (1) shorter.
   (2) longer.
   (3) synthetic.
   (4) natural.
   (5) cross-linked.

4. From a commercial point of view, a major disadvantage of Bakelite was that it was

   (1) a thermosetting plastic.
   (2) a thermoplastic material.
   (3) always a dark color.
   (4) used for clock and radio cases.
   (5) made from petroleum.

Feedback

- If you got all of the answers right...   you're doing great! Concentrate on adding to your knowledge of science.

- If you missed question 1...   you need to improve your ability to understand the main idea of a paragraph.

- If you missed question 2...   you need to learn to take general information and apply it to a specific situation.

- If you missed question 3...   you need to learn to figure out the relationships between ideas.

- If you missed question 4...   you need to learn to evaluate the importance of nonscientific factors in driving science and technology.

PROGRAM 25: Chemistry

Vocabulary for *Chemistry*

acid	a substance with a sour taste and low pH that conducts electricity when dissolved in water and that neutralizes bases
atom	a tiny particle of matter consisting of protons, neutrons, and electrons
atomic number	the number of protons in the nucleus of an element
base	a substance with a high pH that conducts electricity when dissolved in water and that neutralizes acids
chemical reaction	a process in which one substance or set of substances is changed into another substance or set of substances
compound	a substance made of two or more elements chemically combined in exact proportion
covalent bond	the combining of two or more atoms by the sharing of electrons
electron	a negatively charged particle orbiting the nucleus of an atom
element	a substance that cannot be broken down into a simpler substance by chemical means
hydrocarbon	a compound that consists only of carbon and hydrogen atoms
ion	an atom or molecule with an electric charge
ionic bond	the combining of two or more atoms by transferring electrons
mixture	a substance made up of two or more different substances that are not chemically combined; for example, salt water
molecule	a group of two or more atoms held together by covalent bonds; see *covalent bond*
neutron	a neutral particle in the nucleus of an atom
periodic table	a chart in which the elements are arranged according to atomic weight and the number of electrons in their outer shells
polymer	a compound that has very large molecules made up of thousands of smaller, identical molecules joined together
proton	a positively charged particle in the nucleus of an atom
states of matter	the different forms substances can take: solid, liquid, or gas

➡ NOW WATCH PROGRAM 25:

At first, the many terms introduced in this program may seem confusing. Focus on these important concepts as you watch: What is matter made of? What happens when substances combine chemically? The workbook lesson and online activities will help you build your familiarity with atoms, molecules, elements, mixtures, compounds and chemical reactions.

After you watch the program, work on:

- pages 205–220 in this workbook
- Internet activities at http://www.pbs.org/literacy

AFTER YOU WATCH

25

Chemistry

On the following pages, you will learn more about the ideas discussed in the video program and have an opportunity to develop and practice your GED science skills.

Key Points to Think About

In the video program, you explored:
- The structure and states of matter.
- The behavior of elements when they bond and react.
- Different types of substances, such as, mixtures, solutions, acids, bases, and salts.

On the GED Science Test:
- You will be expected to know some basic facts about the composition and properties of matter.
- You should know how to evaluate whether the information you are given can support a conclusion.
- You will be given passages to read and diagrams, charts, and graphs to interpret.

As you work through the lesson for Program 25:
- Concentrate on mastering basic concepts, not memorizing details.
- Remember that in science, observation of the behavior of matter leads to hypotheses that help explain what is happening.
- Relate what you are learning to your own life, not just to the GED Science Test.

The Structure of Matter

WORKPLACE LINK: Marcy has a part-time job filling and selling balloons. The balloons are filled with helium, a gas that's lighter than air. A co-worker tells her that helium is an element. Marcy wants to learn more about the elements.

Elements and Compounds

An **element** is a substance in which all the **atoms,** or tiny particles, are of the same kind. An element cannot be broken down into a simpler substance by chemical means. In ancient times, scientists thought there were only four elements: earth, water, fire, and air. Today 103 elements are recognized internationally, and scientists claim to have made 6 more. Of these, only 92 occur naturally on Earth. Some elements are gold, copper, carbon, sodium, oxygen, helium, mercury, and chlorine.

Elements combine with each other to produce **compounds.** In a compound, two or more elements are chemically united in exact proportion. For example, water is a compound that consists of two parts of the element hydrogen and one part of the element oxygen. So each **molecule** of water contains two atoms of hydrogen and one atom of oxygen. Because the different atoms in a compound always exist in the same proportions, chemists can write formulas that show the composition of a compound. The formula for water is H_2O. Some familiar compounds are shown in the table below.

> Scientists use symbols to refer to the elements. For instance, oxygen is O. Hydrogen is H. Sodium is Na.

Compound	Chemical Formula	Composition
Salt	NaCl	One atom of sodium (Na) and one atom of chlorine (Cl)
Sugar	$C_6H_{12}O_6$	Six atoms of carbon (C), twelve atoms of hydrogen (H), and six atoms of oxygen (O)
Chalk	$CaCO_3$	One atom of calcium (Ca), one atom of carbon (C), and three atoms of oxygen (O)

SKILL PRACTICE

Write *Element* if the substance is an element, *Compound* if it is a compound.

_____ 1. Oxygen (O)

_____ 2. Methane (CH_4)

_____ 3. Copper (Cu)

_____ 4. Carbon dioxide (CO_2)

_____ 5. Helium (He)

_____ 6. Uranium (U)

_____ 7. Nitric acid (HNO_3)

_____ 8. Neon (Ne)

Answers and explanations start on page 266.

Atoms

An **atom** is a tiny particle of matter consisting of still smaller particles—protons, electrons, and neutrons. Every atom has a nucleus, which contains protons and neutrons. Around the nucleus spin electrons. The protons have a positive charge, the electrons have a negative charge, and the neutrons have no charge.

In a particular element, there are the same number of protons and electrons, so an atom of the element is neither positive nor negative in charge. For example, one atom of the element carbon contains six protons and six electrons, and its charge is neutral. The number of protons in the nucleus of an element is called its **atomic number.** Each element has a unique atomic number. The higher the atomic number, the heavier the element. Carbon's atomic number is 6.

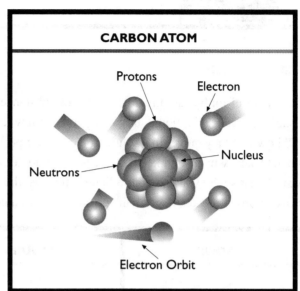

CARBON ATOM

Protons

Electron

Nucleus

Neutrons

Electron Orbit

Atoms have a lot of empty space. Most of the mass of an atom is in its nucleus, which is very small compared to the atom as a whole. Electrons orbit the nucleus at high speed. Because of this speed, an atom behaves as if it is solid. It is similar to the quickly rotating blades of a fan. The blades appear solid and repel other matter, even though there is much empty space between them.

SKILL PRACTICE

Write *True* if the statement is true, *False* if it is false.

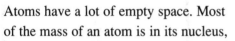

_____ 1. An atom is a tiny particle of matter made up of protons, electrons, and neutrons.

_____ 2. Electrons have a positive charge.

_____ 3. Protons and neutrons make up the nucleus of an atom.

_____ 4. In an element, there are the same number of protons and electrons, producing a negative charge.

_____ 5. The atomic number of an element tells you how many protons are in the nucleus of the atom.

_____ 6. Most of the mass of an atom is in its electrons.

Answers and explanations start on page 267.

COMMUNITY LINK: The city department for which you work watches the temperature forecasts closely. They need to know what type of precipitation to prepare for—ice and snow in freezing temperatures, rain in warmer temperatures.

States of Matter

The **states of matter** are the different forms substances can take—solid, liquid, or gas. Whether a substance is a solid, liquid, or gas depends on how close together its atoms or molecules are and how fast they move. In a solid, molecules are packed tightly together and cannot move very much. That's why a solid keeps its shape. In a liquid, molecules are farther apart and can move easily. That's why you can pour a liquid. In a gas, the molecules are very far apart and they can move in any direction. A gas will spread out to fill a container.

SOLID	LIQUID	GAS

Most substances can exist in either solid, liquid, or gas form, depending on temperature. At low temperatures, substances are solid. If the solid is heated, its atoms begin to move more quickly, and it melts and forms a liquid. If the liquid is further heated until it boils, the atoms absorb even more energy. They move faster, and the liquid forms a gas. At very high temperatures, the electrons of an atom can separate from its nucleus, forming a fourth state of matter, plasma. The sun and other stars are made of plasma.

At room temperature on Earth, most of the 92 elements occur in solid or gas form. Only two elements, bromine and mercury, are liquid at room temperature.

SKILL PRACTICE

**Write *Solid* if the substance is solid, *Liquid* if it is liquid, and *Gas* if it is a gas.
If it consists of more than one state of matter, write all that apply.**

_____ 1. Melted butter

_____ 2. Ice

_____ 3. Carbonated beverage

_____ 4. Air

_____ 5. Mercury in a thermometer

_____ 6. Olive oil

_____ 7. Helium in a balloon

_____ 8. Marble

Answers and explanations start on page 267.

SCIENCE

■ Apply What You Learn

Read the following article about making popcorn. Then answer the questions that follow.

What Makes Popcorn Pop?

The sound of popcorn kernels exploding in the microwave is music to a hungry snacker. But just what is going on inside that microwaveable bag of popcorn to cause these mini-explosions?

Popcorn kernels have an outer layer of cells called the pericarp. The pericarp is hard and water does not pass through it easily. Inside, the kernel is soft and contains some water. When the popcorn is heated, the energy of the water molecules increases and they move apart rapidly. The liquid water turns to steam. Inside the kernel, the pressure builds up until it explodes.

In a bag of popcorn, there are always kernels that do not pop. Sometimes there's a scratch on the pericarp that lets the steam out slowly so the kernel doesn't explode. Sometimes the popcorn is too dry and not enough steam builds up. And sometimes a kernel's pericarp is too moist and soft and it doesn't hold the steam in. Popcorn experts say that a moisture content of 13.5 to 14 percent is ideal for popcorn.

Popcorn is meant to explode, but potatoes are not. If you forget to prick holes in the tough skin of a baking potato, it too will explode when the steam inside creates enough pressure to break the skin.

SKILL PRACTICE

Answer the questions based on the above information.

1. According to the article, what basic principle underlies the popping of popcorn?

   _____

   _____

2. List three things that prevent a kernel of popcorn from popping.

   _____

   _____

Connection

Science and Technology

Changing water to steam provides energy that drives many industrial processes. For example, in most electrical power plants, a fuel such as coal or oil is used to heat water, which produces steam to drive a turbine. The change from water to steam is used in many homes, too, to heat spaces and to cook.

Write a description of at least two ways that steam is used in your home.

Answers and explanations start on page 267.

How Elements Behave

COMMUNITY LINK: Many people in your neighborhood have had their homes tested for radon, an air pollutant. Someone mentions that radon is one of the noble gases—gases that don't react easily with other elements. You decide to find out more about radon.

The Periodic Table

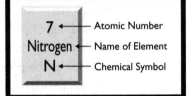

All the elements can be arranged in a **periodic table** in increasing order of atomic number, and according to the number of electrons in their outer shell. When this is done, elements with similar properties are grouped together.

The horizontal rows of the periodic table are arranged in atomic number order with elements having one electron in the outer shell on the left (light metals), through elements having a full eight electrons in the outer shell on the right (noble gases). The vertical columns are called groups or families. Elements in a group show the same or similar properties. A portion of the periodic table is shown here.

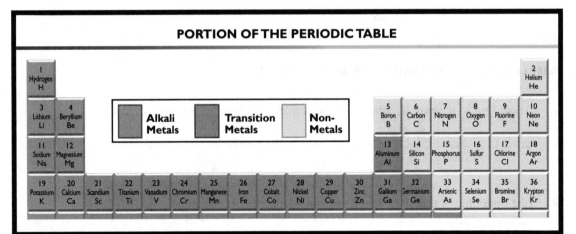

PORTION OF THE PERIODIC TABLE

SKILL PRACTICE

Use the periodic table to answer the following questions.

1. Which element has atomic number 29? _____

2. What type of element is iron? _____

3. Which elements have properties similar to those of nitrogen?

   _____

4. List one element that has one electron in its outer shell. _____

5. List one element that has eight electrons in its outer shell. _____

Answers and explanations start on page 267.

SCIENCE

Chemical Bonds

When two or more elements combine to form a compound, they are held together by chemical bonds. An atom consists of a positively charged nucleus around which orbit negatively charged electrons. Bonding takes place when the electrons of two atoms interact. There are two main types of bonds: covalent bonds and ionic bonds.

In **covalent bonds,** two or more atoms join together by sharing electrons. These joined atoms form a molecule. For example, a water molecule forms when two hydrogen atoms share their single electrons with one oxygen atom, which has six electrons in the outer shell. This is shown on the right:

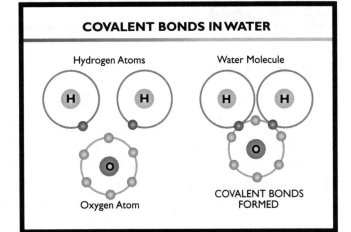

COVALENT BONDS IN WATER

Hydrogen Atoms   Water Molecule

Oxygen Atom

COVALENT BONDS FORMED

In **ionic bonds,** electrons are transferred from one atom to one or more other atoms. For example, when sodium and chlorine come together, each sodium atom loses an electron to a chlorine atom. Because the sodium atom has one fewer electron than proton, it becomes a positively charged **ion.** Because the chlorine atom has one more electron than proton, it

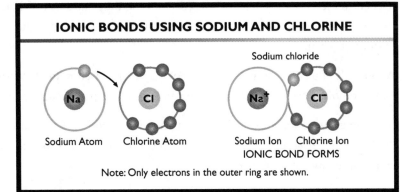

IONIC BONDS USING SODIUM AND CHLORINE

Sodium chloride

Sodium Atom   Chlorine Atom

Sodium Ion   Chlorine Ion
IONIC BOND FORMS

Note: Only electrons in the outer ring are shown.

becomes a negatively charged ion. Positive and negative bodies attract, so the sodium and chlorine ions bond together to make sodium chloride (salt).

SKILL PRACTICE

Answer the questions based on the above information.

1. Ions are atoms with which of the following?

    (1) a single neutron   **(2)** an electric charge   **(3)** a covalent bond

2. In which kind of bond are electrons shared?

    (1) ionic bonds   **(2)** covalent bonds

3. Another compound, lithium fluoride, forms when a lithium atom gives up an electron to a fluorine atom. This is an example of

    (1) ionic bonding.   **(2)** covalent bonding.

Chemical Reactions

When one or more elements and compounds are changed into another set of elements or compounds, a **chemical reaction** has taken place. In a chemical reaction, the substances you start with are called the reactants. The substances into which they change are called the products. The bonds between the reactants are broken and reformed during a chemical reaction. Common chemical reactions include oxidation (burning and rusting) in which a substance combines with oxygen, and digestion, in which foods are broken down by stomach acids into nutrients the body can use.

In order to get a reaction started, activation energy must be applied. This is the amount of energy needed to increase the energy of the reactants so they can react. When you burn a piece of paper, for example, you apply enough heat to get the burning started. Once it has started, the paper will burn on its own.

As a result of a chemical reaction, energy may be released in the form of heat or light. The explosion of fireworks is a dramatic example of this type of reaction, called an exothermic reaction.

Sometimes energy is absorbed during a chemical reaction. For example, when you bake a cake, the liquid batter absorbs heat energy and a solid cake is the product. This type of reaction is called an endothermic reaction.

SKILL PRACTICE

Match each term with its definition.

Term	Definition
_____ 1. chemical reaction	**a.** a reaction in which energy is absorbed
_____ 2. exothermic reaction	**b.** the energy needed to start a chemical reaction
_____ 3. endothermic reaction	**c.** a chemical reaction with oxygen
_____ 4. activation energy	**d.** the substances that result from a chemical reaction
_____ 5. reactants	**e.** a reaction in which energy is released
_____ 6. products	**f.** the substances that combine during a chemical reaction
_____ 7. oxidation	**g.** the changing of one or more substances into different substances

Answers and explanations start on page 267.

■ Apply What You Learn

Read the following article about measuring the heat produced by a chemical reaction. Then answer the questions that follow.

Counting Calories

As every dieter knows, chocolate cake and peanuts have lots of calories, and celery and carrots do not. The energy a food supplies your body can be measured in calories. A calorie is the amount of heat energy needed to raise the temperature of 1 gram of water by 1 degree Centigrade.

Food scientists find out how many Calories a food contains by burning it in a furnace. The heat from the burning food warms a container of water. By measuring the increase in the water's temperature, a scientist can calculate how many Calories the food contains.

You can do a simplified version of this by using the equipment shown in the diagram. First you weigh the water and the food. Then you record the temperature of the water. You set fire to the food, and as it burns, it heats the water in the flask. When the food is completely burned, you again record the temperature of the water. The number of Calories in the food can be calculated using this formula:

Food scientists generally measure energy in Calories (also called kilocalories). One Calorie is equal to 1,000 calories.

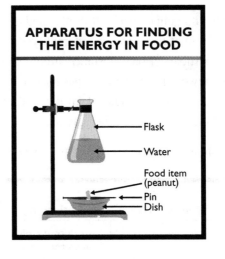

APPARATUS FOR FINDING THE ENERGY IN FOOD

Flask
Water
Food item (peanut)
Pin
Dish

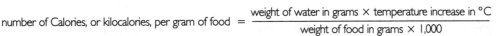

$$\text{number of Calories, or kilocalories, per gram of food} = \frac{\text{weight of water in grams} \times \text{temperature increase in °C}}{\text{weight of food in grams} \times 1{,}000}$$

SKILL PRACTICE

Answer the questions based on the above information.

1. What is a calorie? _____

2. What chemical reaction is taking place during the Calorie test?

    _____

Connection

Science as Inquiry

In the experiment described above, the more heat that is absorbed by the water, the more accurate the results will be. Yet with this equipment, some heat from the burning food will be lost to the surrounding air. What changes could you make in the equipment to increase the accuracy of the results?

▶▶ **For information about the scientific method, see page 274.**

Answers and explanations start on page 267.

How Chemicals Behave

FAMILY LINK: Lila is showing her young son how to mix his favorite powdered soft drink. She measures the correct amount of the powder into a glass and adds water. Her son is impatient, so Lila stirs the drink vigorously so the sugar and flavoring will dissolve faster.

Mixtures

What do gunpowder, soft drinks, and air all have in common? They are **mixtures,** substances made up of two or more different types of particles that are not chemically bonded. In a mixture, the particles of one substance are more or less evenly distributed among the others. For example, gunpowder is a mixture of particles of charcoal, sulfur, and potassium nitrate. Soft drinks are a mixture of water, sugar, flavoring, and carbon dioxide. Air is a mixture of nitrogen, oxygen, carbon dioxide, and other gases.

There are many types of mixtures, some of which are shown in the table below.

Type of Mixture	Description	Example
Solution	A solute dissolves in a liquid, called the solvent	Salt water (salt dissolved in water); carbonated drink (carbon dioxide gas dissolved in water)
Colloid	Tiny particles are scattered evenly through a liquid or gas	Smoke (solid particles in air); butter
Suspension	Small particles (larger than those in a colloid) are scattered evenly through a liquid or gas	Muddy water

The contents of mixtures can be separated by mechanical means. Paper coffee filters, for example, separate coffee grounds from water. Evaporation separates sea salt from seawater. Magnets can separate iron filings from sand.

SKILL PRACTICE

Match each type of mixture with an example of it.

Type of Mixture	Example
_____ **1.** solution	**a.** homogenized milk, which has tiny fat droplets dispersed in water
_____ **2.** colloid	**b.** hot tea with sugar
_____ **3.** suspension	**c.** fog, which has small particles of matter suspended in air

Answers and explanations start on page 267.

Acids and Bases

One of the key characteristics of an **acid** is its sour taste. We eat some mild acids like lemon juice and vinegar, but other acids are poisons, and still others can cause skin burns. When an acid is dissolved in water, it forms a solution that conducts electricity. When an acid is placed on litmus paper, the paper turns pink-red.

Acids have many uses. Sulfuric acid is used in the manufacture of fertilizers, steel, and petroleum products. In watered-down form, sulfuric acid is used in car batteries. Other acids include nitric acid, used to make drugs and explosives, and hydrochloric acid, used in metalworking and food processing.

Bases are the opposite of acids. Many are highly reactive and corrosive. Caustic soda, ammonia, and lime are examples of these. Other bases are mild. For example, milk of magnesia is a mild base that we take to soothe an acid upset stomach. Like acids, when a base is dissolved in water, it conducts electricity. When a base is placed on litmus paper, the paper turns blue.

A measure known as pH indicates how acidic or basic a solution is. The pH scale goes from 1, a strong acid, to 7, neutral (water), to 14, a strong base.

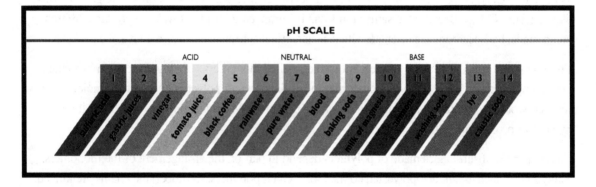

When an acid and base are mixed together, a chemical reaction occurs and they neutralize each other. Both lose their properties and form water and a salt.

SKILL PRACTICE

Write *True* if the statement is true, *False* if it is false.

_____ **1.** Most acids have a sour taste.

_____ **2.** Sulfuric acid is used in the manufacture of fertilizers and in diluted form in car batteries.

_____ **3.** When an acid is dissolved in water, it conducts electricity, but when a base is dissolved in water, it becomes a salt.

_____ **4.** When you mix an acid and a base together, you get water and a salt.

_____ **5.** Milk of Magnesia soothes an acid stomach because acids and bases neutralize one another.

_____ **6.** A substance that measures 13 on the pH scale is a strong acid.

Answers and explanations start on page 267.

Hydrocarbons and Polymers

Organic chemistry is a branch of chemistry that involves the study of compounds containing the element carbon. One type of organic compound includes **hydrocarbons,** which consist only of carbon and hydrogen atoms. Hydrocarbons are found in oil, natural gas, coal tar, and petroleum products, such as plastics.

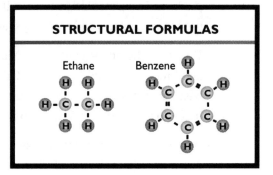

STRUCTURAL FORMULAS

Ethane   Benzene

Some hydrocarbons have carbon atoms arranged in chains, such as methane (CH_4) and ethane (C_2H_6). Other hydrocarbons have their carbon atoms arranged in a ring, like benzene (C_6H_6). Because the same atoms can be arranged in different ways to produce different compounds, hydrocarbons are often identified by structural formulas like those above.

Polymers are formed when two or more molecules, called monomers, join together, often in a chain. For example, ethene (C_2H_4) is a monomer that forms the polymer polyethylene, a chain molecule. Rubber, wool, and cellulose are naturally occurring polymers. Manmade polymers include all plastics, nylon, Styrofoam, and Teflon.

The properties of substances made of polymers depend in part on the arrangement of the monomers. Many fibers, such as silk and polyester, contain long-chain polymers. In rubber, the chains are kinked. When you stretch a piece of rubber, the kinks straighten out, but when you let it go, they snap back, kinking up again. In Plexiglas and melamine, the monomers are linked together in all directions, forming a network that makes the polymer strong and stiff.

SKILL PRACTICE

Choose the correct answer.

1. What are compounds consisting only of hydrogen and carbon called?

    (1) carbons   **(2)** hydrocarbons   **(3)** monomers

2. Chemists identify hydrocarbons by structural formulas because different hydrocarbons contain the same atoms that

    (1) kink and unkink.   **(2)** are manmade.   **(3)** are arranged in different ways.

3. A large molecule that is made up of repeating smaller molecules (or monomers) is called a

    (1) polymer.   **(2)** hydrocarbon.   **(3)** carbon.

SCIENCE

Answers and explanations start on page 267.

■ Apply What You Learn

Read the following article about one use of acids and bases. Then answer the questions that follow.

Soap vs. Grease and Dirt

Did you know that a pleasantly scented bar of soap is made from a fatty acid and a base? People have been making soap for hundreds of years by boiling animal fat, ashes (which contain the base lye), and water.

Today, manufacturers make soap by heating fat or vegetable oil with a strong base, such as caustic soda, dissolved in water. They add salt to make the soap come out of the solution. They may add perfume, dyes, and cold cream. Then they shape it into bars, or make it into other forms of soap like liquid soap or shaving cream. The quality and properties of a soap depend mainly on the type of fat or oil used in its manufacture.

Soap removes grease and dirt because it contains molecules that act as a link between water and dirt particles, loosening them from the surface to be cleaned. One end of the soap molecule is attracted to water, and the other end is attracted to nonsoluble substances like grease. When soap dissolves, its molecules surround a patch of dirt or grease and attach themselves to it. The surface of the grease or dirt patch is now covered by water-soluble soap molecules, so the dirt lifts off and can be rinsed away.

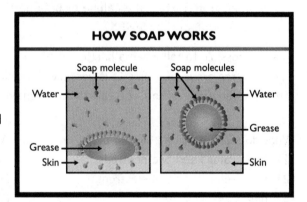

SKILL PRACTICE

Answer the questions based on the above information.

1. What are soaps made from? _____

   _____

2. How do soaps work to remove dirt or grease? _____

   _____

C o n n e c t i o n

Science in Personal and Social Perspectives

Plastics are everywhere in modern life—used in health care, manufacturing, recreation, household and personal items, and so on. In fact, we take them for granted. Take a moment to think about how the invention of at least one plastic item has improved or affected modern life. Then write a paragraph describing the impact this plastic product has had on our world.

DIRECTIONS: Read the passage. Then answer the questions that follow.

Some atoms are unstable and their nuclei decay, giving off subatomic particles and rays. This process is called radioactivity. There are three types of radiation:

- Alpha particles consist of two neutrons and two protons. They don't have much energy and can be stopped by a sheet of paper. When an atom emits alpha particles, its atomic number changes, and so it becomes a different element.

- Beta particles consist of high-speed electrons or positrons, a type of antimatter. Beta particles are produced when a proton turns into a neutron, or a neutron turns into a proton. These particles will penetrate paper but are stopped by aluminum. Beta radiation also changes the atomic number of the element.

- Gamma rays consist of electromagnetic radiation of very high frequency. Gamma rays penetrate farther than alpha or beta particles and can be stopped only by a thick layer of steel or lead.

It's not possible to tell when a particular atom of an element will decay. However, given a large group of atoms, it is possible to predict when half of them will decay. The time required for half of a radioactive element to decay is called its half-life.

1. What do alpha particles consist of?
(1) two protons and two neutrons
(2) two protons and two electrons
(3) high-speed positrons
(4) high-speed electrons
(5) high frequency electromagnetic waves

2. In the early 1900s, many scientists and workers who used radioactive materials died of radiation-related illnesses. These deaths were caused by a failure to
(1) get regular medical checkups.
(2) test the effects of radioactivity on living things before using radioactive materials.
(3) protect scientists and workers from alpha particles.
(4) determine the material's half-life.
(5) detect which materials were radioactive and which were not.

3. Alpha and beta radiation change one element into another because the number of
(1) protons in the nucleus changes.
(2) electrons in the outer shell changes.
(3) positrons in the atom changes.
(4) protons increases.
(5) gamma rays increases.

4. Strontium-85 has a half-life of 65.2 days. If you have 10 grams of Strontium-85, how much will be left after 65.2 days?
(1) 20 grams
(2) 10 grams
(3) 5 grams
(4) 2.5 grams
(5) none

SCIENCE

Read the passage and study the diagram. Then answer the questions that follow.

One of NASA's newest robotic probes is a spacecraft powered by an ion engine. Deep Space 1 produces a small stream of electrically charged atoms, called ions. These leave the engine, creating tiny amounts of thrust. The thrust increases the speed of the spacecraft by about 30 feet per second each day. Eventually, Deep Space 1 will travel at 8,000 miles per hour.

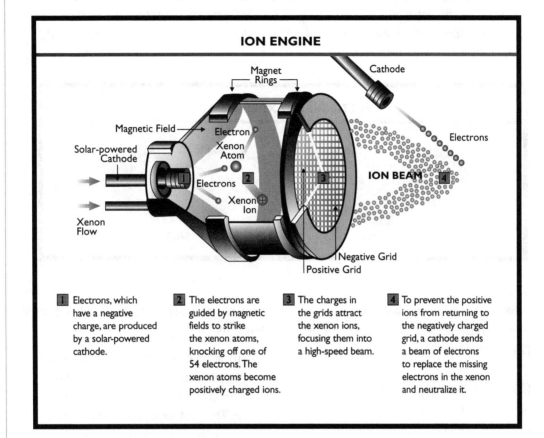

ION ENGINE

1 Electrons, which have a negative charge, are produced by a solar-powered cathode.

2 The electrons are guided by magnetic fields to strike the xenon atoms, knocking off one of 54 electrons. The xenon atoms become positively charged ions.

3 The charges in the grids attract the xenon ions, focusing them into a high-speed beam.

4 To prevent the positive ions from returning to the negatively charged grid, a cathode sends a beam of electrons to replace the missing electrons in the xenon and neutralize it.

5. According to the diagram, what fuel powers the ion engine?
   (1) xenon gas
   (2) electron beams
   (3) ion beams
   (4) liquid oxygen
   (5) rocket fuel

6. Which of the following is the basic principle underlying the ion engine?
   (1) Positive ions are attracted to a negative grid, producing thrust.
   (2) Atoms have negatively charged electrons orbiting their nuclei.
   (3) Xenon is a heavy, inert gas with 54 electrons.
   (4) Burning fuel produces heat, light, and thrust.
   (5) Cathodes produce streams of electrons.

7. Conventional rockets reach high speed by burning almost all their fuel in a few minutes. In contrast, ion engines reach high speed by gradually adding momentum over a long period of time. For what type of mission are ion engines best suited?
   (1) brief orbital missions
   (2) conventional aircraft
   (3) planet surface exploration
   (4) crewed space missions
   (5) long-term space missions

8. When is a positive xenon ion produced?
   (1) when a neutron is removed
   (2) when a proton is removed
   (3) when an electron is removed
   (4) when a magnetic field is generated
   (5) when a positive grid is activated

Read the passage and study the diagram. Then answer the questions that follow.

Antifreeze is a substance added to liquid to lower its freezing point or raise its boiling point.

A science class did an experiment to determine whether salt is an antifreeze. They floated two ice cubes in a bowl of cold water. They placed a matchstick on each ice cube. Then they sprinkled salt on one ice cube but not the other. After a few minutes, the ice on each side of the matchstick on the salted ice cube had melted, leaving a raised ice ridge under the matchstick. On the unsalted ice cube, the matchstick was level with the cube's surface.

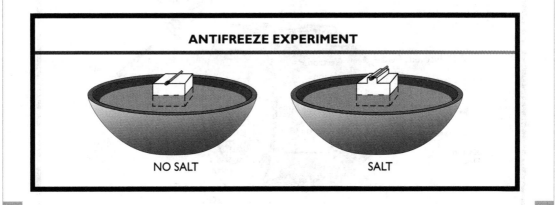

ANTIFREEZE EXPERIMENT

NO SALT   SALT

9. Which of the following conclusions is supported by the data from this experiment?
   (1) Antifreeze lowers the freezing point of a liquid.
   (2) Antifreeze raises the boiling point of a liquid.
   (3) Salt lowers the freezing point of water.
   (4) Salt raises the boiling point of water.
   (5) Friction from a matchstick causes ice to melt.

10. Which of the following experiments would give the best data on the effect of salt on the freezing point of water?
   (1) Record the temperatures at which salt water and plain water freeze.
   (2) Record the amount of time it takes for salt water and plain water to freeze.
   (3) Record the quantity of ice formed after a given amount of time
   (4) Repeat the ice cube/matchstick experiment but use more ice cubes.
   (5) Repeat the ice cube/matchstick experiment but measure the quantity of melted ice.

Read the passage. Then answer the question that follows.

In grain elevators, grain dust is in suspension in the air. The grain dust can catch fire when a spark ignites it. The first explosion shakes loose more dust, which in turn ignites. Pressure builds up inside the building, which then explodes.

11. Which of the following would not help prevent grain elevator explosions?
   (1) venting the elevator to release pressure
   (2) removing foreign matter and broken kernels before grain storage
   (3) spraying oil on conveyors to reduce dust
   (4) making the elevator more airtight
   (5) installing dust collection systems using bag filters.

Answers and explanations start on page 267.

SCIENCE

Fasten your seat belt and get ready to find out a little bit about the science behind a rollercoaster ride, a space shuttle launch, a singer's voice, and an MRI. In this program you'll see how the study of the relationships between matter and energy affect our lives in many ways.

Physics

OBJECTIVES

1. Learn about the laws of motion, work, and heat.
2. Understand the properties and behaviors of waves.
3. Explore magnetism, electricity, and nuclear physics.

A skateboarder oils the skateboard's ball bearings to reduce friction and improve performance. A bass player uses a tiny computer to make sure the instrument is in tune. A student flips open a solar powered calculator to get the electrical current flowing. All of this technology is an application of physics, the study of the relationships between matter and energy.

Since physics is an important part of the GED Science Test, learning the concepts of physics will help you excel on the test. Learning about physics will also enrich your understanding of everyday events.

On the following pages, you will find a brief exercise called *Sneak Preview*. It is designed to introduce you to the topics that will be featured in the video program and the corresponding lesson. After you complete the exercise and check your answers, turn to the vocabulary page. There you will find terms that will help you better understand the video and the lessons that follow. After reviewing page 224, you will be ready to watch Program 26.

For additional practice, visit *LiteracyLink* online at http://www.pbs.org/literacy.

Sneak Preview

This exercise previews some of the concepts from Program 26. After you answer the questions, use the chart on page 223 to help set your learning goals.

WORKPLACE LINK: George works in a factory where the noise can literally be deafening. He and the other workers are required to wear protective gear to reduce the sound that reaches their ears.

If you dislike someone's favorite music, you may be tempted to call it noise. But is it really noise? No, because there is a physical difference between noise and music. The sound **waves** of noise are spiky and irregular. In contrast, the sound waves of music are regular and gently curving.

One type of noise is electrical noise. In all matter, electrons move around randomly, producing sound waves of noise. Most of the time we don't notice this noise. However, we do notice it when it interferes with a regular signal. For example, electrical noise can disturb radio, cell phone, and television transmissions. The disturbance may come from the sun's radiation, a bolt of lightning, or an electric motor starting up. The signal-to-noise ratio is a measure of the effectiveness of electronic stereo and communications devices in filtering out noise. The higher the ratio, the clearer the signal.

Noise pollution is any sound that has too much energy. Generally, this energy is related to loudness. Sound energy is measured in decibels (dB). A quiet room has a decibel level of about 38, and conversation is about 60 dB. Engines are very loud: a vacuum cleaner is about 70 dB, truck traffic about 80 dB, and jet planes from 120 to 150 dB. Any sound with a decibel level above 130 has vibrations strong enough to permanently damage hearing.

Answer these questions based on the reading above.

1. What is the main idea of the last paragraph?

    (1) Noise consists of musical sounds that are too loud.
    (2) Noise pollution is a serious problem today because of modern engines.
    (3) There are different types of noise, including sound noise and electrical noise.
    (4) Sounds over 130 dB can damage human ears.
    (5) Noise pollution consists of sounds that have too much energy, or loudness.

2. Which of the following can be inferred from information in the article?

    (1) Classical music is much more pleasant than rock music.
    (2) Electrical noise is produced by randomly moving electrons.
    (3) Noise is louder than music of all types.
    (4) Noise pollution has increased since engines were invented.
    (5) Noise pollution is the number one environmental problem in cities.

3. When Marla plays the radio in her kitchen, the reception fades out for a few seconds when the ignition on the oil burner in the basement turns on. What causes the poor reception?

    (1) sound noise
    (2) electrical noise
    (3) a transmission signal
    (4) noise pollution
    (5) problems at the radio station

4. Why is it generally more pleasant to listen to loud music than to equally loud noise?

    (1) Loud music has gently curving, regular sound waves.
    (2) Loud music has irregular, spiky sound waves.
    (3) Loud music has a low decibel level.
    (4) Loud noise has a low decibel level.
    (5) Loud noise can damage your hearing, but loud music cannot.

Feedback

- If you got all of the answers right...   you're doing great! Concentrate on adding to your knowledge of science.

- If you missed question 1...   you need to improve your ability to understand the main point of a paragraph.

- If you missed question 2...   you need to learn how to "read between the lines" of a passage and infer things not directly stated.

- If you missed question 3...   you need to learn to apply general information to a specific situation.

- If you missed question 4...   you need to learn to analyze the relationships among ideas.

Vocabulary for *Physics*

acceleration	any change in an object's speed or direction of motion
amplitude	in a wave, the distance between its crest (high point) and its midpoint
circuit	a complete path along which electric current flows
diffraction	the spreading of a wave after the wave passes through a gap in a barrier
electricity	a flow of charged particles, usually electrons
electromagnetic radiation	a wave motion of electric and magnetic fields; for example, visible light, radio waves, and X rays
energy	the ability to do work; see *work*
force	the pushes and pulls that act on matter; for example, gravity
frequency	the number of waves that pass a given point in a given time
heat	a form of energy that is transferred from one object to another when there is a difference in temperature
inertia	the tendency of an object at rest to remain at rest and the tendency of an object in motion to remain in motion unless acted upon by a force
kinetic energy	the energy of an object in motion
machine	a device that changes the amount of force used to do a given amount of work, usually by increasing the distance involved
magnetism	force that results from the movement of electric charges
mass	the amount of matter an object contains
nuclear fission	the production of large amounts of energy by splitting the nuclei of heavy atoms
potential energy	the energy of an object at rest
reflection	the bouncing of a wave off a surface
refraction	the bending of a wave when it passes from one substance to another
wave	a disturbance or displacement that repeats itself
wavelength	the distance between two consecutive waves
work	in physics, work is done when an object on which a force is acting moves in the direction of that force

➡ NOW WATCH PROGRAM 26:

As you watch, think about the special physics definitions of such familiar terms as work, energy, and waves. Also pay attention to the many useful applications of physics. Don't try to memorize all the facts, formulas, and scientific laws that are introduced; the workbook and online activities will help you review these.

PBS LiteracyLink®

After you watch the program, work on:

- pages 225–240 in this workbook
- Internet activities at http://www.pbs.org/literacy

AFTER YOU WATCH

26

Physics

On the following pages, you will learn more about the ideas discussed in the video program and have an opportunity to develop and practice your GED science skills.

Key Points to Think About

In the video program, you explored:

- The laws of motion, work, and heat
- The properties and behavior of waves
- Electricity, magnetism, and nuclear fission and fusion

On the GED Science Test:

- You will be expected to know some basic facts about the interaction of matter and energy.
- You should know how to recognize cause-and-effect relationships.
- You will be given passages to read and diagrams, charts, and graphs to interpret.

As you work through the lesson for Program 26:

- Concentrate on mastering basic concepts, not memorizing details.
- Remember that in science, general laws can be applied to specific situations.
- Relate what you are learning to your own life, not just to the GED Science Test.

Physical Laws

COMMUNITY LINK: Your state may lose some federal highway money because not enough drivers and passengers are buckling up. You lead a campaign to enforce your state's seat belt laws, but first you find out why seat belts work to reduce injury and death.

The Laws of Motion

The laws of motion explain how objects move in response to the **forces**—the pushes and pulls—around them. Sir Isaac Newton first stated three laws of motion more than three hundred years ago.

Newton's First Law: An object at rest remains at rest unless acted upon by a force. An object in motion remains in motion at constant speed in a straight line unless acted upon by a force. These tendencies are called **inertia,** and they underlie the use of seat belts and air bags. When a car stops suddenly because a force has been applied (the brakes or a collision), its motion is suddenly slowed or stopped. But nothing has acted on the car's occupants. They keep moving forward until acted upon by a force—either a seat belt, air bag, or windshield.

Newton's Second Law: You can measure a force by multiplying the mass of an object by its acceleration—the rate at which it changes speed. A tractor trailer truck accelerating has far more force than a VW Beetle accelerating.

Newton's Third Law: For every force exerted by a first object, there is an equal and opposite force exerted by a second object. In other words, for every action there is an equal and opposite reaction. When a batter makes contact with a ball, the ball exerts a force on the bat, while the bat exerts a force on the ball.

SKILL PRACTICE

Answer the questions based on the above information.

1. When a large sport utility vehicle collides with a small car, the car usually sustains more damage. Which law of motion helps explain this fact? _____

2. The weight of a ship pushes down on the water, and the water pushes up on the ship. Which law of motion helps explain this fact? _____

3. A bullet may travel fast and far, but if it hits nothing, friction slows it and gravity brings it down. Which law of motion helps explain this fact? _____

Answers and explanations start on page 268.

SCIENCE

Work

In physics, **work** is done when an object on which a force is acting moves in the direction of that force. For example, if you are lifting a carton and the carton moves up, you do work on the carton. On the other hand, if you are simply holding the carton in your arms, no work is being done despite the effort it takes to hold it. That's because the carton is not moving.

You can think of work as a means of transferring energy from one system to another. When you push the carton along the floor, the carton gains energy. At the same time, you lose energy in the effort to push it.

Energy also has a special meaning in physics. It is the ability to do work. Energy is conserved, which means that the total amount of energy never changes, but it is converted from one form to another. If an object is moving, like a sliding carton, it has kinetic energy. If it is stationary, like a carton in your arms, its energy is called potential energy. When you let go of the carton, the carton falls and its potential energy becomes kinetic energy.

Machines are objects designed to change the amount of force required to do a given amount of work. Usually a machine reduces the force required to produce work by increasing the distance involved. For example, an inclined plane (ramp) reduces the effort needed to lift an object like a carton to a given height. It does this by increasing the distance the object must travel up the slope. Whether you use the ramp or lift the carton, the amount of work you do to move the carton remains the same.

A. WORK

B. NO WORK

C. WORK USING A MACHINE

SKILL PRACTICE

Write *True* if the statement is true, *False* if it is false.

_____ 1. In physics, work is done only when an object moves.

_____ 2. An object in motion has potential energy; when it stops it has kinetic energy.

_____ 3. If you push a car and it moves forward, you do work on the car, but if you push it and it does not move, you do no work.

_____ 4. A machine is designed to reduce the amount of effort required to do work by increasing the distance the moving object travels.

Answers and explanations start on page 268.

Heat

What happens to frozen food when you take it out of the freezer and put it on a counter? In a few hours, it probably thaws. Heat energy from the air is transferred to the frozen food until the food reaches room temperature. When the food is the same temperature as the surrounding air, heat transfer stops. The system is in equilibrium.

Heat is a form of energy that is transferred from one object to another when there is a difference in temperature. Heat always travels from hotter objects to cooler ones unless energy is added to change the direction of flow.

Heat is stored in matter in the form of motions and vibrations of molecules. When matter gains heat energy, its molecules vibrate and move more, and it expands. When it loses heat energy, matter usually contracts. When enough heat is gained or lost, the matter changes state—from gas to liquid, for example.

There are three main ways that heat can travel: by electromagnetic radiation as in sunlight, by conduction through a material of any type, and by convection in a liquid or gas.

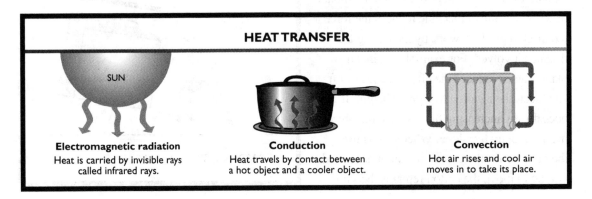

HEAT TRANSFER

Electromagnetic radiation
Heat is carried by invisible rays called infrared rays.

Conduction
Heat travels by contact between a hot object and a cooler object.

Convection
Hot air rises and cool air moves in to take its place.

SKILL PRACTICE

Answer the questions based on the above information and diagrams.

1. What kitchen item cooks food mainly by conduction?

    (1) frying pan   **(2)** microwave oven

2. Pulling down window shades on summer afternoons helps keep a house cooler by slowing heat transfer through

    (1) convection.   **(2)** electromagnetic radiation.

Answers and explanations start on page 268.

■ Apply What You Learn

Read the following article about parachutes. Then answer the questions that follow.

Why Do Parachutes Sometimes Collapse?

When a parachute comes out of its container, its shape changes from a log to a streamer to a half-cup in a matter of seconds. The flow of air into and around the chute changes during the various phases of flight. When the parachute first opens, it captures air, creating greater pressure inside the parachute than above it. This difference in pressure creates drag and slows the parachute.

By the time the parachute is fully open, a great deal of energy has been transferred to the air. This creates a wake—downward moving turbulent air—above the chute. As the parachute slows, air from the wake can push on the chute and make it collapse. This also happens with some large parachutes made of light, new synthetic fabrics. The large area gives the chute great braking power, but sometimes the air rushes around the edge of the chute over the top, collapsing it.

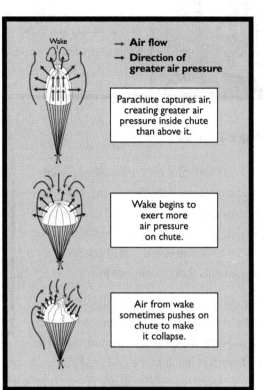

Wake

→ **Air flow**
→ **Direction of greater air pressure**

Parachute captures air, creating greater air pressure inside chute than above it.

Wake begins to exert more air pressure on chute.

Air from wake sometimes pushes on chute to make it collapse.

SKILL PRACTICE

Answer the questions based on the above information.

1. Why do parachutes slow a person or object's descent?

   _____

   _____

2. Why do parachutes sometimes collapse?

   _____

   _____

Connection

History and Nature of Science

Isaac Newton was one of history's greatest scientists, making contributions to many fields. Use an online encyclopedia or other reference source to make a list of three things Newton studied.

Answers and explanations start on page 268.

Waves

SCIENCE

What Is a Wave?

When we think of waves, most of us picture the rolling waves of the ocean surf. However, there are other waves all around us—sound waves, light waves, and radio waves, to name just a few. All **waves** are disturbances or displacements that repeat themselves.

Waves have several characteristics. The **amplitude** of a wave is the distance between its high point, the crest, and its midpoint. The

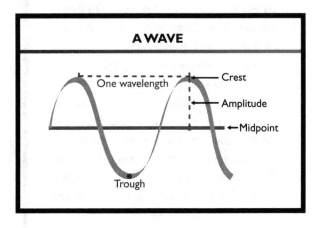

A WAVE

One wavelength — Crest
— Amplitude
← Midpoint
Trough

wavelength is the distance covered by one complete cycle—crest to crest or trough to trough. The number of waves that pass a given point in a given time is the **frequency.**

Amplitude, wavelength, and frequency affect the way we perceive waves. For example, the pitch of a sound—whether it is high or low—depends on frequency and wavelength. High pitched sounds have short wavelengths and high frequency; low pitched sounds have long wavelengths and low frequency. Loud sounds have a large amplitude, and quiet sounds have a smaller amplitude.

Music sounds good to us because the pitches of notes have a mathematical relationship with one another. For example, on a piano middle C is the pitch with a sound wave having a frequency of 261.6 hertz (Hz). The C above middle C has a frequency exactly twice that of middle C. Doubling the frequency of a note raises its pitch by one octave.

SKILL PRACTICE

Match each term with its definition.

Term	Definition
_____ **1.** wave	**a.** distance between crest and midpoint
_____ **2.** amplitude	**b.** a disturbance or displacement that repeats itself
_____ **3.** wavelength	**c.** distance covered by one complete wave cycle
_____ **4.** frequency	**d.** number of waves passing a point in a given time

Answers and explanations start on page 268.

How Waves Interact with Matter

Waves break on shore because they have met a barrier that slows them down. In this case, the sloping land is the barrier. When any type of wave meets a substance or barrier, its movements change.

When a wave passes from one substance into another of a different density, it is **refracted,** or bent. For example, when a sound wave enters a wall, it is refracted. When it reenters the air it is refracted back to its original direction of travel. Ordinary white light traveling through a prism is refracted into different colors (wavelengths) of the spectrum.

When a wave bounces off a barrier, as a sound wave bounces off a cliff, it is **reflected.** We can see objects that do not produce light because light waves reflect off them. Smooth, shiny objects like mirrors are good reflectors.

A wave that passes through a small gap in a barrier is **diffracted.** It spreads out after it passes through the gap. After sound passes through a narrow slit, its long waves spread out more than its short waves.

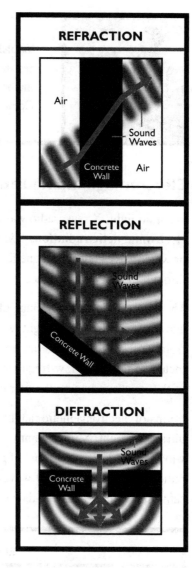

REFRACTION

REFLECTION

DIFFRACTION

SKILL PRACTICE

Write *Refraction, Reflection,* or *Diffraction* to identify the type of wave behavior described below.

_____ **1.** In a pair of eyeglasses, light is bent as it enters the lens and bent again as it passes through air into the eye.

_____ **2.** When you hear a large group of people in a room beyond a narrow open doorway, the sounds are jumbled and confused.

_____ **3.** In a car's rearview mirror, you can see objects behind you.

_____ **4.** After a rain shower, a rainbow appears in the sky.

_____ **5.** You can see the moon even though it gives off no light.

Answers and explanations start on page 268.

Electromagnetic Radiation

What do light, X rays, radio waves, and microwaves have in common? They are all forms of **electromagnetic radiation,** a wave motion of electric and magnetic fields. Unlike sound waves or water waves, electromagnetic radiation does not have to travel through a material. It can travel through the vacuum of space.

The spectrum is the total range of electromagnetic radiation with waves of different wavelengths and frequencies. Visible light was the first part of the spectrum to be discovered. Its colors range from violet at the high frequency end (wavelength about 400 nanometers, or billionths of a meter) to red at the low frequency end (wavelength about 650 nm). You can see the visible part of the spectrum in a rainbow or through a prism.

Forms of electromagnetic radiation with wavelengths shorter than that of violet light are ultraviolet light, X rays, gamma rays, and cosmic rays. Forms of electromagnetic radiation with wavelengths longer than that of red light are infrared light, microwaves, radar, and television and radio waves. Regardless of wavelength and frequency, all electromagnetic radiation travels at the same speed in a vacuum—the speed of light.

ELECTROMAGNETIC SPECTRUM

Cosmic Rays	Gamma Rays	X-rays	Ultra-Violet	Visible Light	Infrared	Microwaves	Radar	Television	Radio

.01 nm   1 nm   100 nm   1 mm   1 cm   1 m   1 km

SKILL PRACTICE

Write *True* if the statement is true, *False* if it is false.

_____ 1. You can see all types of electromagnetic radiation.

_____ 2. Microwaves have a longer wavelength than radio waves.

_____ 3. Cosmic rays can travel through the vacuum of space, but radar, television, and radio waves cannot.

_____ 4. All electromagnetic radiation travels at the speed of light in a vacuum.

Answers and explanations start on page 269.

■ Apply What You Learn

Read the following article about laser light. Then answer the questions that follow.

Laser Light

Burning matches, fluorescent light bulbs, and the sun all emit light that's a mix of colors: different wavelengths, amplitudes, frequencies, and directions. What's unique about laser light is that it consists of rays of a single wavelength, amplitude, frequency, and direction. In addition, all the waves are in step with one another. This coherence is what gives laser light its power.

Lasers have many uses in medicine. In surgery, lasers can cut and they can cauterize, or seal, incisions. They are especially useful in eye surgery. An eye surgeon can correct some vision problems caused by irregularities in the shape of the eyeball. He or she can reattach portions of the retina that have become detached. Lasers are also used in cosmetic surgery. They can remove age spots, warts, wrinkles, and tattoos. In dentistry, lasers have begun to replace drills to vaporize cavities instead of grinding them out.

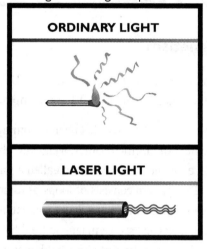

There are many other uses for lasers. For example, in construction, lasers are used to check alignment because their beams are perfectly straight. In stores, lasers are used to read product bar codes. Lasers now manufacture and read music, video, and computer CDs. And lasers are used to create dramatic light shows.

SKILL PRACTICE

Answer the questions based on the above information.

1. What makes laser light different from normal white light? _____

   _____

2. Name three uses for laser light. _____

   _____

 Connection

Science as Inquiry

See for yourself the advantages of laser light over ordinary light. Shine a flashlight in a dark room. Note how the beam of light spreads over a circular area and loses its power after a short distance. Then imagine laser light that has beams so coherent that scientists can shoot a single beam to the moon, and a mirror on the moon reflects it back to Earth!

 **For information about the scientific method, see page 274.**

Answers and explanations start on page 269.

Magnetism, Electricity, and Nuclear Physics

FAMILY LINK: Sarah's little boy was playing with a set of magnets near the family VCR. Later, Sarah couldn't get the VCR to work—all she got was snow on the screen. The repair person told her the magnets had interfered with the magnetic tape heads.

Magnetism

Magnets are everywhere in daily life. Besides the horseshoe-shaped magnets that kids play with, there are magnets in TVs, VCRs, computers, and telephones, to name just a few.

Magnetism is the force that results from the movement of electric charges. Magnetic objects produce magnetism in a pattern called a magnetic field. This pattern consists of loops of force that pass through the magnetic object and extend away from it. You can "see" a magnetic field by placing iron filings on a sheet of paper held over a strong magnet. The filings will arrange themselves along the lines of force. These lines are concentrated at the ends of the magnet, called the poles.

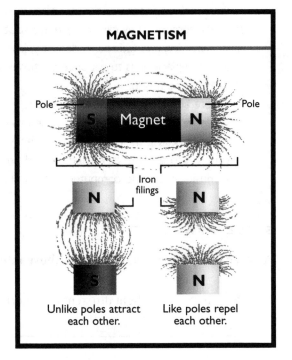

Every magnet has two poles, north and south. Like poles repel each other, and unlike poles attract each other.

There are two types of magnets—permanent magnets and electromagnets. A bar magnet is a permanent magnet. If you stroke a piece of iron or steel with a bar magnet, the metal will become magnetic, too. An electromagnet is made by winding a coil of wire around a bar of iron and passing an electric current through the wire, producing a magnetic field. When the current is turned off, the magnetic field stops.

SKILL PRACTICE

Write *True* if the statement is true, *False* if it is false.

_____ **1.** The north poles of two magnets attract one another.

_____ **2.** Most magnets have two south poles.

_____ **3.** Electromagnets can be turned on and off.

_____ **4.** The force of magnetism works only when two magnetic objects are touching.

Answers and explanations start on page 269.

Electricity

A bolt of lightning, the static crackle of a wool sweater, and the power that turns the lights on are all forms of electricity. **Electricity** is the flow of charged particles, usually electrons. Positively charged particles, like protons, repel one another, and negatively charged particles, like electrons, also repel one another. But positive and negative charges attract. Electrons, being lighter than protons, tend to jump from areas of negative charge to areas of positive charge.

In a battery, chemical energy is used to produce areas of positive and negative electric charge. One terminal has a positive charge, and the other has a negative charge. There is a potential difference between the terminals. When a material that conducts electricity, such as a copper wire, is connected to the two terminals, electric charge will flow along the conductor between the terminals. Because this current flows in one direction, it is called direct current.

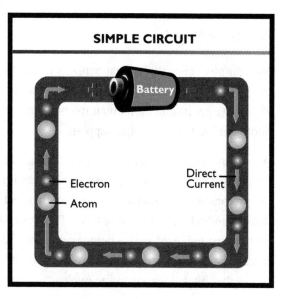

Electricity and magnetism are closely related to one another. A changing magnetic field causes current to flow. Likewise, the movement of charged particles (electric current) creates a magnetic field. This interrelationship between electricity and magnetism is put to work in an alternator.

In an alternator, a coil of wire is mounted between two poles of a magnet so it can be spun around. The magnetic field points first one way and then the other. The changing magnetic field produces a current that flows through the coil. The current travels first one way, then the other. This is called alternating current. It is the type of current used in households.

A circuit is a complete path of electrical conductors through which an electric current can flow. If the path is broken by an open switch, a disconnected wire, or the broken filament in a burned-out light bulb, then the current stops flowing.

SKILL PRACTICE

Match each term with its definition.

Term	Definition
_____ 1. electricity	**a.** a current that goes in one direction
_____ 2. circuit	**b.** a device that uses chemical energy to produce electrical energy
_____ 3. battery	**c.** a current that changes direction
_____ 4. alternating current	**d.** a complete path along which current flows
_____ 5. direct current	**e.** the flow of electrons from one atom to another

Answers and explanations start on page 269.

Nuclear Physics

Nuclear physicists study what happens inside the nucleus of an atom. Since an atom's nucleus is roughly 40 thousand million millionths of an inch in diameter, it is much too small to see. Physicists get information about the nucleus and its particles by smashing it and studying the photographic traces of what happens.

A nucleus is made of particles called protons and neutrons, which are similar to one another except that protons have a positive charge and neutrons have no charge. The positive charges of the protons would tend to repel one another, but instead the nucleus is held together in a very dense bundle by a very strong force. Protons and neutrons are themselves made of even smaller particles called quarks, also held together by the strong force. The strong force is much greater than the electrical forces that bind electrons to the nucleus.

When a heavy nucleus is bombarded with free neutrons, the nucleus splits. The breaking of the strong force releases energy. This form of nuclear energy is called **nuclear fission.** Controlled fission reactions are used in nuclear power plants to produce energy.

Another form of nuclear energy is called fusion. In fusion, two light nuclei combine to form a heavier nucleus, releasing energy. The sun and other stars produce energy through fusion. So far no one has been able to develop a practical system that creates a stable fusion reaction that produces more energy than it consumes.

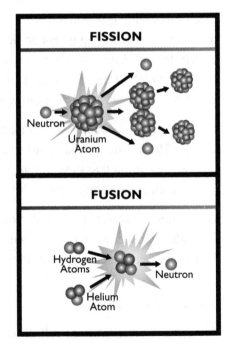

SKILL PRACTICE

Fill in the blank with a word that makes the sentence correct.

1. Nuclear physicists study the _____ of an atom by smashing it.

2. In nuclear _____, two light nuclei combine, producing energy.

3. In nuclear _____, a heavy nucleus splits, producing energy.

Answers and explanations start on page 269.

■ Apply What You Learn

Read the following article about nuclear wastes. Then answer the questions that follow.

Nuclear Wastes

What should be done with the used fuel from nuclear power plants? This waste material stays radioactive for hundreds, sometimes thousands, of years. That means it is emitting particles and waves that can be harmful to human health. The safe disposal of radioactive waste is a major problem.

When used fuel rods are first removed from a reactor, they are placed in cooling ponds until their temperature drops and they can be more safely handled. In some countries, used fuel is transported to a reprocessing plant to extract still-usable uranium and plutonium. In other countries, reprocessing is illegal because the possibility of a toxic spill is thought to be too dangerous. Still, whether the fuel has been reprocessed or not, the waste is still radioactive.

Waste with low levels of radioactivity, such as clothing used at a nuclear power plant, can simply be buried. But waste with high levels of radioactivity must be sealed to prevent radiation from leaking into the environment. Usually the waste is placed in sealed containers deep underground. It is buried in hard rock, such as granite, that will not move. If the rocks moved or cracked, the containers might break, releasing radioactive matter into the ground.

SKILL PRACTICE

Answer the questions based on the above information.

1. Why are nuclear wastes dangerous?

   _____

2. How is low-level radioactive waste disposed of?

   _____

3. How is high-level radioactive waste disposed of?

   _____

━━━━━━━━━━━━━━ Connection

Science in Personal and Social Perspectives

Imagine that a utility company wants to build a nuclear power plant in your community. The community is torn—the new plant would mean new jobs, but it would also cause environmental concerns. Citizens are invited to a question-and-answer session with a company spokesperson. List three questions you would ask the spokesperson.

Answers and explanations start on page 269.

DIRECTIONS: Read the passage and study the diagram. Then answer the questions that follow.

An airplane flies because the air pressure below its wings is greater than the air pressure above its wings, causing lift. The shape of the wing causes the difference in air pressure. The top part is curved, so air flowing over it must speed up to travel the greater distance. The fast flowing air causes a drop in air pressure. The bottom is flat, so the air speed is slower. The slower flowing air is under greater pressure. The difference in pressure between the air above and under the wing causes lift. As a plane increases its speed to take off, the air flow over the wings increases lift enough to counteract the force of gravity (measured by the plane's weight) holding the plane on the ground.

Besides lift and weight, airplanes are acted upon by the forces of thrust and drag. Thrust is the force that propels the plane forward in the air. It is provided by the airplane's engines, either by means of a propeller or a jet.

Counteracting thrust is a type of friction called drag. Drag is created because an airplane is moving through a substance, air, and it must push the air aside in order to pass.

A pilot's job is to use these four forces to fly a plane. For example, by controlling wing and tail surfaces and the propulsion system, the pilot can increase thrust or reduce drag to accelerate. He or she can slow the plane by lowering the wing flaps and landing gear to increase drag or by reducing the power in the engines.

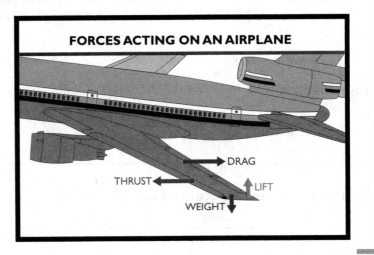

FORCES ACTING ON AN AIRPLANE

1. Which of the following is not one of the major forces acting on an airplane at takeoff?
   (1) thrust
   (2) drag
   (3) gravity
   (4) magnetism
   (5) lift

2. Which of the following actions would increase the speed of an airplane?
   (1) decreasing the flow of fuel to the engine
   (2) pulling up the landing gear
   (3) using one engine rather than all engines
   (4) letting down the wing flaps
   (5) letting down the landing gear

3. Which of the following is necessary for an airplane to take off?
   (1) Lift must be greater than weight.
   (2) Lift must be greater than thrust.
   (3) Lift must be greater than drag.
   (4) Drag must be greater than thrust.
   (5) Thrust must be greater than lift.

4. For what reason do commercial airliners fly at high altitudes where the air is thin?
   (1) to increase lift
   (2) to reduce thrust
   (3) to increase weight
   (4) to reduce drag
   (5) to increase friction

Read the passage. Then answer the questions that follow.

To get images of soft tissue, physicians can use a diagnostic tool called magnetic resonance imaging (MRI). Here is how it works.

The charged particles in atoms—the electrons and protons—are always spinning, producing a magnetic field. Usually, the spins are in random directions. Inside an MRI machine, however, a powerful magnetic field causes the proton spins of hydrogen atoms, which are everywhere in the body, to line up with it. The machine then emits radio waves of about 40 million hertz. This frequency switches the magnetic poles of the hydrogen protons. When the waves are turned off, the magnetic poles of the protons flip back, emitting radio signals. The MRI machine records the radio signals and converts them into an image of the tissue. Because the amount of hydrogen in different types of tissue is different, the image can distinguish one type of tissue from another, providing an excellent diagnostic tool.

5. MRI technology uses
   (1) heat and motion.
   (2) X rays and film.
   (3) magnetic fields and radio waves.
   (4) gamma rays and beta particles.
   (5) ultrasound.

6. Before undergoing an MRI, patients must remove all metal jewelry and braces and must inform technicians of metal implants such as pins used in repairing fractures. Why?
   (1) Metal is uncomfortable to the patient.
   (2) Metal can be overheated during the MRI.
   (3) Metal would interfere with the magnetic fields.
   (4) Metal would interfere with the hydrogen atoms.
   (5) Metal can scratch the inside of the machine.

7. MRI machines are extremely expensive to buy and operate. When they first came out, hospitals and medical offices rushed to buy them. However, in many areas today, hospitals and medical offices share the use of a centrally located machine. Why?
   (1) to provide better patient care
   (2) to make diagnoses more accurate
   (3) to make access to MRIs more convenient for patients
   (4) to make access to MRIs more convenient for physicians
   (5) to reduce the cost of using MRI technology

Read the passage. Then answer the question that follows.

In quantum mechanics, one important idea is called the uncertainty principle. This principle states that it is impossible to know both where a subatomic particle is and how fast it is moving. When we try to measure a particle's position and speed, we disturb it in some way.

8. Which of the following statements is implied by the uncertainty principle?
   (1) Data obtained from particle experiments may be unreliable.
   (2) Physicists will never discover any subatomic particles.
   (3) Quantum mechanics has no uses.
   (4) Electrons orbit the nucleus of an atom.
   (5) All measurements are accurate.

Read the passage and study the table. Then answer the questions that follow.

The static coefficient is the amount of friction force to be overcome in order to get an object moving. To calculate the force needed to move an object, use this formula:

weight of object × static coefficient = force needed to move the object

For example, for rubber on wet concrete, the static coefficient is 0.7. That means you have to apply a force of 70 pounds to get a 100-pound rubber block moving.

Approximate Static Coefficients

0.1	ice on ice
1.0	rubber on dry concrete
0.7	rubber on wet concrete
0.01	lubricated ball bearings
0.04	Teflon on steel

9. How many pounds of force are needed to get a 100-pound block of ice moving on ice?
   (1) 1
   (2) 10
   (3) 40
   (4) 70
   (5) 100

10. In which of the following situations is there the <u>least</u> friction?
    (1) getting ice moving on ice
    (2) getting rubber moving on dry concrete
    (3) getting rubber moving on wet concrete
    (4) getting lubricated ball bearings moving
    (5) getting Teflon moving on steel

Read the passage and study the diagram. Then answer the question that follows.

An electric circuit is a complete path through which an electric current can flow. If current flows through several resistances, such as light bulbs, one after another, the circuit is wired in series, and the lights will be dim. If each light bulb has its own connection to the power source, the circuit is wired in parallel and all the lights will be bright.

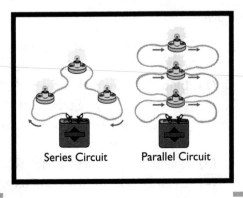

Series Circuit   Parallel Circuit

11. Which of the following statements is supported by the evidence in the passage and diagrams?
    (1) If you unscrew one of the bulbs in the parallel circuit, the others will stay lit.
    (2) If you unscrew one of the bulbs in the series circuit, the others will stay lit.
    (3) Bulbs in a parallel circuit are dimmer than the same bulbs in a series circuit.
    (4) A battery is the only type of power source used in parallel circuits.
    (5) A battery is the only type of power source used in series circuits.

Answers and explanations start on page 269.

Science Practice Test

DIRECTIONS: Choose the one best answer to each question.

<u>Questions 1 and 2</u> refer to the following information.

Despite prevention efforts, HIV infections continue to increase worldwide. HIV, the virus that causes AIDS, spreads in bodily fluids exchanged mainly through sexual contact and intravenous drug use.

Selected Regions	Total with HIV/AIDS 1998	Percent of Adults Infected
Sub-Saharan Africa	22.5 million	8.00%
South and Southeast Asia	6.7 million	0.69%
Central and South America	1.4 million	0.57%
North America	890,000	0.56%
Western Europe	500,000	0.25%

1. Approximately how many people are infected with HIV in North America?
   (1) 500,000
   (2) 890,000
   (3) 1.4 million
   (4) 6.7 million
   (5) 22.5 million

2. Which of the following statements is best supported by the information given?
   (1) People in Sub-Saharan Africa who have more than one sexual partner have the greatest chance of contracting HIV.
   (2) The spread of HIV has slowed in Western Europe and North America.
   (3) HIV probably originated in Africa and spread outward to other regions.
   (4) Intravenous drug use is the primary means by which HIV is spread.
   (5) In Africa the main mode of transmission is heterosexual sex.

Question 3 refers to the following graph.

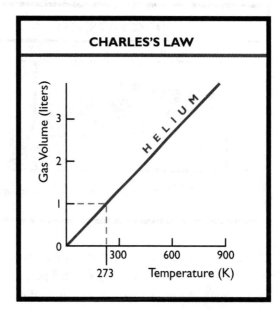

3. According to Charles's Law, the volume of a gas varies directly with the temperature if the pressure of the gas remains constant.

   Which of the following is an example of this gas law?
   (1) Canisters of liquid oxygen are sealed under pressure.
   (2) A balloon filled with helium will rise because it is lighter than air.
   (3) A can of soda will burst if heated to a certain temperature.
   (4) Carbon monoxide is a gas with no color or smell.
   (5) Water evaporates to form steam.

Questions 4 through 6 refer to the information below.

In the 1950s, the Army Corps of Engineers built 15-foot high levees along a stretch of the Snake River in Wyoming. The levees were intended to protect farms from flooding.

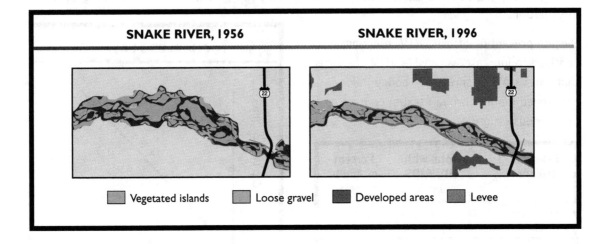

Before the levees, the Snake flowed through five or six shifting channels. There were many wooded islands, and the spring flooding created ponds, wetlands, and marshes that supported many plants and animals. Now the river's energy is confined to one or two channels. As a result, vegetation is destroyed at a much faster rate than it can grow. The surrounding flood plain now remains dry. The cottonwoods and willows are dying out.

In the late 1990s the Army engineers and local officials tried to restore at least part of the river's natural flow. They placed lattices of logs and cable in the river to catch debris and silt, hoping to create islands. They dug new channels to disperse the river's energy. These actions may restore some of the ecosystem, at least between the riverbanks.

4. Why did the Army Corps of Engineers build levees along a stretch of the Snake River?
   (1) to protect farm property
   (2) to provide water for irrigating crops
   (3) to provide a source of drinking water
   (4) to prevent flooding upstream
   (5) to protect endangered species

5. Which one of the following was an intended result of building the levees?
   (1) the bareness of the riverbank
   (2) the destruction of habitat
   (3) real estate development in the flood plain
   (4) the destruction of islands in the river
   (5) the stopping of floods on the flood plain

6. Which of the following is the most likely reason that the restoration plan for the Snake did not include tearing down the levees?
   (1) Tearing down levees is an expensive demolition task.
   (2) Creating new river channels makes tearing down levees unnecessary.
   (3) There is now much valuable real estate in the flood plain.
   (4) Highway 22 might be closed if the river flooded.
   (5) Making islands in the river is a more effective way to restore the ecosystem.

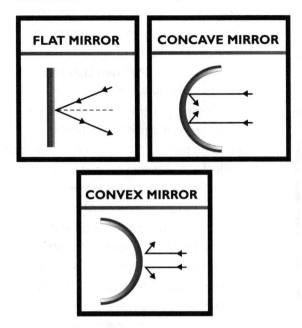

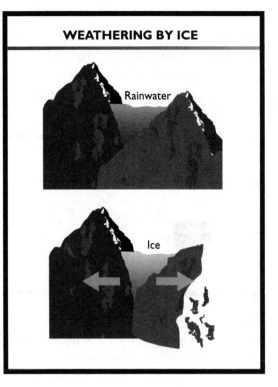

7. Mirrors reflect light. Flat mirrors reflect undistorted images, concave mirrors magnify images, and convex mirrors give a reduced image of an object.

   Which of the following is an example of a convex mirror?
   (1) a dressing room mirror that gives an undistorted image
   (2) a funhouse mirror that magnifies some areas and reduces others
   (3) a car's rear view mirror in which objects appear farther away than they really are
   (4) a makeup mirror that magnifies the face to make applying makeup easier
   (5) a telescope mirror, which enlarges the images of distant objects

8. Glaciers form when more snow falls each year than melts. Some of the ice in glaciers is thousands of years old. In which of the following subject areas would evidence from glaciers be most useful?
   (1) the history of Earth's climate
   (2) the composition of ocean water
   (3) the long-term weather forecast
   (4) marine life in the Arctic and Antarctic
   (5) the extent of the ozone layer

9. Weathering refers to the process by which rock disintegrates. Ice is one of the main causes of weathering. Rain fills cracks, then expands when it freezes. This expansion causes rock to crack.

   Which of the following is an example of weathering caused by ice?
   (1) The limestone facades of buildings dissolve through the action of acid rain.
   (2) The bed of a river changes position as it flows across a plain.
   (3) Sidewalks crack because of rapid heating and cooling.
   (4) Potholes form in roads and highways over the course of a winter.
   (5) Sand is moved from one beach to another by ocean waves and currents.

SCIENCE PRACTICE TEST

Questions 10 and 11 refer to the following information.

In 1908, Ernest Rutherford bombarded a very thin sheet of gold foil with tiny alpha particles. Most particles went right through the sheet, but a few bounced back to the source and a few were deflected at an angle.

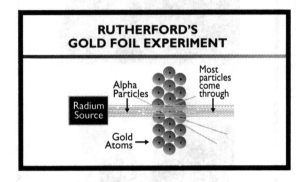

RUTHERFORD'S GOLD FOIL EXPERIMENT

From this, Rutherford concluded that atoms were mostly empty space, with a dense nucleus and electrons in orbit "far" from the nucleus.

10. Which of the following is evidence supporting Rutherford's conclusion that atoms consist mostly of empty space?
 (1) Alpha particles are a form of radiation.
 (2) Radium was used as a source of alpha particles in the experiment.
 (3) Some alpha particles were deflected or bounced back.
 (4) Most alpha particles went right through the gold foil.
 (5) Gold can be beaten into extremely thin sheets.

11. At the time of Rutherford's experiment, it was known that alpha particles were related to helium atoms but had a positive charge. Rutherford's experiment showed that alpha particles were actually helium nuclei, not helium atoms. They penetrated gold foil because they
 (1) had a positive electrical charge.
 (2) were emitted by radium.
 (3) were radioactive.
 (4) had electrons.
 (5) were smaller than atoms.

12. Parkinson's disease is a condition in which a person slowly loses muscle control until movement is impossible. An experimental treatment consists of injecting healthy brain cells from aborted fetuses into the brains of Parkinson's patients. The healthy cells may take over some brain function, relieving the symptoms. Forty Parkinson's patients volunteered for a study to test the effectiveness of this treatment. All underwent brain surgery. At random, 20 received the healthy cells, and 20 received nothing. Critics of the study claim that it is unethical to perform "sham surgery" on patients because surgery always has risk and in these 20 cases, it had no benefit.

Which of the following statements expresses an opinion rather than a fact?
 (1) Parkinson's disease is a condition in which a person slowly loses muscle control.
 (2) A new treatment involves injecting healthy brain cells into the brains of Parkinson's patients.
 (3) Forty Parkinson's patients volunteered to take part in a study testing the effectiveness of the new treatment.
 (4) All the patients had surgery, but only half of them were injected with the healthy brain cells.
 (5) Performing surgery on patients when there is risk but no personal benefit is unethical.

13. The gene that controls blood clotting is on the X chromosome, one of the two sex chromosomes. When this gene is defective, it can cause hemophilia, a disease in which the blood does not clot. Hemophilia usually affects men, because they inherit one X and one Y chromosome. If their X chromosome carries the hemophilia gene, they will have hemophilia. Women do not usually suffer from hemophilia because they inherit two X chromosomes. Even if one of their X chromosomes carries the hemophilia gene, the other usually has a normal blood clot gene, so they are normal.

Which of the following statements is supported by this information?
(1) Most people who suffer from hemophilia are women.
(2) Although a woman may not have hemophilia, she can pass the disease to her children.
(3) Hemophilia can be corrected by splicing the normal gene into the X chromosome.
(4) Women inherit one X chromosome and one Y chromosome from their parents.
(5) Men inherit an X chromosome from their mother and an X chromosome from their father.

14. In electrical conductors, charged particles called electrons flow easily and carry an electric current. Electrical insulators are materials that do not conduct electricity well. What is the function of electrical insulators?
(1) to increase the voltage
(2) to confine the flow of electricity
(3) to alternate the direction of an electric current
(4) to slow the electric current
(5) to generate an electric current

Question 15 refers to the following graph.

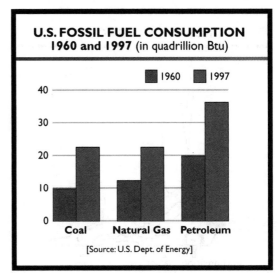

U.S. FOSSIL FUEL CONSUMPTION
1960 and 1997 (in quadrillion Btu)

[Source: U.S. Dept. of Energy]

15. In the period shown by this graph, what happened to U.S. consumption of natural gas?
(1) It increased.
(2) It decreased.
(3) It was much greater than consumption of petroleum.
(4) It was much less than consumption of coal.
(5) It was the most-consumed fossil fuel.

16. White blood cells come in different sizes and shapes. They circulate in the blood, but they can also change shape, squeezing through capillary walls to destroy germs. What might happen if a person had a low white blood cell count?
(1) Not enough oxygen would be delivered to the body's cells.
(2) Not enough carbon dioxide would be removed from the body's cells.
(3) Blood would not clot at the site of a cut.
(4) Blood pressure would increase.
(5) The body's ability to fight infection would decrease.

Question 17 refers to the following diagram.

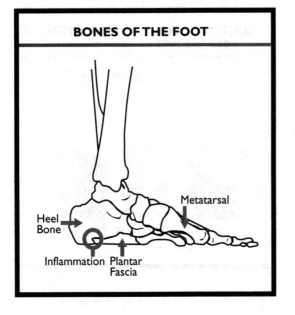

BONES OF THE FOOT

Heel Bone

Metatarsal

Inflammation Plantar Fascia

Question 19 refers to the following graph.

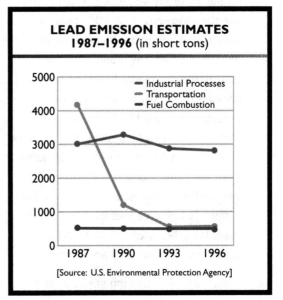

LEAD EMISSION ESTIMATES
1987–1996 (in short tons)

— Industrial Processes
— Transportation
— Fuel Combustion

[Source: U.S. Environmental Protection Agency]

17. Plantar fasciitis is an inflammation of a band of fibrous tissue that runs from the heel to the toes. It is usually caused by overuse. Which of the following is most likely to be a symptom of plantar fasciitis?
    (1) heel pain
    (2) aching shins
    (3) sore ankles
    (4) pain along the upper part of the foot
    (5) sore calf muscles

Question 18 refers to the following diagram.

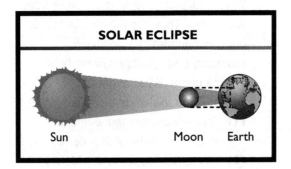

SOLAR ECLIPSE

Sun

Moon   Earth

18. What happens during a solar eclipse?
    (1) Earth casts a shadow on the moon.
    (2) The moon casts a shadow on Earth.
    (3) Earth casts a shadow on the sun.
    (4) The sun casts a shadow on the moon.
    (5) The moon casts a shadow on the sun.

19. Which of the following was the most likely cause of the drop in lead emissions from transportation?
    (1) an increase in air travel
    (2) an increase in the number of automobiles
    (3) a decrease in the number of automobiles
    (4) the switch to unleaded gasoline
    (5) the invention of new industrial processes

20. Heat is a form of energy stored as the vibrations and movements of atoms. The amount of vibration determines the temperature of an object. Larger objects contain more heat energy than smaller objects at the same temperature.

    Which of the following has the most heat energy?
    (1) a pint of water at room temperature
    (2) a gallon of water at room temperature
    (3) a pint of boiling water
    (4) a gallon of boiling water
    (5) a gallon of water heated by the sun

SCIENCE

21. Mistletoe grows on the branches of trees. It produces its own food by photosynthesis, but it gets its water and minerals from the trees. Which term best describes the relationship between mistletoe and the trees on which it grows?

(1) photosynthesis, in which green plants make their own food

(2) respiration, in which organisms produce energy from food

(3) parasitism, in which one species lives in or on another, taking from it but giving nothing in return

(4) predation, in which one species hunts and feeds on another species

(5) symbiosis, in which two species both benefit from their close association

Question 22 refers to the following drawing.

22. Which of the following statements is supported by the drawing of the potted plant?

(1) Growth stops when the roots fill the pot.

(2) Potted plants flower only when fertilized.

(3) Roots grow downward no matter the position of the plant.

(4) Clay pots are better for plants than plastic pots.

(5) Potting soil is a mixture of humus and sand.

Question 23 refers to the following table.

Broad Area of Life Science	Subject of Study
Genetics	Genes and inheritance
Botany	Plants
Zoology	Animals
Microbiology	Microscopic organisms
Physiology	Functions of organisms

23. Dr. Edward O. Wilson is one of the world's foremost experts on ants. Which of the following is Dr. Wilson's field of study?

(1) genetics   **(4)** microbiology

(2) botany   **(5)** physiology

(3) zoology

24. In 1915, Alfred Wegener, a German scientist, suggested that the continents originally had formed one land mass. They had broken into plates and were drifting apart. Wegener thought that the continental crust floated on top of the stationary ocean crust, causing the continents to move.

By the 1960s, advances in technology led to the discovery of sea floor spreading, in which molten material comes up from the mantle through the crust, forming new crust. Sea floor spreading showed that ocean crust, as well as continental crust, was moving.

Wegener was correct in proposing that the continents had drifted. In what area was he <u>incorrect</u>?

(1) proposing that the oceanic crust was stationary

(2) proposing that there was originally one land mass

(3) hypothesizing that the continents were still moving

(4) assuming that the continents had moved in the past

(5) explaining how Earth originally formed

Question 25 refers to the following diagram.

Question 27 refers to the following table.

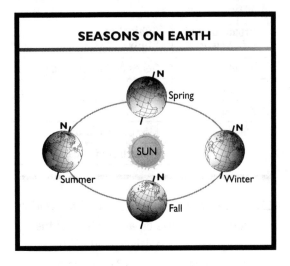

SEASONS ON EARTH

Planet	Gravity Compared to Earth's Gravity
Mercury	0.38
Venus	0.9
Earth	1
Mars	0.38
Jupiter	2.87
Saturn	1.32
Uranus	0.93
Neptune	1.23
Pluto	0.03

25. The seasons are caused by the tilt of Earth's axis and its motion around the sun. Which of the following statements correctly describes the northern half of Earth?
   (1) It tilts toward the sun in winter.
   (2) It tilts toward the sun in summer.
   (3) It gets no sunlight in winter.
   (4) It gets no sunlight in fall.
   (5) It never tilts toward the sun.

26. Mountains, deserts, and oceans are some of the physical barriers that prevent organisms from spreading to new locations. Which of the following is an example of an organism reaching a place that it ordinarily could not reach?
   (1) Dandelion seeds are carried several miles by the wind.
   (2) A coconut shell floats down a stream to a spot on the bank.
   (3) A sycamore burr gets caught on an animal's fur and later falls off.
   (4) A berry is eaten by a mouse, which later passes the seeds in its droppings.
   (5) A cutting of a new plant is brought home by a tourist from overseas.

27. On a planet with greater gravity than Earth, an object will seem to be heavier. For example, a person who weighs 100 pounds on Earth would weigh 287 pounds on Jupiter.

   Which of the following statements is supported by the information given?
   (1) A person weighs more on Earth than he does on Saturn.
   (2) The gravitational pull of the sun keeps the planets in orbit.
   (3) The force of gravity on Neptune is greater than the force of gravity on Saturn.
   (4) Prolonged exposure to low gravity weakens bones and muscles.
   (5) Mercury and Mars exert about the same gravitational pull.

Question 28 refers to the following map.

KEY

Rain

Snow

Clouds

Temperature
in degrees
Fahrenheit

high°F/low°F

Seattle 74°/55°
Boston 63°/53°
Detroit 66°/48°
New York 67°/55°
Chicago 70°/40°
Washington D.C. 68°/52°
Salt Lake City 80°/56°
Denver 79°/47°
St. Louis 71°/54°
Los Angeles 83°/65°
Phoenix 90°/75°
Dallas 81°/57°
Atlanta 70°/52°
Tropical Storm
Miami 88°/75°

28. A family is traveling to Boston for a short vacation. According to the weather map, they should pack each of the following items <u>except</u>
   (1) an umbrella.
   (2) long-sleeved shirts.
   (3) snowboots.
   (4) long pants.
   (5) raincoats.

29. Byproducts of burning fossil fuels include nitrogen oxides—air pollutants that cause respiratory problems. An analysis of air in enclosed ice skating rinks found that the levels of nitrogen oxides were dangerously high because of the fuel used in the ice resurfacers. Propane produced the most nitrogen oxides. Gasoline was the second-highest contributor.

   To achieve the greatest decrease in nitrogen oxide levels, what form of power should ice skating rinks use for their ice resurfacers?
   (1) fossil fuels
   (2) propane
   (3) gasoline
   (4) electricity
   (5) diesel fuel

30. A researcher did a study to see whether doing stretches improves strength as well as flexibility. Participants in Group A were guided by an instructor. They worked out on 13 standard weight-training machines, and did six stretches after the weight exercises. Participants in Group B worked out on their own on the 13 weight machines and did no stretches. After 10 weeks, Group A increased their strength by about 54 percent, compared to 29 percent for Group B. The researcher concluded that weight exercises plus stretching improve strength more than weight exercises alone.

What aspect of the study's design casts doubt on the researcher's conclusion that stretching improves strength?
   (1) One group of participants had an instructor's help and the other did not.
   (2) One group of participants did stretches and the other did not.
   (3) Strength cannot be measured reliably in this type of study.
   (4) Both groups exercised for only 10 weeks.
   (5) Both groups used standard weight-training equipment.

SCIENCE PRACTICE TEST

249

Answers and explanations start on page 250.

Science Practice Test Answers and Explanations

1. **(2) 890,000** According to the table, 890,000 people in North America are infected with HIV.

2. **(1) People in Sub-Saharan Africa who have more than one sexual partner have the greatest chance of becoming infected with HIV.** Because 8 out of 100 people in this region are already infected, the chances of sexual contact with an infected person are greater here.

3. **(3) A can of soda will burst if heated to a certain temperature.** As the temperature of a soda increases, the volume of the dissolved carbon dioxide gas also increases until the can bursts. This choice is the only one that involves the relationship of temperature, pressure, and volume of a gas.

4. **(1) to protect farm property** The levees were intended to protect farmland from floods.

5. **(5) the stopping of floods on the flood plain** The only result that was intended was that floods stopped.

6. **(3) There is now much valuable real estate in the flood plain.** After the levees were built, real estate development spread in the area (see 1996 map). If the levees were torn down, these areas would flood, destroying property. This is the most likely reason that tearing down the levees is not part of the restoration plan.

7. **(3) a car's rear view mirror in which objects appear farther away than they really are** If an object appears to be farther away than it really is, that means its image in the mirror is reduced, a characteristic of convex mirrors.

8. **(1) the history of Earth's climate** Studying the layers of ice in a glacier provides evidence about precipitation and temperature over thousands of years.

9. **(4) Potholes form in roads and highways over the course of a winter.** Potholes begin when water freezes and expands, breaking part of the road surface. None of the other examples of weathering is caused by ice.

10. **(4) Most alpha particles went right through the gold foil.** The particles went through the foil because they had the space to do so. This was evidence for Rutherford's conclusion that atoms are mostly empty space.

11. **(5) were smaller than atoms.** Because the alpha particles are just the nuclei of helium atoms, they are tiny and dense. Thus they can penetrate the gold foil, passing through the empty spaces between the gold atoms' nuclei and their electrons.

12. **(5) Performing surgery on patients when there is risk but no personal benefit is unethical.** Of the five statements, this is the only opinion; it cannot be proved true or false. Note that choice (5) expresses one opinion. Many people hold the opposite opinion. They believe that as long as the volunteers are aware that they might not receive the brain cells and are aware of the risks of surgery, the study is ethical.

13. **(2) Although a woman may not have hemophilia, she can pass the disease to her children.** This may happen if the woman has the gene for hemophilia on one of her X chromosomes. None of the other statements is supported by the information given.

14. **(2) to confine the flow of electricity** An insulator, such as the plastic covering on a wire, serves to confine the flow of electricity to where it is wanted.

15. **(1) It increased.** The graph shows that the consumption of natural gas increased between 1960 and 1997.

16. **(5) The body's ability to fight infection would decrease.** According to the information given, the function of white blood cells is to destroy germs. Thus if a person had fewer than the normal number of white blood cells, his or her ability to fight infection would decrease.

17. **(1) heel pain** The diagram shows an inflammation, or swelling, in the heel, so the heel is likely to be painful.

18. **(2) The moon casts a shadow on Earth.** According to the diagram, during a solar eclipse the moon is between the sun and Earth, casting its shadow on a small area of Earth.

19. **(4) the switch to unleaded gasoline** As more newer-model cars that use unleaded gasoline were driven, the emissions of lead from transportation decreased.

20. **(4) a gallon of boiling water** Of all the choices, the highest temperature would be that of boiling water. Since a gallon of boiling water is larger than a pint of boiling water, the gallon of boiling water has the most heat energy.

21. **(3) parasitism, in which one species lives in or on another, taking from it but giving nothing in return** The mistletoe is taking water and minerals from the tree, but the tree gets nothing in return.

22. **(3) Roots grow downward no matter the position of the plant.** Even though the plant is on its side, the roots are growing downward because of the force of gravity.

23. **(3) zoology** Ants are animals, so Dr. Wilson is a zoologist.

24. **(1) proposing that the oceanic crust was stationary** Wegener believed that the continental crust floats on top of oceanic crust, which he thought was stationary. This turned out to be incorrect, because scientists found evidence that both the ocean and continental crusts are moving.

25. **(2) It tilts toward the sun in summer.** According to the diagram, the northern half of Earth tilts toward the sun during summer.

26. **(5) A cutting of a new plant is brought home by a tourist from overseas.** Without human technology, this plant would not have made it across the ocean.

27. **(5) Mercury and Mars exert about the same gravitational pull.** According to the table, these planets have about 0.38 the gravity of Earth.

28. **(3) snowboots.** The weather map shows that Boston is in the midst of a tropical storm and has a low temperature of 53 degrees Fahrenheit. With this temperature, it is unlikely to snow.

29. **(4) electricity** All of the other choices are fossil fuels, the burning of which gives off nitrogen oxides. Only electricity would not pollute the air in the rink.

30. **(1) One group of participants had an instructor's help and the other did not.** Because one group had help as well as did stretches, the results of the study are inconclusive. The better performance of Group A might have resulted from doing the stretches or the guidance of an instructor.

Circle the question numbers that you got incorrect. Use this information to determine the skills and content areas in which you need more work.

	Comprehension	Application	Analysis	Evaluation
Life Science	1, 4	21, 23, 26	5, 12, 16, 17	2, 6, 13, 22, 30
Earth and Space	15, 18, 25	9, 28	19	8, 24, 27
Chemistry		3	11, 27	10
Physics	14	7	20	

Social Studies Answer Key

SOCIAL STUDIES

PROGRAM 16: PASSING THE GED SOCIAL STUDIES TEST

Understanding What You Read:

Comprehension
GED Practice, page 13
(3) Human groups moved from place to place to find food. The passage states that agriculture led to permanent settlements. This implies that before agriculture developed, people moved from place to place in order to find new sources of food.

Using What You Read: Application
GED Practice, page 14
(5) senator or representative Because Ms. Mendez is under 35 and was not born in the United States, she cannot run for President or Vice President. Since Ms. Mendez has been a citizen for 12 years and is over 30 years old, she is eligible to run either for the Senate or for the House of Representatives.

Thinking About What You Read: Analysis
GED Practice, page 15
(3) the first visit to China by a U.S. president, in 1972 Since the question involves foreign policy achievements, you can eliminate options 1, 4, and 5 because they involve national events. Option 2 can be eliminated because invading Cambodia was not a significant foreign policy achievement, as indicated by the massive protests staged after the invasion.

GED Practice, page 16
(3) The ban on cell phones while driving is simply a matter of common sense. This is not a fact. The other choices are all facts—they can be proven.

GED Practice, page 17
(2) The cost of attending the University of Rhode Island is about $8,000 higher for out-of-state students than for Rhode Island residents. Compare the cost of tuition, room, and board for residents and nonresidents at the University of Rhode Island. Out-of-state students pay about $8,000 more. The other choices are not supported by the information in the graph.

Judging What You Read: Evaluation
GED Practice, page 18
(4) It is not sincerely interested in the taxpayer. In the second panel, even though the IRS agent has adopted a big smile, he is still treating the taxpayer exactly the same—poorly.

GED Practice, page 19
1. **(4) Workers think it is too risky to leave a job without having another.** A lower quit rate indicates that workers are being more cautious. They are less willing to risk being unemployed, so they remain in their old jobs while looking for new jobs.
2. **(3) ambition** A worker who has the confidence to quit a job before having another job is probably ambitious and wishes to succeed in the future. He or she may have the other values, too, but this behavior is not evidence of those values.

Interpreting Social Studies Graphics
GED Practice, page 20
(5) 1990 The difference between receipts and outlays in 1990 was about $200 billion, the greatest gap for all the years shown.

GED Practice, page 21
(4) 1933 to 1947 During the Great Depression and World War II, immigration decreased. The other periods do not show prolonged decreases in immigration.

GED Practice, page 22
(3) New South Wales To find the capital, look at the legend to see the symbol for the capital. Then look for that symbol on the map. Canberra, the capital of Australia, is located in New South Wales.

GED Practice, page 23
1. **(3) Great Dividing Range** Ski resorts are generally located in the mountains, and the map shows that the Great Dividing Range is a mountain range running up and down the eastern part of Australia.
2. **(4) Darling River valley** A river valley is a good place for a farm, since it provides a source of water.

GED Practice, page 24

(1) Women are tough enough to serve in the armed forces partly because they often deal with opposition from male soldiers. The cartoon shows that the female soldier regards the male recruiter/trainer as an enemy, and she thinks her dealings with him help prepare her for meeting an enemy in a combat situation.

PROGRAM 17: THEMES IN U.S. HISTORY

A Multicultural Nation
Skill Practice, page 30
1. Native Americans originally came from Asia and moved to North and South America in search of food.
2. They came from England and Africa.
3. The English (or the British) were the largest group. Note that the British include people from England, Scotland, and Ireland. There are many reasons why this group would have been the largest. People in Great Britain would have been most likely to hear of the colonies or to know people there. British people might feel most comfortable moving there because they would be able to speak the language, know the customs followed in the colonies, and be familiar with the laws and political institutions of the colonies.
4. Native Americans are not included.

Skill Practice, page 31
1. Many Irish left Ireland because of lack of land for farming, the failure of the potato crop, and starvation. They came to America because they hoped to have greater opportunities here.
2. The difference between the way the two men are dressed indicates that some Irish immigrants prospered in the United States.
3. Their hope was to return to Ireland after they made their fortune in America.

Skill Practice, page 32
1. **False** Most of the immigrants who settled the colonies were European.
2. **True**
3. **False** People today immigrate for similar reasons to those of immigrants more than 100 years ago.

Skill Practice, page 33
1. Some people feel that immigrants take away jobs and that immigrants use up the country's resources.
2. Some people feel that immigrants take jobs that other Americans do not want to do and that they have the potential of contributing to the country in many ways.
3. Either answer is acceptable. Sample answer 1: Those who want to limit immigration have the strongest argument, because this country cannot support all the people who want to come here. Sample answer 2: Those who want unlimited immigration have the strongest argument, because immigrants work hard and help create economic opportunities for everyone.

The Math Connection, page 33
Dominican Republic: 6.4 percent; El Salvador: 2.2 percent; Mexico: 14 percent; Philippines: 6.7 percent; Vietnam: 5.1 percent

Work and Working
Skill Practice, page 34
Statements 1 and 4 should have checkmarks because they are true.

Skill Practice, page 35
1. The Industrial Revolution was a time of change in how and where people worked, brought about because of the invention of many large, labor-saving machines. It began in Great Britain.
2. They hoped to get jobs in factories.
3. The number of Americans working in manufacturing grew and the percentage of Americans working on farms dropped. Between 1820 and 1860, agriculture jobs fell by 12.18 percent and manufacturing jobs grew by 6.2 percent.

Skill Practice, page 36
1. **F**
2. **O**
3. **F**
4. **O**
5. **O**

Skill Practice, page 37
1. To work for higher wages and shorter workdays
2. To lower their costs, especially the cost of labor
3. You should infer that living and working conditions are not as good as they are in the United States, since employers located their businesses there in order to cut labor costs.

Technology Connection, page 37
Answers will vary. A list of health hazards related to working with computers and keyboards might focus on eyestrain, carpal tunnel syndrome, and back problems. Solutions might include adjusting behavior, such as taking breaks, maintaining good posture, doing exercises to combat the problems, and using typing pads or specially built desks or chairs to minimize problems.

Rights and Freedoms of Americans
Skill Practice, page 38
1. a
2. b
3. d
4. c

Skill Practice, page 39
1. abolitionists
2. they were afraid Lincoln would try to end slavery and thus ruin their economy.
3. to keep all the states as part of one nation.
4. slavery was abolished.
5. the rights of African Americans.

Skill Practice, page 40
1. Voting is a right that was not always granted women in the United States.
2. white males
3. the Nineteenth Amendment
4. 18 to 20-year-olds

Skill Practice, page 41
1. It means that if one person can have a right taken away, all of us can have that right taken away.
2. Its purpose is to make sure that the rights spelled out in the Bill of Rights are guaranteed to all Americans.
3. It joined the battle against segregation and participated in the civil rights movement.

Writing Connection, page 41
Answers will vary but should list cases in which a person's rights have been violated and/or cases in which someone is discriminated against because of age, gender, or religion.

A World Power Emerges
Skill Practice, page 42
1. **F** Some of the land was added as a result of war.
2. **T**
3. **F** Before the United States made the Louisiana Purchase, Native Americans occupied the land west of the Mississippi River.
4. **T**
5. **T**

Skill Practice, page 43
1. **O**
2. **F**
3. **F**
4. **O**

Skill Practice, page 44
1. **b**
2. **a**
3. **c**

Skill Practice, page 45
Statements 1, 2, and 4 should have checkmarks because they are true.

Science Connection, page 45
Answers will vary. Sample answer: to produce electricity; to power some submarines and ships; used as nuclear radiation in medicine, industry, and science.

GED Practice, pages 46–48
1. **(4) a windmill that pumped water for irrigation** With irrigation, more land could be planted for farms and the watered crops would grow better. The refrigerated cars allowed more food to come to market without spoiling, but did not make the farms themselves more productive.
2. **(4) The population rose steadily.** The figures show a steady increase in the total population.
3. **(2) 1920** According to the graph, the population of urban and rural dwellers was about 55,000,000, for a total of about 110,000,000.

4. **(4) The actual number of American farmers declined from 1790 to 1940.** Although the percentage of farmers decreased during that period, the actual number of farmers did not.

5. **(3) the growth of western railroads between 1880 and 1930** Both the years and the subject matter are identified in the titles of the maps.

6. **(4) Most were located along the eastern edge of the region on the map.** In general, the cities along the western states' easternmost border—Kansas City, Fargo, and Omaha— were the cities from which rail lines spread into the nation's interior plains. These were the starting cities for the railroads already built in 1880. Cities in the central West, the Northwest, or the Southwest did not enjoy as much railroad activity.

7. According to the map, by 1880 San Francisco was the West Coast city with the greatest number of railroads. It also had a railroad line that ran almost directly eastward.

8. **(2) Railroad lines greatly increased in the 1800s and early 1900s.** The maps show that many railroad lines were built throughout the West in 50 years.

9. **(3) renouncing any enemy of the United States** The oath discusses renouncing allegiance to other countries and renouncing allegiance to other leaders, but it does not mention renouncing enemies of the United States.

10. **(5) Germany, Mexico, and the Philippines** The countries contributing the largest number of naturalized citizens are: Mexico with 969,704; Germany with 512,018; and the Philippines with 492,214.

11. **(3) approximately one-half** The passage states that there were about 20 million foreign-born people living in the United States in 1990; 7,996,998 is about 8 million; 8 million out of 20 million is closest to half.

12, **(3) loyalty to the United States and willingness to obey U.S. laws** These are the values supported in the oath. Neither love of any country nor willingness to work hard are addressed.

PROGRAM 18: THEMES IN WORLD HISTORY

Technology and Development
Skill Practice, page 54
1. Without the Nile, the great Egyptian civilization could not have existed.
2. Irrigation improved harvests, allowing Egypt's population to grow.
3. Mesopotamia and China
4. Irrigation led to the development of flourishing civilizations.

Skill Practice, page 55
1. The Agricultural Revolution was a period beginning in the 1700s when many improvements were made in farming methods.
2. Before the Agricultural Revolution, farmers generally followed a three-crop rotation system in which one field in three was left fallow every year. After the Agricultural Revolution, farmers used a four-crop system, planting turnips, legumes, and grains. These crops each used different nutrients and replenished the soil in different ways, so that the land did not have to be left fallow.
3. Bigger, stronger animals were bred. Also, the turnips and clover of the four-crop rotation increased the amount of feed grown for animals. With this system, there was enough food to feed animals through the winter so that farmers did not have to slaughter their animals in the fall.

Skill Practice, page 56
1. **F** According to the map, France took control of Indochina in 1859.
2. **T**
3. **T**
4. **T**

Skill Practice, page 57
1. **F**
2. **O**
3. **O**

Reading Connection, page 57
Answers will vary. Sample answer: *Perpetually* means "all the time."

Nation Building and Nationalism

Skill Practice, page 58

Statements 3 and 4 should be checked because they are true.

Skill Practice, page 59

1. It was divided into small, independent, locally governed political units.
2. Answers include having a common religion, language, ethnic heritage, and/or culture; having a desire to drive away a common enemy.
3. Answers will vary, and should include three of the following: Estonia, Lithuania, Poland, Cumans Territory.

Skill Practice, page 60

Statements 2, 3, and 4 should have checkmarks because they are true.

Skill Practice, page 61

1. Most formed in the mid-1900s from the colonies that Europeans had carved in the late 1800s.
2. Most of the political boundaries in Africa do not encompass a set of compatible ethnic groups or groups with a common culture, language, religion, or history, as they do in Europe.
3. The mixing of incompatible ethnic groups in a single country and the splitting of one ethnic group into two or more countries has caused hostility among nations and political instability.

Math Connection, page 61

You should have two or more examples. If you have trouble finding Roman numerals, look at the end of the credits of many movies, in advertisements in magazines, at the copyright pages of very old books, and on the cornerstones of some buildings. Sample answers: MCM = 1900 and MMC = 2100. Note that IX = 9, XL = 40, and XC = 90.

The Democratic Impulse

Skill Practice, page 62

1. Citizens were free native-born males over 18 years of age.
2. With this system, everyone had equal opportunity to hold office.
3. With ostracism, Athenian citizens had a way to get rid of people they felt were politically dangerous to the city-state for a period of time.
4. Athens was a democracy; José would have had more influence on his government than he had in his homeland of Cuba.

Skill Practice, page 63

1. O
2. F
3. O
4. F

Skill Practice, page 64

1. Europe and Asia
2. the 1940s
3. Under communism, people had few rights and freedoms. People protested and slowly the communist governments began to lose hold, the countries opened their borders, and the communist governments were replaced with democracies.

Skill Practice, page 65

1. **F**   Chinese troops fired upon Chinese protesters.
2. **T**
3. **T**

Writing Connection, page 65

Answers will vary. Sample Answer: Dear family: I am willing to risk my life for freedom if it means my children will get to live in a democracy.

GED Practice, pages 66–68

1. **(3) More new inventions could rely on the steam engine as a power source.** Many other inventions used the steam engine as a power source, such as Richard Trevithick's steam locomotive, constructed in 1804.
2. **(1) Abraham Darby** Darby's method used coke, from coal, rather than charcoal, from trees, for iron refinement.
3. **(5) the eighteenth and nineteenth** The Industrial Revolution spanned the 1700s and 1800s.
4. **(5) New inventions were one of the main causes of the Industrial Revolution.** It was the continued fast pace of the development of new inventions that actually created the Industrial Revolution.
5. **(1) Most of the people were Protestants.** The passage does not discuss choices 2 and 3. Choice 4 is false because the people formed political unions with their neighbors. Choice 5 is false because Northern Ireland is on an island (Ireland) separate from the other neighbors.
6. **(2) Northern Ireland** The map shows that Northern Ireland has the smallest land area of any part of the British Isles. It is just over 5,000 square miles in area; Wales is next at about 8,000 square miles.

7. **(4) The Irish Republic wanted to become a part of the United Kingdom.** The Irish Catholics in the republic did not want to be connected with the Protestant-led United Kingdom.

8. **(1) the American Revolution** In the American Revolution during the 1770s, the British colonists resisted British rule, just as the Irish Catholics did in the 1800s.

9. **(5) about 200 percent** It started out at $1,600 and increased $3,200 to $4,800.

10. **(4) More nations in Asia will adopt democracy than will those in Africa.** The strong economic development in East Asia conflicts with choices 2 and 3. Choices 1 and 5 are unlikely with Africa facing crises on many fronts. Choice 4 is correct because it echoes the opening sentence that "democracy and a strong economy go hand in hand."

11. **(2) Most gained economic stability.** The passage states that leaders worked on economic growth.

12. **(3) The Chinese will adopt democracy.** Choice 3 is correct because it follows the historical pattern described in the passage. Choice 1 is unlikely because the United States has had many more years of economic stability than China. Based on information in the passage, choices 2 and 4 are unlikely if the nation is in an economic growth period. Choice 5 is unrelated to democracy and economic growth.

PROGRAM 19: ECONOMICS

Government's Role in the Economy
Skill Practice, page 74
1. b
2. a
3. c

Skill Practice, page 75
1. To remain competitive with cheaper imported goods, American companies are moving production overseas to take advantage of lower production costs there.
2. The steelmaking industry, because it uses columbium and manganese, both imported from Brazil, a major supplier.
3. Sample answer: The exporting nation can raise prices very high, especially if the importing nation has few other sources to which it can turn for the particular resource.

Skill Practice, page 76
Statements 2 and 3 should have checkmarks because they are true.

Skill Practice, page 77
1. Sample answer: Child-care costs can use up too large a chunk of the minimum-wage worker's paycheck to make it worthwhile to work.
2. Sample answer: Some state governments are giving subsidies or tax credits to businesses that employ people formerly on welfare.
3. Sample answer: Working people can put more money back into the economy, in both spending and savings, than can those on welfare.

Technology Connection, page 77
Aside from looking at your state's home page, you may also find relevant information at the Council of State Governments home page (http://www.csg.org). Answers will vary but should include information you gather from the Internet about your state's policy on welfare and work.

Factors Influencing Jobs and Wages
Skill Practice, page 78
1. The demand for travel agents was reduced as people made their own travel arrangements. Meanwhile, the supply of travel agents remained relatively high, so Margaret had difficulty finding another job in her field.
2. The most money is made by people with advanced degrees.
3. Wages generally are higher when demand for the goods being produced is high. An employer may offer high wages to attract qualified workers. Plus high demand usually allows the producer to make a profit, some of which can be passed on to the workers. Generally, the more education a person has, the higher the wages.

Skill Practice, page 79
Statements 2 and 3 should have checkmarks because they are true.

Skill Practice, page 80
1. They offer their labor.
2. It will be among the fastest-growing fields.
3. Sample answer: We both are trying to improve our skills to help make ourselves more desirable in the job market. As a result, we both hope that we will be more likely to find a good job.

Skill Practice, page 81
1. **O**
2. **F**
3. **O**
4. **F**

Math Connection, page 81
Subtract to find the number of years spent working if the average person works to age 65.
high school/GED: 65-18 = 47
associate's degree: 65-21 = 44

high school/GED—47 × $21,431 = $1,007,257
associate's degree—44 × $23,862 = $1,049,928

The Roles of Individuals in the Economy
Skill Practice, page 82
Statements 1, 3, and 4 should have checkmarks because they are true.

Skill Practice, page 83
1. Individuals borrow money when their earnings and their savings are not enough to meet their wants and needs. Businesses borrow money to expand or improve their businesses.
2. They spend the most on housing; they save and invest 4.9 percent.
3. Many answers are possible. Sample answers: Increased saving and investing could encourage business growth by making more money available for business loans. Increased saving and investing could slow down economic growth by slowing spending.

Skill Practice, page 84
1. **F**
2. **O**
3. **O**
4. **F**

Skill Practice, page 85
1. Consumers' money is limited, so producers must compete for buyers. One of their tools is advertising their product.
2. Advertising can educate consumers on issues such as safety, nutrition, and the availability of certain products.
3. Advertisers can encourage consumers to borrow to meet their wants and needs; they can encourage many consumers to buy one brand of product over another or to demand certain safety features or standards for a product.

Math Connection, page 85
Television = 0.235 = 23.5%
Newspapers = 0.22 = 22.0%
Direct Mail = 0.197 = 19.7%

GED Practice, pages 86–88
1. **(4) the number of high school graduates**
Tough economic times can affect this number because some students are forced to quit school and go to work to help their families. However, it is not a reliable measure in the same way as the consumer price index, inflation, unemployment rate, and the gross domestic product.
2. **(2) The rate fell slowly.** That is the trend illustrated by the graph's unemployment figures. The other answers are not consistent with the trend shown in the graph.
3. **(3) It affects the value of the dollar.** Inflation affects the buying power of the dollar. During inflation, a dollar purchases fewer products than in non-inflation times.
4. **(5) Growth was slow but steady.** As measured in constant dollars, the GDP showed slow, steady growth; unemployment rates showed a slow decline; the consumer price index showed little change.
5. **(2) It has dropped steadily.** According to the text, union membership has been in decline since its high in 1954.
6. **(3) Because of the loss of profits business owners experience during a strike, they sometimes will give in to worker demands to get them back on the job.** Usually businesses lose profits immediately at the onset of a strike. This immediate profit loss can induce business owners to be willing to give in to some of the workers' demands.
7. **(3) Multiply the 60,580,000 days idle by 8 hours in a workday.** According to the table, the total number of days idle in 1960 was 60,580,000. To find the number of hours lost you first need to figure out the number of hours in a work day. According to the passage, a work week has 40 hours, so a single work day has 8 hours (40 hours divided by 5 days of work). Multiplying 60,580,000 days idle by 8 hours per day gives you the total number of hours lost (484,640,000 hours).
8. **(2) Wages might go down, causing businesses to remain or move back to the United States.** Nonunion members generally receive lower wages than union members. Since wages are lower in some other countries and this has caused American businesses to locate many production plants overseas, a cut in labor costs might induce such businesses to stay in the United States, or to move back here.
9. **(2) the effectiveness of the EPA's work** The graph shows change in pollution levels. Since the levels are declining, the graph shows the EPA's effectiveness. There are no pollution levels given on the graph, and information about safety and EPA budget are not given.

10. **(1) Without regulations, a higher population would cause an increase in pollution.** If the population remained stable, it is reasonable to assume that the pollution levels would remain fairly stable. Although these EPA-sponsored improvements are dramatic, they are even more dramatic when the population increase is taken into account.

11. **(2) Improvement was greatest in toxic releases.** According to the graph, toxic releases dropped by about 40 percent during the time span covered.

12. **(3) To show that the EPA has been effective despite continued increases in manufacturing.** The graph shows that the GDP has risen dramatically over the period of the EPA's existence. Without regulations, it is reasonable to believe that pollution levels would rise as manufacturing levels rise. Therefore, a rise in manufacturing levels accompanied by a lowering of pollution levels indicates strong success in government regulation.

PROGRAM 20: CIVICS AND GOVERNMENT

A Constitutional System
Skill Practice, page 94
1. They wanted to form one nation and clearly define the government's role.
2. Compromise allowed all 13 states to reach agreement on the plan for the new government.
3. The following answers all explain how the Constitutional Convention shows democracy in action: there were representatives from all 13 states; the delegates debated, compromised, and voted to come up with the Constitution; the Constitution had to be ratified by a large majority of the states.

Skill Practice, page 95
Statements 1, 2, and 3 should have checkmarks because they are true.

Skill Practice, page 96
1. **T**
2. **T**
3. **F** A bill can become law without the support of both Congress and the president. For example, the president can veto a bill, and Congress can pass it through an override.
4. **F** Congress approves treaties made by the president.

Skill Practice, page 97
1. **O**
2. **F**
3. **O**
4. **F**
5. **F**

Writing Connection, page 97
There are many possible answers. Sample answer: Supporters may have felt women were citizens and so should have a citizen's right to vote. Opponents may have felt women did not have enough formal education to cast an educated vote. Since passage of the Nineteenth Amendment, politicians must appeal to both men and women to ensure their election.

Federal and State Governments
Skill Practice, page 98
1. There are many possible answers. Sample answer: the powers necessary to provide for the welfare of the nation and its citizens
2. Both have projects and services that need to be funded by their citizens.
3. That part of the government would depend on the other part of the government to provide funds for its programs and so would have reduced power.

Skill Practice, page 99
1. **F**
2. **O**
3. **O**
4. **F**
5. **F**

Skill Practice, page 100
1. They provide the day-to-day services needed by a state's citizens.
2. The number of counties has essentially stayed the same for more than 50 years; the number of school districts has steadily decreased.
3. Sample answer: Using local libraries, driving and parking on local streets, garbage collection, and community health services.

Skill Practice, page 101
Statement 2 should have a checkmark because it is true.

Reading Connection, page 101
The following are the most plausible answers: The area's major state highway is going to be repaved: state government's Department of Transportation. Someone has been tampering with mailboxes: national government's U.S. Postal Service.

Rights and Responsibilities

Skill Practice, page 102
1. F
2. O
3. O
4. O
5. F

Skill Practice, page 103
1. Sample answer: If Americans do not fulfill their responsibilities, their democracy will suffer since democracy is government by the people. The end of their democracy could mark the end to many of the rights guaranteed by that government.
2. Some possible reasons include lack of knowledge of the issues or the candidates, lack of time or ability to get to the polls.
3. Citizens have the duty to defend the country, to go to court if called, and to pay taxes.

Skill Practice, page 104
1. Agree
2. Disagree
3. Agree
4. Disagree
5. Disagree

Skill Practice, page 105
1. Political parties work to win elections, while interest groups work to influence specific government policies.
2. Sample answer: They give information to government officials about issues of interest to the public.
3. Sample answer: Interest groups consist of members with strong opinions on issues; other groups have differing opinions on the same issue.

Technology Connection, page 105
Sample answer: I do not think we should use electronic vote counting until we can guarantee that the votes would be protected from tampering.

GED Practice, pages 106–108
1. **(3) a member of Congress**   Although others may suggest ideas for bills, the bills themselves must be introduced by a congressional representative.
2. **(3) A bill rarely reaches the president worded the same way as when it was introduced.**   The chart shows that debate and compromise are part of the legislative process.
3. **(4) after the president signs it**   The chart shows that the president signing the bill into law can be the last step in the legislative process.

4. **(1) Congress's ability to pass laws is limited by the complexity of the bill-to-law process.**   Although choices 3 and 5 also are true, they do not represent a summary of the information in this passage.
5. **(2) to help the president carry out the duties of the executive branch**   The passage says that the departments advise the president, while the agencies help carry out the work of the executive branch. Both these services help the president carry out his or her duties.
6. **(3) State, Defense, and Commerce**   The State Department works toward friendly relationships with other nations, the Defense Department protects the country against hostile attack, and the Commerce Department deals with matters of international trade.
7. **(4) during an economic depression**   Such bleak economic times would affect the nation's finances, and that is the area of concern of the Treasury Department.
8. **(1) The executive branch has grown in size and responsibilities.**   The chart shows a steady increase in the number of departments, and their names indicate the widening scope of the responsibilities of the executive branch.
9. **(2) education and highways**   The national government spends 0.2% of its budget on education and 0.3% of its budget on highways.
10. **(2) The states hold most of the responsibility for education.**   Of the remaining answers, choices 1 and 4 cannot be proven by the graphs; choice 3 is wrong; and choice 5 is an opinion.
11. **(1) Utilities are the responsibility of the state and local governments.**   According to the graphs, the national government allots no money to providing utilities.
12. **(1) Government in the United States is based on federalism.**   The graphs illustrate this point. It can be inferred that if all the power lay with the national government, all the expenditures would be made by the national government, rather than by the national, state, and local governments.

PROGRAM 21: GEOGRAPHY

Places and People

Skill Practice, page 114
Statements 2 and 4 should have checkmarks because they are true.

Skill Practice, page 115
1. Possible answers include the following: local television and radio programs, local newspapers and magazines, stores, theaters, roadways, parks, and any other urban feature.
2. Sample answer: the city of Atlanta itself, the state of Georgia, and the Cotton Belt
3. the southern United States

Skill Practice, page 116
1. F
2. O
3. F
4. O

Skill Practice, page 117
1. b
2. a
3. c

Writing Connection, page 117
Sample answers: The plains are flat with few hills. Mountains are the tallest of hills, and their tops are often covered with snow.

Geography and Human Interaction
Skill Practice, page 118
1. O
2. F
3. F
4. O
5. O

Skill Practice, page 119
1. Their nation has not been fully industrialized, and they often grow crops both for themselves and for export.
2. Manufacturing costs are lower in developing countries.
3. New manufacturing jobs in urban areas have brought people from the rural areas to the cities.
4. Sample answers: Developing nations will not produce enough food for themselves and will need to import more agricultural products. Job opportunities in industrialized countries will go down sharply.

Skill Practice, page 120
Statements 1, 2, and 5 should have checkmarks because they are true.

Skill Practice, page 121
1. c
2. a
3. b

Science Connection, page 121
Sample answer: I predict the first to be built would be the 200-story skyscrapers, because that would be based on technology that already exists. I predict that the space station would be second, because people have been working on this for several decades. I predict that the domed structures in the Arctic would be last.

Environments and Social Development
Skill Practice, page 122
1. People wear appropriate clothing, and they build shelters or housing suited for the climate of their region.
2. The Plains Indians sewed buffalo skins to make teepees because buffalo were plentiful and trees (for wood) were not.
3. The area is very mountainous and difficult to travel in, so it is sparsely settled. The region has several large National Parks. People interested in hiking, skiing, mountain climbing, and vacationers are most likely to visit the area.

Skill Practice, page 123
1. b
2. d
3. a
4. c

Skill Practice, page 124
1. F
2. F
3. O
4. O
5. O

Skill Practice, page 125
Statements 1 and 2 should have checkmarks because they are true.

Writing Connection, page 125
Answers will vary. Sample Answer: Letters may include the fact that the region has flooded before and that floods will continue to affect the area in the future.

1. **(3) the Pacific coast off South America** The map shows El Niño near the western coast of South America in the Pacific Ocean.

2. **(3) People have little control over some weather-related events.** Although people can affect and even control many changes in their environment, they have little ability to affect the onset of El Niño.

3. **(4) El Niño has caused flooding in every continent.** According to the map, although flooding was widespread, it did not occur everywhere in the world. In fact, some places experienced a drought.

4. **(1) People will have time to prepare for its impact.** Although people cannot control the weather, the effects of El Niño can be limited somewhat by advance preparation.

5. **(3) about 30 percent** According to the diagram, 30 percent of the sun's light is reflected back into space by clouds.

6. **(3) decrease electricity use** According to the text, over half of all electricity in the United States is generated from the burning of coal, resulting in the release of carbon dioxide.

7. **(5) solar heating** Solar heat is the only option listed that does not have a negative impact on the atmosphere.

8. **(5) Polar ice caps will shrink, causing flooding along sea coasts.** In time, the polar ice caps will melt, raising ocean levels and causing coastal flooding.

9. **(2) Since 1974, nations have continued to use reserves and discover new ones.** Since oil is a nonrenewable resource, any oil used depletes a country's oil supplies and any oil discovered adds to the reserve.

10. **(2) Australia has no known oil reserves.** In the 100 or so years of oil mining, no nation with oil reserves has yet used them up, so the best answer is that Australia has no known oil reserves. The map is a map of the world and shows all the hemispheres.

11. **(1) Venezuela** On this map, Venezuela is the biggest country in South America.

12. **(3) Iraq wanted to take over the vast oil fields of Kuwait and gain power or income from selling the oil.** The map shows Kuwait to be much bigger than Iraq, so it has larger oil reserves than Iraq does. Since Iraq is a Middle Eastern country, much of which has a warm desert climate, it would be unlikely that Iraqis would need the oil for home heating. It is much more reasonable to infer that the Iraqis would want to take control of the oil fields for economic (or other political) reasons.

Science Answer Key

PROGRAM 22: PASSING THE GED SCIENCE TEST

GED Practice, page 151
(2) Supervise young children when they eat.
According to the passage, many ordinary foods give young children problems because they do not have all their teeth. Therefore, supervising children when they eat is the most effective way to preventing choking accidents. Choice (3), cutting food into small pieces, is not the best answer because one characteristic of choking hazards is that they are small.

GED Practice, page 152
(1) For every action there is an equal and opposite reaction. The force of the jet of gas exiting the rear of the rocket results in forward motion, an equal and opposite reaction. Although all of the other choices are true statements of scientific principles, they do not apply to the forward movement of a rocket.

GED Practice, page 153
(3) continue to increase. There are a huge number of baby boomers, and improvements in nutrition and health continue. So it's likely that the number of elderly people will continue to increase in the foreseeable future.

GED Practice, page 154
(5) observation Both Polly Murray and Allen Speere used observation—looking at what was happening to the children of the town—to collect most of their data.

GED Practice, page 155
(1) increase the number of green plants Because green plants take in carbon dioxide during photosynthesis, an increase in the number of green plants should lead to a decrease in the amount of carbon dioxide in the atmosphere. Choice (5) is not practical; it would not be possible, nor would it be desirable, to eliminate all of the decomposers from the planet.

GED Practice, page 156
(5) methyl anthranilate The color purple is associated with grape, so the chemist is most likely to use methyl anthranilate, which smells like grape.

GED Practice, page 157
(4) The United States produces more energy than any other nation shown. According to the graph, the United States produces about 72 quadrillion Btus of energy, more than any other nation shown on the graph.

GED Practice, page 158
(2) 1988 to 1989 Between 1988 and 1989 the number of deaths from congestive heart failure fell. You can tell because the line on the graph slopes downward instead of sloping upward or staying horizontal during that period.

GED Practice, page 159
(3) carbohydrates. According to the circle graph, carbohydrates make up about 65 percent (sugar and other carbohydrates) of the nutrients in the cookie, the greatest amount.

GED Practice, page 160
(2) triceps relaxes. According to the diagram, when the biceps contracts, the triceps relaxes, thus enabling the arm to bend at the elbow.

PROGRAM 23: LIFE SCIENCE

Similarities in Living Things
Skill Practice, page 166
1. b   4. a
2. c   5. f
3. e   6. d

Skill Practice, page 167
1. photosynthesis
2. chloroplasts
3. light reactions
4. dark reactions
5. cellular respiration

Skill Practice, page 168
1. The DNA duplicates itself and then separates.
2. (3) telophase
3. It has the same genetic material as the mother cell.

Skill Practice, page 169
1. Their cells are capable of dividing only about 50 times. After that, they break down, and the organism dies.
2. Answers will vary. Sample answer: Yes, because the possible benefits of this research outweigh the negative aspects of using a cell that has the potential for life.

History and Nature of Science, page 169

Answers will vary. Sample answers:

1. Today most people are immunized against diseases that commonly killed children and young people earlier in the century.
2. Today antibiotics and other medicines can cure certain illnesses that were not curable earlier in the century.
3. Today people are better informed about good nutrition and exercise habits, so they take better care of themselves and are likely to live longer.

Diversity in Nature
Skill Practice, page 170

1. a
2. Will must have inherited a recessive gene for blue eyes from each of his parents.

Skill Practice, page 171

1. (2) have offspring with his or her characteristics.
2. In different environments, different variations are more useful, so individuals with those variations are most likely to survive and reproduce.
3. fossil evidence and structural evidence

Skill Practice, page 172

1. **True**
2. **False** Fungi are listed in the Multicellular section of the chart.
3. **False** A species is a group of organisms that resemble one another and that can interbreed and produce fertile offspring. Different species are found within each kingdom.
4. **True**
5. **True**

Skill Practice, page 173

1. drugs that kill bacteria
2. (2) evolution

Science as Inquiry, page 173

Answers will vary. Sample answer:
You could grow the bacteria that cause ear infections and then add the new antibiotic to some of them. Then you would see whether the bacteria to which you added the antibiotic developed differently from the bacteria you left alone. If the antibiotic killed the bacteria, you would conclude that it is effective for use against the bacteria that cause ear infections. If it did not, you would conclude that the antibiotic does not work against the bacteria that cause ear infections.

Organisms and Their Environments
Skill Practice, page 174

1. a community of plants, animals, and other organisms together with the nonliving things in the environment
2. (1) the Douglas fir
3. to recycle dead animal and plant matter to provide nutrients for plants

Skill Practice, page 175

1. **True**
2. **True**
3. **False** White blood cells produce antibodies to fight off antigens.
4. **False** Vaccinations prompt the immune system to build antibodies to a particular antigen.
5. **True**

Skill Practice, page 176

1. Human activity destroys habitats, pushing species out of the ecosystem and upsetting its balance.
2. The cougar posed a threat to human life and livestock.
3. Restrictions were placed on hunting cougar, deer, and elk. The population of deer and elk increased, so the cougar population increased, too.

Skill Practice, page 177

1. otter fur
2. He filled a small pool with water, added motor oil, and dumped in a few pounds of hair stuffed in tights to see whether it would absorb the oil.
3. Answers will vary. Sample answers: Collecting and transporting enough hair might be a problem. Safely disposing of the oil-soaked hair also might be a problem.

Science in Personal and Social Perspectives, page 177

Answers will vary. Sample answer: The building of new houses and shopping malls destroys the habitat of birds, small animals, and other wildlife in my area.

GED Practice, pages 178–180

1. **(1) measure the oxygen given off during the day and during the night** Without actually measuring the amount of oxygen in the air around the plants both day and night, Ingenhousz would not have had the evidence he needed to reach the conclusion that plants did not give off oxygen at night.
2. **(5) Jason, because there are too few plants to make any difference** The levels of carbon dioxide and oxygen will not change enough to warrant removing the plants.
3. **(5) to cheer them up** A plant in a room will make little difference in the oxygen and carbon dioxide levels.

SCIENCE

4. **(4) decrease for men; increase for women**
   The present trend for men is downward; the
   trend for women is upward.
5. **(2) mRNA** The messenger RNA, also called
   the sense strand, moves from the nucleus into
   the body of the cell.
6. **(2) the sense strand's coded sequence.**
   Particular codes attract particular building
   blocks of protein.
7. **(1) To work, an antisense drug must target a
   particular sequence of mRNA** Particular
   sequences are associated with particular proteins,
   so the antisense drug must be an exact match.
8. **(3) the young form of an animal** Beetles are
   insects, insects are animals, and the larvae are
   the young form of insects as indicated by their
   position in the beetle life cycle, described in
   the passage.
9. **(3) The beetles have evolved to eat soybeans
   as well as corn.** This means they also lay
   their eggs in the soybean field, which next
   year is planted with corn, whose roots are
   eaten by the rootworms.
10. **(3) rootworms eating the corn roots** The
    rootworms weaken the roots so that the corn
    falls over in the wind.
11. **(1) apply pesticides to both soybean and
    corn fields** This is the only measure that will
    save next year's corn crop.

PROGRAM 24: EARTH AND SPACE SCIENCE

Earth's Place in the Universe
Skill Practice, page 186
1. elliptical
2. irregular
3. spiral

Skill Practice, page 187
1. **True**
2. **True**
3. **False** According to the table, Uranus has 17
   known satellites.
4. **False** If you look in the column marked "Day
   Length," you will see there is no pattern of
   increasing day length the farther from the Sun the
   planet is. For example, Mercury, which is closest
   to the Sun, has a day that lasts 59 Earth days.
   In contrast, Jupiter, which is much farther from
   the Sun, has a day that lasts only about 10 hours.
5. **True**

Skill Practice, page 188
1. c   5. f
2. e   6. d
3. a   7. b
4. g

Skill Practice, page 189
1. about once every 300,000 years
2. to take a census of asteroids and comets whose
   orbits cross Earth's orbit

Science in Personal and Social Perspectives, page 189
Answers will vary. Sample answer: I believe that we
are fascinated by "doomsday" scenarios because they
are out of our control. Our society has gained control
over most of Earth's disasters. We can predict and
prepare for most weather-related disasters. We can
escape and contain other disasters such as fire and
flood. However, we cannot fully prepare for a disaster
from outer space. This frightens and fascinates us.

The Changing Earth
Skill Practice, page 190
1. Transform
2. Subduction
3. Spreading

Skill Practice, page 191
1. (2) heat and pressure
2. a. sedimentary   b. igneous
3. Sedimentary rock, because other types of rock
   and sedimentary rock are eroded to form new
   sedimentary rock.

Skill Practice, page 192
1. **True**
2. **False** According to the first paragraph of the
   article, only 3 percent of Earth's water is fresh
   water and less than $\frac{1}{2}$ of 1 percent of Earth's
   water is drinkable and obtainable.
3. **True**
4. **True**
5. Sample diagram:

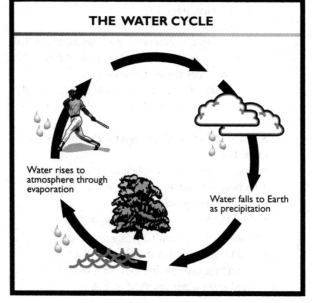

THE WATER CYCLE

Water rises to atmosphere through evaporation

Water falls to Earth as precipitation

Skill Practice, page 193

1. Scientists needed a safe way to explore an active volcano.
2. a. new laser technology
   b. how to program a robot to do routine tasks in dangerous conditions

Science as Inquiry, page 193

Answers will vary. Sample answer:
Observation: A robotic explorer could be used to make observations by collecting data from places too dangerous for humans.

People and the Environment
Skill Practice, page 194

1. The atmosphere traps heat from the sun, thereby warming Earth's surface.
2. Increased burning of fossil fuels and slash-and-burn agriculture both add to the amount of carbon dioxide in the atmosphere.
3. United States, former USSR, China, Japan, Germany

Skill Practice, page 195

1. **True**
2. **False** According to the first paragraph of the article, coal, oil, and natural gas are more concentrated sources of energy.
3. **True**
4. **True**
5. **False** Fossil fuels are used to make much of our electricity. If the supply of fossil fuels runs out, we will not be able to make electricity unless we find another energy source to do so.

Skill Practice, page 196

1. **c**   3. **d**
2. **b**   4. **a**

Skill Practice, page 197

1. 13 to 20 feet
2. Its collapse would raise sea level so much that a lot of low-lying coastal areas would be flooded, destroying communities.
3. evidence of marine life in sediments under the ice sheet within the last two million years

Science in Personal and Social Perspectives, page 197

Answers will vary. Sample answers:
Two possible effects of rising sea levels:
• communities would flood
• drinking water would be contaminated

Possible ways to combat rising sea levels:
• build levees or dikes to hold back the water
• rebuild the community, moving it farther inland
• build extra water purification plants

GED Practice, pages 198–200

1. **(2) the amplitude of seismic waves** A seismograph is an instrument that measures the amplitude, or size, of seismic waves.
2. **(1) greater because San Francisco has increased in population and size** San Francisco was a much smaller city with far fewer people in 1906. A similar earthquake there today would do much more damage and kill more people, despite improved construction techniques.
3. **(3) 100 millimeters** A line drawn from 100 kilometers on the distance scale through 5.0 on the magnitude scale crosses the amplitude scale at 100 millimeters.
4. **(1) the amounts of energy they released.** The Richter Scale estimates the force, or energy, of an earthquake.
5. **(1) a shrinking red giant.** The diagram shows that a white dwarf is the stage after red giant.
6. **(4) The life cycle of the solar system is tied to that of our star, the sun.** Since the sun will eventually run out of fuel, the solar system will also come to an end.
7. **(2) Gravity causes the particles to come together.** The gravitational attraction of the particles for one another eventually causes them to draw near one another, forming a star.
8. **(5) red giant.** The diagram shows that the sun will eventually become a red giant.
9. **(3) to cut the cost of satellite launches** The primary point of the new launching technology is to save money on fuel by shortening the distance rockets travel and giving them an extra boost from the rotation of Earth.
10. **(1) is relatively close to the equator.** Florida is closer to the Equator than any other place in the mainland United States.
11. **(1) decreased in most states.** The passage states that emissions have decreased in 41 (out of 50) states.

PROGRAM 25: CHEMISTRY

The Structure of Matter
Skill Practice, page 206

1. Element
2. Compound
3. Element
4. Compound
5. Element
6. Element
7. Compound
8. Element

Skill Practice, page 207
1. **True**
2. **False** Electrons have a negative charge.
3. **True**
4. **False** Since there are the same number of protons and electrons, the positive charges and negative charges cancel one another out, producing no charge.
5. **True**
6. **False** Most of the mass of an atom is in the nucleus, which consists of protons and neutrons.

Skill Practice, page 208
1. Liquid
2. Solid
3. Liquid, gas
4. Gas
5. Liquid
6. Liquid
7. Gas
8. Solid

Skill Practice, page 209
1. Wording will vary. Heat turns moisture in the popcorn kernel to steam. The particles in a gas are much farther away from one another than the particles in a liquid, so in an enclosed space they will exert more pressure. Eventually this pressure causes the kernel to explode.
2. a scratch on the pericarp, too much moisture in the pericarp, too little moisture in the kernel

Science and Technology, page 209
Answers will vary. Sample answer:
In my furnace, the natural gas burner heats water, and steam fills the pipes and radiators in the apartment, heating it. In the kitchen, I use steam to cook vegetables. Steam also tells me when water is boiling in the tea kettle, because it causes a whistling sound as it escapes through the hole in the spout.

How Elements Behave
Skill Practice, page 210
1. Copper (Cu)
2. transition metal
3. phosphorus and arsenic
4. hydrogen, lithium, sodium, or potassium
5. helium, neon, argon, or krypton

Skill Practice, page 211
1. (2) an electrical charge
2. (2) covalent bonds
3. (1) ionic bonding.

Skill Practice, page 212
1. g
2. e
3. a
4. b
5. f
6. d
7. c

Skill Practice, page 213
1. the amount of energy needed to raise 1 gram of water 1 degree Centigrade
2. burning (oxidation)

Science as Inquiry, page 213
Answers will vary. Sample answer:
Enclose the space between the burning food and the flask of water with a cylinder of aluminum foil to prevent the heat from escaping into the surrounding air.

How Chemicals Behave
Skill Practice, page 214
1. **b**
2. **a**
3. **c**

Skill Practice, page 215
1. **True**
2. **True**
3. **False** When an acid or a base is dissolved in water, it conducts electricity.
4. **True**
5. **True**
6. **False** A substance that measures 13 on the pH scale is a strong base.

Skill Practice, page 216
1. (2) hydrocarbons
2. (3) are arranged in different ways.
3. (1) polymer.

Skill Practice, page 217
1. fat (or oil or fatty acid), base (for example, lye or caustic soda), and water
2. Wording will vary. When the soap dissolves, one end of the soap molecules attaches to the grease or dirt. The other end is attracted to water, so soap molecules lift the grease or dirt up from the surface being cleaned.

Science in Personal and Social Perspectives, page 217
Answers will vary. Sample answer:
Plastic saved my uncle's life. He had heart surgery, and doctors used plastic heart valves to repair his heart. His immune system did not reject the plastic. Today he is healthy.

GED Practice, pages 218–220
1. **(1) two protons and two neutrons** Alpha particles consist of two protons and two neutrons, according to the first bulleted item in the passage.

2. **(2) test the effects of radioactivity on living things before using radioactive materials.** Until years of scientific and industrial use had passed, the effects of radioactivity were not known. No systematic effort was made to find out its effects before radioactive substances were used.

3. **(1) protons in the nucleus changes.** A change in the number of protons means a change in the atomic number, which means that another element has formed.

4. **(3) 5 grams** Half will be left after one half-life period of 65.2 days. 10 grams divided in half is 5 grams.

5. **(1) xenon gas** Arrows on the left side of the diagram indicate that xenon, a gas, flows into the engine to power it.

6. **(1) Positive ions are attracted to a negative grid, producing thrust.** By directing the positive ions out the back of the rocket using the negative grid, a flow of ions produces thrust.

7. **(5) long-term space missions** It takes quite a while for the momentum of the spacecraft to increase so that it is traveling quickly. Thus an ion engine would be practical only on missions that last a long time.

8. **(3) when an electron is removed** A positive ion exists when there are more protons than electrons, producing a net positive charge. Since a neutral xenon atom has an equal number of protons and electrons, knocking an electron off will make a positive xenon ion.

9. **(3) Salt lowers the freezing point of water.** The melting of only the salted ice indicates that salt lowers the freezing point of water, causing the ice to melt.

10. **(1) Record the temperatures at which salt water and plain water freeze.** Measuring and comparing the temperatures will give you specific data on the effect of salt on water's freezing point.

11. **(4) making the elevator more airtight** This would make the situation worse because more pressure would build up inside the elevator if it were more airtight, making an explosion more likely.

PROGRAM 26: PHYSICS

Physical Laws
Skill Practice, page 226
1. **second law:** force equals mass times acceleration. The large sport utility vehicle has a far greater mass than the small car, so it will apply more force to the car than the car will apply to the SUV.

2. **third law:** for every action there is an equal and opposite reaction. For the force exerted by a first object (ship on water), there is an equal and opposite force exerted by the second object (water on ship).

3. **first law:** a body in motion tends to stay in motion unless a force acts upon it. The forces of friction and gravity act on the bullet, causing it to slow down and eventually drop to the ground.

Skill Practice, page 227
1. **True**
2. **False** The energy of an object in motion is kinetic energy, and the energy of an object at rest is potential energy.
3. **True**
4. **True**

Skill Practice, page 228
1. (1) frying pan
2. (2) electromagnetic radiation.

Skill Practice, page 229
1. The chute traps air, increasing air pressure inside and creating drag to slow the parachute.
2. Sometimes the air above the parachute has more pressure than the air inside, especially when the chute has a turbulent wake. Then the wake can push down on the parachute, collapsing it.

History and Nature of Science, page 229
Answers will vary. Answers can include any three of the following topics: light, gravity, astronomy, or mathematics.

Waves
Skill Practice, page 230
1. **b**
2. **a**
3. **c**
4. **d**

Skill Practice, page 231
1. **Refraction** The light is passing from air into a plastic or glass lens, which has a different density. It then emerges back into air before entering the eye and bending again.
2. **Diffraction** When waves pass through a small opening like a narrow doorway, the different wavelengths get mixed up and travel at different rates, making the sound jumbled.
3. **Reflection** Light bounces off a mirror, so you can see objects that reflect light.

4. **Refraction** White sunlight travels through water droplets in the air and is refracted into the different colors of the spectrum.
5. **Reflection** Sunlight reflects off the moon, making the moon visible.

Skill Practice, page 232
1. **False** The only type of electromagnetic radiation you can see is visible light.
2. **False** Radio waves have a longer wavelength than microwaves.
3. **False** All electromagnetic radiation can travel through a vacuum.
4. **True**

Skill Practice, page 233
1. In laser light, all the waves have the same wavelength, amplitude, direction, and frequency and they are in step with one another. Normal light consists of a mix of different wavelengths, amplitudes, frequencies, and directions.
2. Any three of the following: eye surgery, cosmetic surgery, dentistry, construction, reading product bar codes, making or reading CDs, light shows.

Magnetism, Electricity, and Nuclear Physics
Skill Practice, page 234
1. **False** The north poles of two magnets repel one another.
2. **False** Magnets have a south pole and a north pole.
3. **True**
4. **False** Magnetism can work when objects are touching and when they are at a distance.

Skill Practice, page 235
1. e
2. d
3. b
4. c
5. a

Skill Practice, page 236
1. nucleus
2. fusion
3. fission

Skill Practice, page 237
1. Nuclear wastes remain radioactive for hundreds or thousands of years, emitting particles that are harmful to people and the environment.
2. It is buried.
3. It is placed in a cooling pond, then placed in sealed containers and buried deep in rock.

Science in Personal and Social Perspectives, page 237
Questions will vary. Sample questions:
1. What is the utility company's track record for nuclear power plant safety?
2. What does the company plan to do with the toxic waste from the nuclear power plant?
3. What type of jobs will be available to local workers? How many jobs will be available?

GED Practice, pages 238–240
1. **(4) magnetism** Magnetism is the only force not mentioned in the paragraph or diagram. It can act on the metal of an airplane, but has no significant effect on an airplane at takeoff.
2. **(2) pulling up the landing gear** This is the only choice that decreases drag, which would increase speed.
3. **(1) Lift must be greater than weight.** Until lift exceeds weight, the plane stays on the ground.
4. **(4) to reduce drag** At high altitudes, the air is thinner, so there is less friction to slow the plane's forward motion.
5. **(3) magnetic fields and radio waves.** According to the passage, the MRI uses magnetic fields and radio waves to produce images.
6. **(3) Metal would interfere with the magnetic field.** Because metals can be magnetized, they cannot go into the MRI machine because they will change the magnetic fields.
7. **(5) to reduce the cost of using MRI technology** Because the machines are so expensive, hospitals and medical groups found ways to cut the cost of purchasing them by sharing access to machines.
8. **(1) Data obtained from particle experiments may be unreliable.** Because measurement of a particle disturbs it, data from particle experiments may not be entirely accurate.
9. **(2) 10** Using the formula, 0.1×100 pounds $= 10$ pounds.
10. **(4) getting lubricated ball bearings moving** The ball bearings have the lowest static coefficient of any of the objects listed in the table, so the least force is required to get them moving.
11. **(1) If you unscrew one of the bulbs in the parallel circuit, the others will stay lit.** Since each bulb has its own connection to the power source, breaking the circuit by unscrewing one bulb will not affect the other bulbs; they will stay lit.

Reference Handbook

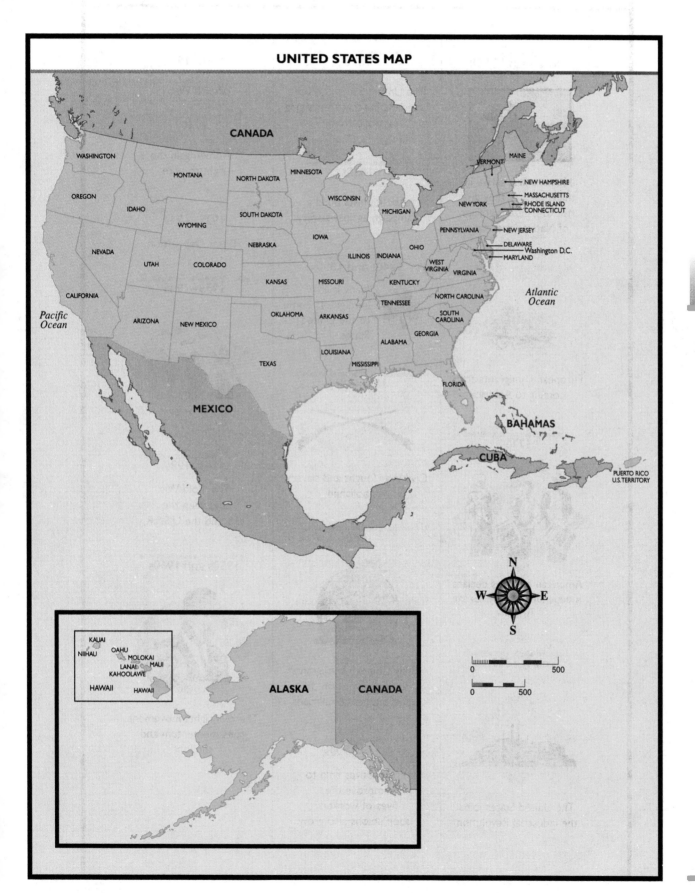

UNITED STATES MAP

CANADA

WASHINGTON

MONTANA

NORTH DAKOTA

MINNESOTA

VERMONT   MAINE

NEW HAMPSHIRE

OREGON

IDAHO

SOUTH DAKOTA

WISCONSIN

MICHIGAN

NEW YORK

MASSACHUSETTS

RHODE ISLAND
CONNECTICUT

WYOMING

IOWA

PENNSYLVANIA

NEW JERSEY

NEVADA

UTAH

NEBRASKA

COLORADO

ILLINOIS INDIANA

OHIO

WEST
VIRGINIA

VIRGINIA

DELAWARE
Washington D.C.
MARYLAND

CALIFORNIA

KANSAS

MISSOURI

KENTUCKY

NORTH CAROLINA

*Atlantic
Ocean*

*Pacific
Ocean*

ARIZONA

NEW MEXICO

OKLAHOMA

ARKANSAS

TENNESSEE

SOUTH
CAROLINA

GEORGIA

ALABAMA

TEXAS

LOUISIANA

MISSISSIPPI

FLORIDA

MEXICO

BAHAMAS

CUBA

PUERTO RICO
U.S. TERRITORY

N
W   E
S

KAUAI
NIIHAU   OAHU
MOLOKAI
LANAI   MAUI
KAHOOLAWE
HAWAII   HAWAII

ALASKA   CANADA

0   500

0   500

271

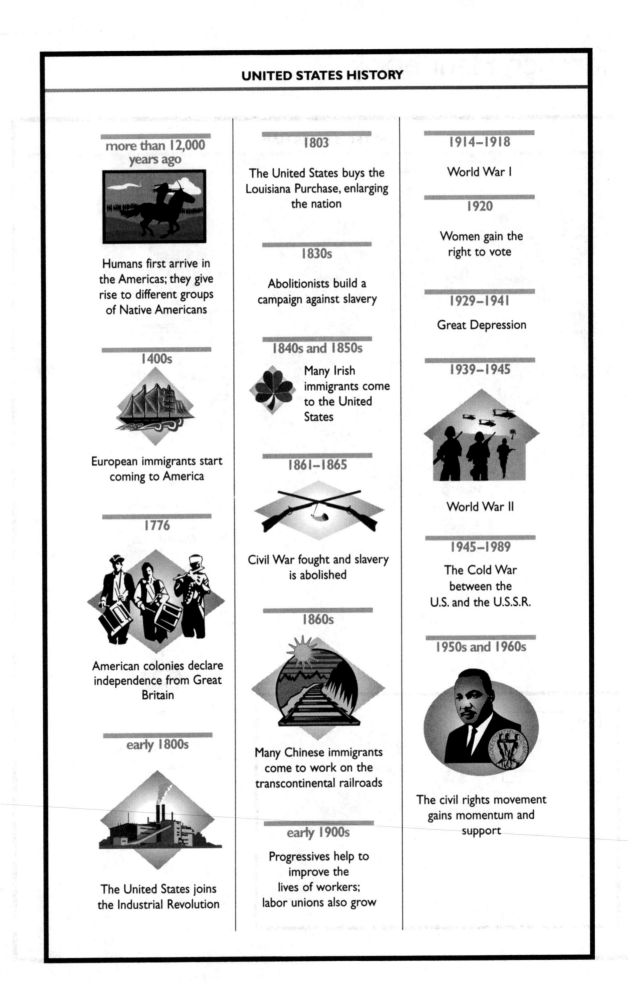

more than 12,000 years ago

Humans first arrive in the Americas; they give rise to different groups of Native Americans

1400s

European immigrants start coming to America

1776

American colonies declare independence from Great Britain

early 1800s

The United States joins the Industrial Revolution

1803

The United States buys the Louisiana Purchase, enlarging the nation

1830s

Abolitionists build a campaign against slavery

1840s and 1850s

Many Irish immigrants come to the United States

1861–1865

Civil War fought and slavery is abolished

1860s

Many Chinese immigrants come to work on the transcontinental railroads

early 1900s

Progressives help to improve the lives of workers; labor unions also grow

1914–1918

World War I

1920

Women gain the right to vote

1929–1941

Great Depression

1939–1945

World War II

1945–1989

The Cold War between the U.S. and the U.S.S.R.

1950s and 1960s

The civil rights movement gains momentum and support

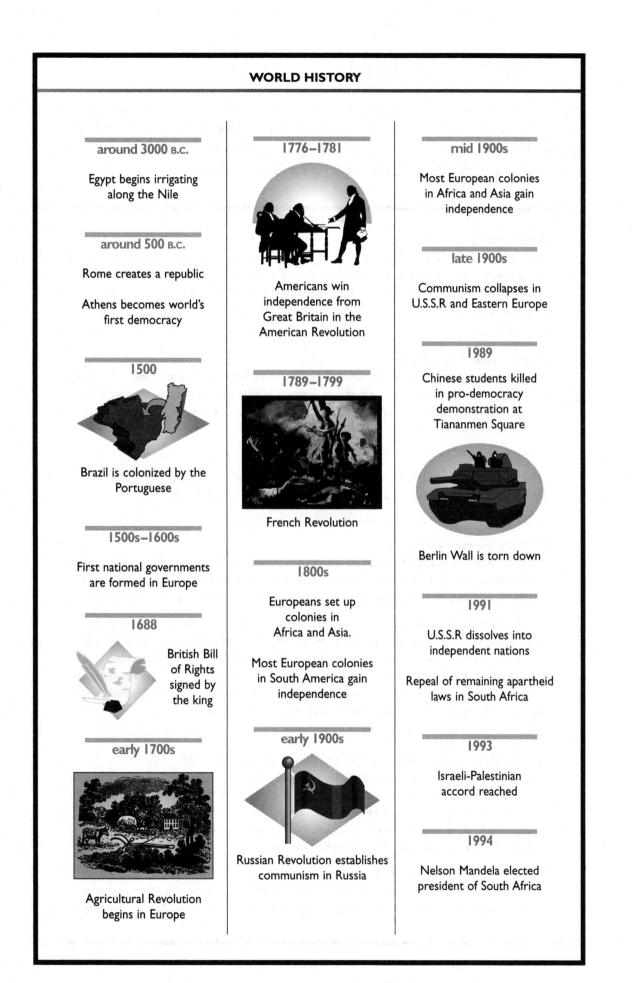

around 3000 B.C.

Egypt begins irrigating along the Nile

around 500 B.C.

Rome creates a republic

Athens becomes world's first democracy

1500

Brazil is colonized by the Portuguese

1500s–1600s

First national governments are formed in Europe

1688

British Bill of Rights signed by the king

early 1700s

Agricultural Revolution begins in Europe

1776–1781

Americans win independence from Great Britain in the American Revolution

1789–1799

French Revolution

1800s

Europeans set up colonies in Africa and Asia.

Most European colonies in South America gain independence

early 1900s

Russian Revolution establishes communism in Russia

mid 1900s

Most European colonies in Africa and Asia gain independence

late 1900s

Communism collapses in U.S.S.R and Eastern Europe

1989

Chinese students killed in pro-democracy demonstration at Tiananmen Square

Berlin Wall is torn down

1991

U.S.S.R dissolves into independent nations

Repeal of remaining apartheid laws in South Africa

1993

Israeli-Palestinian accord reached

1994

Nelson Mandela elected president of South Africa

Scientific Method

The scientific method refers to the processes scientists use when they add to the body of scientific knowledge. There are several steps in the scientific method. We will describe each step and illustrate it with research conducted by Dr. Derek Denton of the University of Melbourne in Australia. He studied the role of salt in high blood pressure.

STEP 1. Identify a problem.
Hypertension, or high blood pressure, is a serious disease affecting millions of people. It has many contributing causes: genetic factors, lack of exercise, drinking alcohol, smoking, and diet, including salt intake. However, the role of salt in hypertension has been controversial, and it is not completely understood.

STEP 2. Collect information.
Not everyone who eats a lot of salt develops hypertension. Research on the connection between salt and hypertension has not been conclusive. Some scientists think that calcium or potassium shortages cause hypertension, not salt. Still, most doctors prescribe low-salt diets to their patients along with medication to control high blood pressure.

STEP 3. Form a hypothesis, or theory, based on the information gathered.
Hypothesis: Adding salt to the diet will cause an increase in blood pressure.

STEP 4. Test the hypothesis.
Dr. Denton had to find a way to test the hypothesis without dealing with complicated human diets and life styles. He also had to consider the ethical problems that arise when humans are the subjects of experiments. Thus Dr. Denton turned to chimpanzees, the species most similar to humans.

He and his colleagues worked with a group of 26 chimpanzees at a research center in Gabon. All were healthy and all had normal blood pressure. Half of the chimps were given a high-salt diet for 20 months, and half remained on their normal, low-salt diet. Most animals in the group on the high-salt diet experienced a significant rise in blood pressure. None of the animals in the low-salt group had a rise in blood pressure. Six months after the chimps on the high-salt diet resumed a normal diet, their blood pressure had returned to normal.

STEP 5. Draw conclusions based on the data that was gathered.
Dr. Denton and his colleagues concluded that changes in the chimpanzees' salt intake caused changes in blood pressure. When salt was added to the chimps' diet, blood pressure rose in almost all of them. When salt was removed from their diet, blood pressure fell. Some of the chimps were more sensitive to salt than others. This is similar to humans, some of whom can eat a lot of salt without it affecting their blood pressure.

Dr. Denton did not extend his conclusions to humans. The number of chimps studied was too small. In addition, the causes of human high blood pressure are complex. Still, the chimpanzee study helped clarify the relationship between a high-salt diet and increased blood-pressure levels.

Glossary

abolitionist: a person who fought to end slavery

acceleration: any change in an object's speed or direction of motion

acid: a substance with a sour taste and low pH that conducts electricity when dissolved in water and that neutralizes bases

adapt: to adjust

amendment: an addition or change, especially to a law or legal document, such as the Constitution of the United States

amplitude: in a wave, the distance between its crest (high point) and its midpoint

apprentice: a young person who works for a period of years to learn a skill or trade from a craftsperson

atmosphere: the layer of gases around Earth

atom: a tiny particle of matter consisting of protons, neutrons, and electrons

atomic number: the number of protons in the nucleus of an element

base: a substance with a high pH that conducts electricity when dissolved in water and that neutralizes acids

bill: a proposed law

cell: the basic living unit of all organisms

cell membrane: the structure surrounding a cell that allows substances to pass in and out

cell wall: a cellulose structure surrounding the cell membrane in a plant cell

cellular respiration: the process by which cells use oxygen to release energy from glucose

checks and balances: a system by which each branch of government can limit the powers of other branches

chemical reaction: a process in which one substance or set of substances is changed into another substance or set of substances

chloroplasts: in plant cells, the green structures that absorb the sun's energy, enabling the plant to produce sugar

circuit: a complete path along which electric current flows

city-state: a city and its surrounding territory

classification: the identification, naming, and grouping of organisms into a formal system

climate: average weather conditions over a long period of time

colony: a settlement with close political ties to its parent country; colonists live in these settlements

communism: a system of government led by followers of a single party with state ownership of almost all property

commute: to travel back and forth from home to a workplace regularly

compound: a substance made of two or more elements chemically combined in exact proportion

consumer: one who buys a product or service from someone else

covalent bond: the joining of two or more atoms by the sharing of electrons

credit: money available to borrow with the promise of repayment

crust: the top, rocky layer of Earth

debit card: a card that subtracts money directly from a checking account

delta: silt-built land at the mouth of a river

demand: what consumers or businesses will buy of a particular good or service at a given price

democracy: a system of government in which people have many political and economic choices

developing nation: a country that has not yet fully industrialized its economy

dictatorship: a government in which the leader holds absolute power

diffraction: the spreading of a wave after the wave passes through a gap in a barrier

DNA: deoxyribonucleic acid; the molecule that carries genetic instructions

downsize: to decrease the number of employees for economic reasons

earthquake: movement of Earth's crust caused by shifting plates

ecosystem: a community of plants, animals, and other organisms along with the nonliving things in the environment

electricity: a flow of charged particles, usually electrons

electromagnetic radiation: a wave motion of electric and magnetic fields; for example, visible light, radio waves, and X rays

electron: a negatively charged particle orbiting the nucleus of an atom

element: a substance that cannot be broken down into a simpler substance by chemical means

embargo: a ban, often enforced by a government, on trade with one or more nations

energy: the ability to do work; see *work*

environment: the geography of the immediate surroundings

ethnic: relating to a person's race or place of origin

evolution: the process by which the genetic makeup of a population changes over a period of time

export: to sell goods produced in one's own country to people and businesses in other countries

fallow: the state of farmland purposely left idle during the growing season

fault: crack in Earth's crust

federalism: a government system in which the national government and the state governments share power

feudal: concerning the relationship between a lord and his land tenants, called vassals

floodplain: the flat land along the course of a stream or river that can flood easily

food web: a feeding pattern that shows the energy transfer throughout an ecosystem

force: the pushes and pulls that act on matter; for example, gravity

fossil fuel: coal, oil, and natural gas; so-called because they form from ancient plant and animal remains

frequency: the number of waves that pass a given point in a given time

galaxy: a huge group of stars, dust, and gas kept together by gravity

gene: a unit of DNA by which traits are passed from parent to offspring

genetics: the scientific study of how traits are inherited

genome: the entire genetic code of an individual or species

greenhouse effect: the atmosphere's role in heating Earth by trapping the sun's energy

gross domestic product: the value of a nation's production of goods and services during a particular year

habitat: the place in an ecosystem where a species lives

heat: a form of energy that is transferred from one object to another when there is a difference in temperature

House of Representatives: the house of the national legislature in which states are represented according to their population

hydrocarbon: a compound that consists only of carbon and hydrogen atoms

immigrant: a person who leaves his or her homeland for a new life in another country

immune system: the body system that attacks disease-causing agents

imperialism: the practice of taking control over nations for their raw materials

import: to bring to one's own country products from another country

indentured: legally bound to work for someone for a certain number of years, generally in exchange for passage to a new homeland

industrialize: to replace human labor with machines

inertia: the tendency of an object at rest to remain at rest and the tendency of an object in motion to remain in motion unless acted upon by a force

inflation: a period during which prices of many items rise sharply and continually

interest group: an organization of people who share a common interest and who work to influence government policies

interest rate: the amount of money a loan will cost, usually given in a percentage of the borrowed money that will be paid back every year

ion: an atom or molecule with an electric charge

ionic bond: the combining of two or more atoms by transferring electrons

irrigate: to water artificially

kinetic energy: the energy of an object in motion

labor union: an organization of workers who try to get better wages, benefits, and working conditions

landform: a physical feature of Earth's surface

legislature: a lawmaking body

levee: artificial banks and walls built to control rivers

light year: the distance light travels in one year (5,880,000,000,000 miles); used to measure huge distances in space

machine: a device that changes the amount of force used to do a given amount of work, usually by increasing the distance involved

magma: molten rock below Earth's surface

magnetism: force that results from the movement of electric charges

manifest destiny: the belief that it is the nation's future to stretch from ocean to ocean

mantle: the layer of Earth below the crust

manufacture: to make or produce goods

mass: the amount of matter an object contains

mitosis: the process by which most cells reproduce; cell division

mixture: a substance made up of two or more different substances that are not chemically combined; for example, salt water

molecule: a group of two or more atoms held together by covalent bonds; see *covalent bond*

monarchy: a government led by a hereditary ruler, either a king or queen

monopoly: a business that is the only one providing a certain good or service

municipality: an urban area, such as a city or village

nation: a community of people who control a specific territory under a government; a country

nationalism: loyalty and devotion to a nation rather than to a local ruler or government

neutron: a neutral particle in the nucleus of an atom

nonrenewable resource: a resource, such as oil and minerals, that is limited in supply and cannot be replaced once it is used up

nuclear fission: the production of large amounts of energy by splitting the nuclei of heavy atoms

nucleus: in a cell, the structure that contains genetic material and controls the cell's activities

ostracism: the act of banishing; in ancient Greece, the act of voting to force a dangerous leader to leave a city state for a period of ten years

override: to overturn; to cancel

patrician: in ancient Rome, a member of one of the oldest and richest families

periodic table: a chart in which the elements are arranged according to atomic weight and the number of electrons in their outer shells

photosynthesis: the process by which green plants use carbon dioxide, water, and energy from sunlight to make their own food

plate: large section of Earth's crust that moves

plate tectonics: a theory explaining how Earth's crust changes over time

political party: a group of citizens with similar opinions on public issues who work together to influence public policy, win elections, and control the government

polymer: a compound that has very large molecules made up of thousands of smaller, identical molecules joined together

potential energy: the energy of an object at rest

Preamble: the introduction to the Constitution

producer: in economics, one who makes a product for others to buy; in life science, an organization that makes its own food (green plants)

progressives: people who worked for the improvement of workers' lives and for other reforms

proton: a positively charged particle in the nucleus of an atom

ratification: the process of approving the Constitution

reflection: the bouncing of a wave off a surface

refraction: the bending of a wave when it passes from one substance to another

region: an area of Earth's surface defined by one or more physical or human characteristics

renewable resource: a resource, such as solar energy, whose supply is limitless

republic: a government in which citizens elect officials to represent them

revolt: to rise up in protest

rock cycle: the processes that change one type of rock to another

secede: to break away from a nation and form a separate nation

segregation: the separation of groups of people, usually by race

self-sufficient: dependent only on oneself for life's necessities

Senate: the house of the national legislature in which states are represented equally

separation of powers: a system by which government power is separated among the branches of government

silt: fine particles of rich soil, sometimes deposited by rivers

solar system: the sun and the objects that revolve around it: planets, their satellites, asteroids, comets, and meteoroids

species: a group of organisms that resemble one another and that produce fertile offspring when they interbreed

states of matter: the different forms substances can take: solid, liquid, or gas

stock market: a place where investors buy and sell shares of stock in major corporations

strike: a work stoppage, intended to force an employer to respond to demands

subduction: the sliding of one plate under another when they collide

supply: what producers will provide of a particular good or service for sale at a given price

tariff: a tax on imported goods

telecommuter: an employee who works at home using an electronic linkup with the office

trust: a combination of several companies that are under one organization's control

veto: to reject something, for example a bill passed by Congress

volunteer: someone who contributes time and skills for no pay

water cycle: the processes by which water moves between the atmosphere, land, and oceans

wave: a disturbance or displacement that repeats itself

wavelength: the distance between two consecutive waves

work: in physics, work is done when an object on which a force is acting moves in the direction of that force

Index

Note to Reader: Words in bold are vocabulary words and bold page numbers contain their definitions.